Homeless Dogs

&

Melancholy Apes

Homeless Dogs

&

Melancholy Apes

HUMANS AND OTHER ANIMALS
in the
MODERN LITERARY IMAGINATION

LAURA BROWN

CORNELL UNIVERSITY PRESS
Ithaca & London

First published 2010 by Cornell University Press
First printing, Cornell Paperbacks, 2017
Printed in the United States of America

Library of Congress Cataloging-in-Publication Data

Brown, Laura, 1949–
    Homeless dogs and melancholy apes : humans and other animals in the modern literary imagination / Laura Brown.
        p. cm.
    Includes bibliographical references and index.
    ISBN 978-0-8014-4828-7 (cloth : alk. paper)
    ISBN 978-1-5017-1355-2 (pbk. : alk. paper)
    1. English literature—History and criticism.   2. American literature—History and criticism.
3. Animals in literature.   4. Human-animal relationships in literature.   5. Pets in literature.
I. Title.
    PR408.A55B76   2010
    823'.009362—dc22   2010010713

Cornell University Press strives to use environmentally responsible suppliers and materials to the fullest extent possible in the publishing of its books. Such materials include vegetable-based, low-VOC inks and acid-free papers that are recycled, totally chlorine-free, or partly composed of nonwood fibers. For further information, visit our website at www.cornellpress.cornell.edu.

For Walter

"I am thinking of aurochs and angels, the secret of durable pigments, prophetic sonnets, the refuge of art."

Vladimir Nabokov, *Lolita*

CONTENTS

PREFACE

This book began in an undergraduate seminar on The Idea of the Pet in Literature and History, a course that I offered in the English Department at Cornell University. Describing the status of "the pet in history" to this group was a straightforward project, compared with our discussions of "the pet in literature." My own interdisciplinary syllabus exacerbated the complexities. I began with historical studies of the lived relationships between humans and other animals in western Europe from the early modern period to the present. And I incorporated materials and information from Cornell's College of Veterinary Medicine, in particular Bernard E. Rollin's textbook, *An Introduction to Veterinary Medical Ethics*, and a discussion with a Cornell colleague, Professor Katherine Houpt, VMD, a veterinary behaviorist and a key figure in Cornell's cutting-edge Animal Behavior Clinic.

In this context, our literary readings had a strangely irrelevant potency and priority. Students experienced the animals represented by William Wordsworth, Matthew Arnold, Jack London, Albert Payson Terhune, James Merrill, and Paul Auster with an immediacy and a poignancy that even Rollin's most needy and Houpt's most misunderstood pets did not inspire. But of course—with Houpt's and Rollin's examples before our eyes—we were repeatedly forced to register the almost unbridgeable distance between "White Fang" or "Lad" and those real animals who share our world. Students quickly found the task of measuring the precise distance between the imaginary and the real nonhuman beings to be exhausting and fruitless. This course tested my ability to grasp and to express the significance of purely literary animals—their vitality in our imagination and their pertinence to our experience. Which literary animal most fully expresses the raw alterity of animal-kind? Which are most evidently people in animal suits? We concluded, first, that neither alterity nor anthropomorphism, in itself, can account for the versatility and complex nature of the imaginary animal, and second, that no singular judgment of the representation of animals can claim to have access to the authentic existences of those real animal beings that Rollin and Houpt documented.

This book builds upon those conclusions about the power and effect of purely imaginary animals. In this context, I do not critique the human-centered assumptions of anthropomorphism, nor am I concerned with the anthropocentrism involved in the human use of other animals to conceive or understand exclusively human issues. This study does not focus on the fundamental alterity of animals, seek access to an authentic approach to animal-kind across that gap of alterity, or bear witness to the lives or the suffering of real animals. It does not take up the post-structuralist topic of the aporia of nonhuman difference, nor does it engage with the so-called posthumanist assertion that the nonhuman resides in the core or at the origin of the human, as an outside that is always already inside and thus generative of a radical means of thinking beyond the human subject and in common with all beings. My analysis throughout this study focuses on the realm of representation. Not that I dismiss the real animals who enter the compass of human experience; this project begins from the historical premise that the encounter with real animals in the eighteenth century generates a novel engagement with animal-kind that continues to shape literary discourse through the modern era. I argue that the imaginary animals created by that engagement provide a new lens through which to examine the significance of the nonhuman being for human identity, human experience, and human history. Within literary texts and forms, these animals offer opportunities for disruption, innovation, and even transcendence. They create new genres, produce strange affiliations, and disturb given norms and hierarchies.

Thus my course on The Pet in Literature and History and its students presented me with the key problematic of this project—the question of the critical significance of the imaginary animal. I would like to express my gratitude for the opportunity to teach that class and my debt to its sponsor, the John S. Knight Institute for Writing in the Disciplines at Cornell University. Furthermore, in 2008–2009 I was a member of the Mellon Humanities Seminar on the topic of "The Human," sponsored by the Andrew W. Mellon Foundation and administered by the College of Arts and Sciences at Cornell. I would like to thank Harry Shaw, then senior associate dean of the college, for this chance for sustained intellectual exchange on the topic, and my fellow participants in the seminar for a year of stimulating discussion. I am also indebted to the College of Arts and Sciences for providing me with research funds to support the publication of this book.

In addition, I have had several occasions to present versions of these materials at the English Department of the University of California at Davis, the English Department of the University of Pennsylvania, and the Long Eighteenth Century seminar at The Huntington Library, cosponsored by the University of Southern California and the University of California at Los Angeles. I would like to thank the audiences at those venues for their invaluable questions and comments, and especially Margaret Ferguson, Chi-ming Yang, Emily Anderson, and Felicity Nussbaum for extending those invitations.

Versions of two chapters of this book have previously appeared in print. A version of chapter 3 is available as "The Lady, the Lapdog, and Literary Alterity" in a special issue of the journal *Eighteenth Century: Theory and Interpretation* (2010) entitled "Brute Enlightenment: Humans, Animals, and Souls in the Eighteenth Century," edited by Lucinda Cole. A version of chapter 4 appears as "Shock Effect: *Evelina*'s Monkey and the Marriage Plot" in a special issue of *The Eighteenth Century Novel* (7: 2010) in honor of John Richetti and edited by George Justice; copyright 2009 AMS Press, Inc., all rights reserved. I am grateful to both of these journals for permission to publish somewhat altered versions of these articles here.

I would like to acknowledge my debt to the staffs and resources of the Flower-Sprecher Veterinary Library at Cornell University, the Mary L. Schofield Collection of Children's Literature in the Rare Books Division of the Stanford University Library, and the American Kennel Club Library. Individual thanks for particular comments, suggestions, and help are due to Bryan Alkemeyer, Felicity Nussbaum, Ana Brown-Cohen, Jonah Brown-Cohen, Wendy Jones, and Mariam Wassif. I am most deeply indebted to Walter Cohen, who is always my first and who will be my last and best reader.

Homeless Dogs

Melancholy Apes

1

SPECULATIVE SPACE

The Rise of the Animal in the Modern Imagination

In his sentimental novel *Melincourt; or, Sir Oran Haut-ton* (1818), Thomas Love Peacock depicts a dramatic rescue. The novel's eligible young heroine, Anthelia, while enjoying the delightful solitude of a bridge over a foaming stream, finds herself trapped on a rock in midtorrent by a sudden deluge. Out of the nearby pine grove a stranger runs with "surprising speed to the edge of the chasm":

> Anthelia had never seen so singular a physiognomy....The stranger seemed interested for her situation....He paused a moment, as if measuring with his eyes the breadth of the chasm, and then returning to the grove, proceeded very deliberately to pull up a pine [which]...he bore...on his shoulders to the chasm: where placing one end on a high point of the bank, and lowering the other on the insulated rock, he ran like a flash of lightning along the stem, caught Anthelia in his arms, and carried her safely over in an instant.[1]

This benevolent, quick moving, and unusually strong being is the figure of the novel's subtitle, Sir Oran Haut-ton, Baronet, whose extraordinary impact extends well beyond the moment of the rescue, and beyond his relationship with the novel's beautiful female protagonist: "The remarkable physiognomy and unparalleled strength of the stranger, caused much of surprise, and something of apprehension, to mingle with Anthelia's gratitude: but the air of high fashion, which characterized his whole deportment, diminished her apprehension, while it increased her surprise at the exploit he had performed" (106–107).

---

[1] Thomas Love Peacock, *Melincourt*, vol. 2 of *The Halliford Edition of the Works of Thomas Love Peacock*, ed. H. F. B. Brett-Smith and C. E. Jones (London: Constable, 1924), 105–106.

In his disturbing, compelling, and extraordinarily fertile capacities within this playful text, Sir Oran can stand for the imaginary animal of eighteenth-century literary culture. Assembled from a wide range of eighteenth-century precedents—images, tropes, arguments, and ideas about animals that circulated in diverse texts, from Edward Tyson's *Anatomy of a Pygmie* (1699) to Edward Kendall's *Keeper's Travels in Search of His Master* (1798)—Sir Oran sums up the historical distinctiveness and the formal complexities of that experimental period that marks the rise of the nonhuman animal in the modern imagination.[2] And, beyond his own period, he provides a perspective on current debates about the nature of the human-animal relationship.

This chapter will explore the extraordinary flexibility of Peacock's portrayal of Sir Oran in order to provide a concrete demonstration of the ways in which the imaginary animal resists any simple positioning or singular interpretation. Sir Oran can help us see that the modern literary imagination represents animals in a manner that does not match up well with the two main positions advanced by critics of the human-animal relationship from the end of the twentieth and the beginning of the twenty-first century—the contrasting positions of anthropomorphism or alterity. I argue here, through a sketch of selected critical works on the animal in the Anglo-American tradition, that opposing claims that see the animal either through the lens of anthropomorphism or of alterity have largely shaped the critical understanding of animal-kind. Literature provides an alternative model. This chapter ends by describing the ways in which the vital new modern experience of the nonhuman animal, generated within the distinctive historical context of the eighteenth century, gives rise to complex and flexible literary fantasies that verge toward the dissonant, the unconventional, the aberrant, and the unbounded.

Sir Oran Haut-ton

The reader has been introduced to Sir Oran in an earlier chapter of Peacock's work, when he appears as the friend of Mr. Sylvan Forester, the eventual love-match of Anthelia and the novel's spokesman for the benefits of nature over the corruptions of civilization as well as for the surpassing virtues of original man. Sir Oran joins Mr. Forester and his guest, Sir Telegraph Paxarett, in an elegant supper on Mr. Forester's estate, Redrose Abbey, a neighboring property to the eligible Anthelia's Melincourt

---

[2] "Nonhuman animal" and "other animal" have become the acceptable phrases to refer to other-than-human animal species. Following Martha Nussbaum's example, I will sometimes use "animal" or "animal-kind" as shorthand for these more accurate but longer phrases. Martha C. Nussbaum, *Frontiers of Justice: Disability, Nationality, Species Membership* (Cambridge, Mass.: Harvard University Press, 2006), 326n.

Castle. Sir Oran, we learn after the conclusion of this meal, is Mr. Forester's protégé, obtained from a sea captain who bought him from "an intelligent negro." Sir Oran had been "caught…very young, in the woods of Angola…and brought…up in [an Angolan family's] cottage as the playfellow of their little boys and girls" (54). As Mr. Forester says, "He is a specimen of the natural and original man—the wild man of the woods; called in the language of the more civilized and sophisticated natives of Angola, *Pongo*, and in that of the Indians of South America, *Oran Outang*" (52).

Sir Oran is a being of natural sentiment and amiable simplicity; he is ingenuous, contemplative, invariably polite, prone to melancholy, and deeply attached to his friends. He is also an instinctually talented musician on the French horn and flute and completely at home in the fashionable world. Mr. Forester has introduced him to the best society, and, he says, "with a view of ensuring him the respect…which always attends on rank and fortune, I have purchased him a baronetcy, and made over to him an estate" (61). Mr. Forester has "also purchased of the Duke of Rottenburgh one half of the elective franchise vested in the body of Mr. Christopher Corporate, the free, fat, and dependent burgess of the ancient and honourable borough of Onevote, who returns two members to Parliament, one of whom will shortly be Sir Oran" (61). A baronet, an MP, a man of feeling, a figure of fashion, and a rescuer of ladies in distress, Sir Oran has only one idiosyncrasy: he has a natural propensity to inebriation. Thus, at the end of the dignified supper with Mr. Forester and Sir Telegraph, where he has behaved with the utmost polite and mannerly attention to Sir Telegraph's comfort, "Sir Oran,…having taken a glass too much, rose suddenly from table, took a flying leap through the window, and went dancing among the woods like a harlequin" (40).

If, for the moment, we take Sir Oran Haut-ton, Baronet, as a compendium of the many materials and effects that created the imaginary animal of eighteenth-century English literature, we can use him to generate a virtual encyclopedia of eclectic references. First, Sir Oran shows us how eighteenth-century writers might evoke animal-kind in order to define and advance prominent concepts of human virtue: in this case the idea of natural sensibility with its signature accoutrements of sympathy, honor, dignity, friendship, contemplation, and melancholy, and its systematic separation from artificial attitudes or civilized structures. These good qualities make Sir Oran "a much better man than many that are to be found in civilized countries" (71). At the same time, however, we might understand Sir Oran as a model for the playful or burlesque or even satiric use of the imaginary animal to undercut such ideals. Such dissonance, as we shall see, is the signature attribute of this prototype. Next, Peacock's classical allusions illustrate the ways in which new depictions of nonhuman animals might lean on antique or established traditions—here the mythological domain of early modern humanism. Sir Oran is represented as an updated version of the sylvan semideity of classical mythology, one "of the very same beings whom the ancients worshipped as divinities under the names of Fauns and Satyrs, Silenus and Pan" (64). Already we can see a tension between Sir Oran as the dignified and contemplative man of feeling, on the one hand, and Sir Oran as a mythological being engaging in his typical "Bacchanalian revelry" as he follows the model of "our friend Pan's attachment to the bottle," on the other (66).[3]

But the catalog of Sir Oran's roles is even more extensive and diverse. Though the river-rescue scene is compatible with the genre of romantic adventure and looks back to the seventeenth-century prose romance, the scene of Sir Oran's election to Parliament as representative of the borough of Onevote—with its political speechifying, public drunkenness, and final mock-epic brawl—is straightforward social satire. Sir Oran's generic affiliations are continuously under revision, and his character slips into and out of burlesque throughout the novel. Meanwhile, though Sir Oran, as "the natural and original man—the wild man of the woods," is defined in relation to a precivilized simplicity, he is also naturally a man of taste and fashion (52): "The theatres [of London] delighted him, particularly the opera, which not only accorded admirably with his taste for music; but where, as he looked round on the ornaments of the fashionable world, he seemed to be particularly comfortable, and to feel himself completely at home" (60). And indeed we see Sir Oran first at Mr. Forester's supper table, where he helps Sir Telegraph "with great dexterity" to a slice of fish and "bow[s] gracefully" as he tosses off the Madeira "with the usual ceremonies" (39). Here, in an allusion to several contemporary travelers' accounts of hominoid apes' behaviors in human settings, the character of Sir Oran suggests that a nonhuman being can perfect the essential arts of human civilization, especially those of the tea and supper table.

At least twice, Sir Oran's appearance generates an ontological shock, a kind of identity crisis, promulgating the idea of human-animal proximity, or the even more surprising notion that a nonhuman being might actually be indistinguishable from a human. When we first see him through Sir Telegraph's eyes, he appears as "that gentleman, sitting under the great oak yonder in the green coat and nankins [who] seems very thoughtful" (37); and again when he first appears to Anthelia she describes him as a "stranger" of "remarkable physiognomy," "unparalleled strength," and "high fashion." Meanwhile, Sir Oran supplies Peacock with an allusion to comparative anatomy, the modern science whose major discoveries regarding the proximity of humankind and the hominoid ape prepared the way for evolutionary thought: "Comparative anatomy shows that he has...in every essential particular, the human form, and the human anatomy" (68). Distinct, but not unrelated, is Peacock's use of Sir Oran to evoke and support a particular interpretation of the Platonistic chain of being; namely, the erosion

---

[3] Marilyn Butler observes the problems generated by the satyr connection, noting the strange inversion in which "the satyr behaves like a gentleman." Marilyn Butler, *Peacock Displayed: A Satirist in His Context* (London: Routledge and Kegan Paul, 1979), 69.

of the idea of the immutable gradations of the chain in favor of the possibility of the transformation of species. Thus Sir Telegraph exclaims: "Your Oran rises rapidly in the scale of being:—from a Baronet and M.P. to a king of the world, and now to a god of the woods" (65). Sir Oran also gives Peacock an opportunity to invoke the major eighteenth-century taxonomists, Carolus Linnaeus and George-Louis Leclerc, Comte de Buffon, and their understanding of the biological classification of the anthropoid ape (62–63).

In addition, Sir Oran embodies the modern question of the role of speech in defining the human, or, more broadly, the nature of language in relation to human and nonhuman being. Peacock's text follows verse and line of contemporary debates on language in recounting that Sir Oran lacks speech but has the physiological organs and full potential for learning to speak, that he does not yet speak because speech is a "highly artificial" and difficult accomplishment of civilized man, that he is an expert musician because music is "more natural to man than speech," and that Mr. Forester is wishing and even expecting "to put a few words into his mouth" (68, 57, 61). But in a very different vein, Sir Oran's failure to speak is seen as a dimension of his "contemplative disposition," which is an allusion to the type of the "mute philosopher," a broad reference to classical traditions of silence from the Stoics to the Pythagoreans (37).[4] For these traditions, of course, silence is a desideratum rather than a defect to be remedied.

Mr. Forester's benevolent adoption and protection of the orangutan references the contemporary humanitarian movements that advocated the custodianship of animals and resulted in proposals for anticruelty legislation and eventually in the founding of the Society for the Prevention of Cruelty to Animals. On the other hand, Sir Oran's love for Anthelia and his catching her in his arms during the river-rescue scene closely reproduce a disturbing contemporary fantasy of ape-human miscegenation, in which orangutan were said to carry off women to "their woody retreats, in order to enjoy them."[5] Indeed, the text specifically signals this anxiety by describing Anthelia's "apprehension" in regard to the orangutan. Even though this apprehension is "diminished" by Sir Oran's reassuring behavior, the idea of inter-species miscegenation and of the violence that would accompany it is a vital contemporary image whose currency strongly affects the significance of this imaginary animal. Furthermore, Sir Oran's obvious attraction to Anthelia throughout the novel, especially notable as he shadows her nature walk, "peeping at her through the trees" (102), and in his final exercise of "boundless" wrath on her abductors in the last scene at Alga Castle, makes him a rival for Anthelia's love (449). Here again, Peacock's

---

[4] Reference to silence also evokes the indigenous stories retailed in earlier travel literature: that the orangutan is a human who refuses to speak to avoid work or slavery. See H. W. Janson, *Apes and Ape Lore in the Middle Ages and the Renaissance* (London: Warburg Institute, 1952), 275, 337.
[5] Edward Long, *The History of Jamaica*, vol. 2 (London: T. Lowndes, 1774), 360.

text plays down the effects of this rivalry; Sir Oran is only a proxy for Mr. Forester, Anthelia's perfect and uncontested future husband. But the notion of the animal proxy for a human lover is another vivid contemporary image, especially relevant to female pet keeping, to which Peacock's orangutan directly alludes.

In short, Peacock's Sir Oran provides an object lesson in the flexibility of the representation of animal-kind in the modern period. In this single imaginary animal we can find an anthropomorphic projection of human virtue as well as a fearful vision of violent alterity. We can read the orangutan as a playful experiment in species transformation, where the human can try on the identity of the nonhuman being and vice versa. We can take Peacock's account of the nonhuman animal as a practical lesson in contemporary taxonomic method and anatomical practice, as an intervention in theories of the nature of language, or as an expression of new conceptualizations of the life sciences that opened avenues for evolutionist thought. Sir Oran stands for the moral good of benevolent custodianship, but also for the sudden, troubling ontological undecidability inherent in the human discovery of the hominoid ape. He foils any attempt to find a coherent meaning in the imaginary animal or to attach a single significance to the appearance of the animal in literary representation.

In this book I will examine many of those eighteenth-century precedents in the representation of imaginary animals that directly inform and anticipate Sir Oran's multiple meanings, including the sometimes extreme anthropomorphism proposed by Jakob de Bondt, Edward Tyson, Richard Blackmore, and Thomas Boreman; the troubling or even terrifying alterities evoked by Alexander Pope, Jonathan Swift, John Arbuthnot, and Edward Long; the negotiations with identity, exchange, and transformation proposed by Jonas Hanway, Sarah Scott, Frances Burney, Susanna Centlivre, and Francis Coventry; the taxonomies laid out by Linnaeus and Buffon; the moral advocacy for animal custodianship asserted by Edward Kendall; and the linguistic theories developed by James Burnet, Lord Monboddo. As we shall see, Peacock self-consciously generates his imaginary orangutan out of these preceding forms and themes: Sir Oran is in this respect true to the eighteenth-century experience of the imaginary animal in all of its complexity. But Sir Oran also projects this experience into the future. Indeed, Sir Oran's successors are uncountable; they constitute a vast realm of literary representation—popular and canonical—that plays out this distinctive modern engagement with images of animal-kind. Among anthropoid apes, for instance, a rapid list of local highlights might include Sir Walter Scott's Sylvan of *Count Robert of Paris* (1832), Edgar Allen Poe's orangutan murderer in *The Murders in the Rue Morgue* (1841), Franz Kafka's Rotpeter in *A Report to an Academy* (1917), Edgar Rice Burroughs's *Tarzan of the Apes* (1914), and of course King Kong of the internationally influential film of that name (1933). The portrayal of the anthropoid ape, however, represents only one stream in a flood of lyrical, narrative, anecdotal, and autobiographical accounts of intimate, immediate, personal, and contemporary interactions with animal-kind. These accounts swell the canonical and popular press from the early nineteenth century onward, from Sarah Trimmer's *Fabulous Histories, Designed for the Instruction of Children, Respecting Their Treatment of Animals* (1796) and Joseph Taylor's *General Character of the Dog* (1804), with its sequels *Canine Gratitude* (1806) and *Four-Footed Friends* (1828); and from William Wordsworth's *Fidelity* (1805) and Elizabeth Barrett Browning's *To Flush, My Dog* (1844); to today's explosion of diverse narrative sub-genres: the rescue-dog stories, detective-fiction dogs, sheepdog trial dogs, supernatural-thriller dogs, and memoirs of dogs, along with the parallel repertory of cat genres, and not to mention the substantial bibliography of imaginative works on pigs, horses, wolves, bears, and birds.[6] This extensive cultural event—the rise of the nonhuman animal in the modern literary imagination—takes its shape in the eighteenth century, in the literature that comprises Sir Oran's immediate predecessors. Those earlier works, fewer and more venturous for their time, can be used to examine some of the core ways in which animals enter the modern imagination and alter its products. And like Peacock's orangutan, these experiments in the portrayal of the nonhuman being are flexible, complex, and resistant to a singular understanding of the status or meaning of the animal. Thus they are not readily contained by the set of positions typical of many of the current approaches to the topic of the human-animal relationship—approaches that often oppose anthropomorphism to alterity, or a human-associated to a human-alienating approach to the nonhuman.

Anthropomorphism and Alienation

The modern understanding of the nonhuman being is often built on this opposition between anthropomorphism and alienation—on the long Western tradition of human-animal dichotomization. Richard Sorabji has provided a full history of "the origins of the Western debate" in his account of the treatment of reason in regard to nonhuman animals in classical philosophy of mind. He argues that Aristotle's denial of reason to animals led to a crisis in the understanding of perception, and thence to "a massive re-analysis of psychological capacities: of perception, of perceptual appearance, of belief, of concept-possession, of memory, of intention and preparation, of anger and other emotions, and of speech."[7] On the other hand, Sorabji shows, the long

---

[6] For a summary of nineteenth-century materials, see Barbara T. Gates, *Kindred Nature: Victorian and Edwardian Women Embrace the Living World* (Chicago: University of Chicago Press, 1998), 220–230, and Teresa Magnum, "Dog Years, Human Fears," in *Representing Animals: Theories of Contemporary Culture*, ed. Nigel Rothfels (Bloomington: Indiana University Press, 2002), 35–47.
[7] Richard Sorabji, *Animal Minds and Human Morals: The Origins of the Western Debate* (Ithaca, N.Y.: Cornell University Press, 1993), 103.

debate generated by the Aristotelian position was variously countered by the views of the Pythagoreans, the Cynics, and the Platonists. Plato's long-standing interest in the idea that animals may be reincarnated humans tended to imply their possession of a rational soul (Sorabji, 10). Similarly, the Pythagoreans and in particular the Pythagorean Empedocles, in opposing meat eating and animal sacrifice, countered the Aristotelian alienation of human from animal by proposing that "we are made of the same elements, one breath permeates us all," and that "we are quite literally akin, because the dog you are beating could be a friend, or presumably a relative, reincarnated." And the Cynic philosopher, Diogenes of Sinope, who went by the nickname of "dog," was an advocate of the claim that animals are superior to humans, a position that is taken up by the Platonist Plutarch (Sorabji, 173, 131, 160).[8]

In the early modern period, the influential positions staked out by Descartes and Montaigne have often been used to map these same contrasting poles for the subsequent debates of modernity. For Descartes, whose central category is the rational soul, the animal is activated solely by "the corporeal and mechanical principle," which he opposes to the "incorporeal principle" or "thinking substance" that defines the human; animals are natural "automatons" for which "we cannot at all prove the presence of a thinking soul."[9] The core test of this difference for Descartes is the capacity for language: "There is no other animal, however perfect and well-endowed it may be, that can [make their thoughts understood in speech]....This shows not merely that the beasts have less reason than men, but that they have no reason at all....Their souls [are] completely different in nature from ours." And the crucial consequence is the exclusion of animal-kind from an afterlife:

[The rational soul] cannot be derived in any way from the potentiality of matter, but must be specially created....After the error of those who deny God,...there is none that leads weak minds further from the straight path of virtue than that of imagining that the souls of the beasts are of the same nature as ours, and hence after this present life we have nothing to fear or to hope for, any more than flies and ants. But when we know how much the beasts differ from us, we understand much better the arguments which prove that our soul

---

[8] James Serpell provides a thumbnail account of the classical and early modern positions on animals, summarizing Richard Sorabji and Keith Thomas, *Man and the Natural World: A History of the Modern Sensibility* (New York: Pantheon, 1983). See Serpell, *In the Company of Animals: A Study of Human-Animal Relationships* (1986; repr. Cambridge: Cambridge University Press, 1996), 147–168. Nussbaum cautions that the intervention of Judeo-Christian views strongly shaped the impact of the classical tradition on animals (328–329).

[9] René Descartes, Letter to More, 5 February 1649, in *The Philosophical Writings of Descartes*, vol. 3, trans. John Cottingham, Robert Stoothoff, and Dugald Murdoch (Cambridge: Cambridge University Press, 1984–1991), 365, 366.

is of a nature entirely independent of the body, and consequently that it is not bound to die with it.[10]

In Montaigne's thought, on the other hand, humans and nonhuman animals are on a path toward convergence. Deeply comparable in sensibility, playfulness, and even communication, these beings are sometimes for Montaigne even difficult to distinguish from one another: "When I play with my cat, who can say that it is not she amusing herself with me more than I with her?...This deficiency that prevents communication between them and us, why is it not in us as much as in them?"[11] And significantly, in describing his sympathetic connection with animals, Montaigne too takes up the notion of the soul:

Pythagoras borrowed the doctrine of metempsychosis from the Egyptians; but since then, it has been accepted by many nations....The religion of our ancient Gauls held that men's souls, being eternal, never ceased to move and change place from one body to another....When I meet, among the more moderate opinions, with arguments whose purpose is to prove the close resemblance between ourselves and animals, and how largely they share in our greatest advantages, and with how much likelihood they are compared to us, I certainly then abate much of our presumption, and readily resign that imaginary sovereignty over other creatures which is attributed to us.[12]

The tendency either to alienation or to association is strongly evident in the modern study of the natural world, from the Darwinian revolution in natural history that generated a new science of human-animal proximity to the rise of ethology and the formulation of behavioral animal studies, whose inductive methodology erects an absolute barrier between animal and human. Sorabji sees Darwin's *Descent of Man* as the modern analogue of Pythagorean ideas of reincarnation, "the claim of literal kinship" between human and animal. Darwin, Sorabji argues, "defends his thesis of the Descent of Man from the apes...by insisting that animals differ from man only in degree. No characteristic, he maintains...is unique to man, not emotion, curiosity, imitation, attention, memory, imagination, reason, progressive improvement, tool use, abstraction, self-consciousness, language, sense of beauty, belief in the supernatural, nor moral sense" (131). On the other hand, speaking for modern behavioral

[10] Descartes, "Discourse on the Method" (1737) in *The Philosophical Writings of Descartes*, vol. 1, 140–141.
[11] Michel de Montaigne, "Apology for Raimond Sebond" (1580) in *The Essays of Montaigne*, vol. 2, trans. George B. Ives (Cambridge, Mass.: Harvard University Press, 1925), 202.
[12] Montaigne, "Of Cruelty" (1580) in *The Essays of Montaigne*, vol. 2, 167.

animal studies, William T. Keeton's basic textbook in biology warns that "we must constantly guard against unwarranted attribution of human characteristics to other species."[13] And John S. Kennedy's polemical reassertion of the argument against anthropomorphism in *The New Anthropomorphism* (1992) enjoins readers: "If the study of animal behaviour is to mature as a science, the process of liberation from the delusions of anthropomorphism must go on."[14]

The alienation of human from animal is further sustained, though in a very different register, by the philosophical problem of the privacy of mind—the skepticism regarding the possibility of knowing what passes in minds not our own. For example, in accounting for the problem of the privacy of pain in "Knowing and Acknowledging" (1969), Stanley Cavell offers his own characterization of the skeptic's real sense of incapacity when encountering another person's feeling. The result is the "gesture towards [the] self": "I am filled with [the] feeling…of our separateness…and I want you to have it too."[15] Descartes himself refers to this impasse as he reflects on his denial of reason to animal-kind: "Though I regard it as established that we cannot prove there is any thought in animals, I do not think it can be proved that there is none, since the human mind does not reach into their hearts."[16] Though for Descartes the privacy of mind does not support (or refute) his conclusion that animals are automata, it sustains affectively the alienation of human from animal that the Cartesian principle argues logically.

Thus, within and also well beyond modern philosophical discourse, the animal mind has been a focus of intense speculation and a test case for thinking about the subjectivity of minds not our own. Thomas Nagel's well-known essay on the importance of subjectivity, "What Is It Like to Be a Bat?" (1974), famously considers the experience of a specific nonhuman being in order to explore the divergence between subjective and objective. On the one hand, as a mammal, the bat approaches proximity to the human in that "we all believe that bats have experience." On the other hand, bats diverge sharply from the human because of their use of echolocation; in this respect they are "a fundamentally *alien* form of life." Thus Nagel argues that we cannot "extrapolate to the inner life of the bat"; it has "a specific subjective character, which it is beyond our ability to conceive." But on the other hand, we can know that "there is something that it is like to be a bat."[17] Nagel's animal example thus provides a paradigm for the importance of the subjective character of experience—in that we know both that it exists and that it is inconceivable.

[13] William T. Keeton, *Biological Science* (New York: W. W. Norton, 1967), 452.
[14] John S. Kennedy, *The New Anthropomorphism* (Cambridge: Cambridge University Press, 1992), 5.
[15] Stanley Cavell, *Must We Mean What We Say?* (1969; repr., Cambridge: Cambridge University Press, 1976), 262–263.
[16] Descartes, Letter to More, in *The Philosophical Writings of Descartes*, vol. 3, 365.
[17] Thomas Nagel, "What Is It Like to Be a Bat?" *The Philosophical Review* 83 (1974): 435–450, 438, 439.

The critical, cultural, and environmental theory of the end of the twentieth and the beginning of the twenty-first century that takes up the issue of animal-kind can also be parsed in terms of this dichotomy between human-associated and human-alienating approaches. A very selective account of this writing can help to illustrate the continuing strength of the dichotomy. In the context of Anglo-American critical theory, the human-alienating perspective is often signaled by the designation of the nonhuman being as the "other." Indeed, the animal-as-other has become a common extrapolation of that very influential human category derived from twentieth-century anthropology and cultural theory. The idea of the "other" reflects the development and manipulation—often through psychoanalysis or Marxist theory—of the Hegelian dialectic between subjective and objective, idea and nature, or master and slave. In all these recent contexts the other usually has a constitutive function in relation to the non-other: the psychic self or the identity of the colonizer is produced through the projection or subjection of the other. Designed originally to define the human self or the claims to power of the human subject, the concept of the other is thus conceived within the realm of human consciousness.

Paul Shepard's *The Others: How Animals Made Us Human* (1996) recruits this idea in support of deep environmentalism. Shepard writes out of "respect for that which is unbridgeable between ourselves and the animals" and describes his position as "an attitude of accepted separateness." But his aim is to demonstrate that the human is ecologically, evolutionarily, cognitively, cosmologically, and psychically created by and through connection with nonhuman animals. His accounts of the human in all these realms serve to "confirm difference in a way that relates us to animals but does not assume that we understand them." The letter signed by *"The Others"* that closes Shepard's book thus adopts an entirely human epistolary discourse to warn: "When we have gone they will not know who they are."[18]

The claim to authenticity is a hallmark of this human-alienating idea of the animal-as-other. Building on the important concept of "becoming-animal" introduced in Gilles Deleuze and Félix Guattari's *A Thousand Plateaus* (1980), Steve Baker has argued that a study of the role of the animal in postmodern visual culture can supply a definition of both the human-animal relationship and the aesthetics of postmodernism. In Baker's analysis, postmodern art is an "unthinking or undoing of the conventionally human." This form of creativity is evident in postmodern representations of animals, which entail a performance of "becoming-animal"—a representation that is "swept up in something of the animal's difference and distance from the human," and that generates a "radical un-humaning of animals" that is "discouraging [of] anthropomorphic

[18] Paul Shepard, *The Others: How Animals Made Us Human* (Washington, D.C.: Island Press, 1996), 5, 7, 333.

identifications" and anthropocentric meanings. By this means, Baker argues, these works of art can obtain access to "the truth and immediacy of these animals" and thus can serve as a direct recording of "precisely that animal's reality." They should be understood then as enacting a literal "sense of responsibility to the animal."[19]

But Donna Haraway's sense of responsibility is directly opposed to the human-alienating scenario. In various ways, her works resist paradigms of radical differentiation. *Primate Visions* (1989) employs the methods of postcolonial studies to expose the modern use of the animal for the ends of capitalism, imperialism, technology, and patriarchy. Evoking Said's orientalism, Haraway argues that modern primatology—"simian orientalism"—can be understood as an appropriation of the ape in the form of the other, an appropriation that has served to constitute modern culture. Haraway's summary statement illustrates the extent of her reliance on the idea of the postcolonial other, which operates in a range of repeated contrasts:

> Primatology has been about the construction of the self from the raw material of the other, the appropriation of nature in the production of culture, the ripening of the human from the soil of the animal, the clarity of white from the obscurity of color, the issue of man from the body of woman, the elaboration of gender from the resource of sex, the emergence of mind by the activation of body.[20]

In this book, Haraway makes clear her "distaste for [these] endlessly socially enforced dualisms" (Haraway, *Visions*, 3). In *When Species Meet* (2008) she moves on to active advocacy of a human-associated approach to the "messmates," "companions," or "partners" of humans among animal-kind. Here, Haraway takes up another concept from postcolonial studies: the mediating paradigms of the contact zone or of transculturation, made influential through the works of Mary Louise Pratt and James Clifford. Haraway designates this human-animal association through the notion of "becoming with"—a phrase that expresses a "coshaping" of identities and behaviors, and which refers to complexity, reciprocity, "intra- and interaction," and "multispecies knots."[21] "Becoming with" is based in touch, in "the making each other available to events," and in the inheritance of common histories, and it results in "accountability, caring for, being affected, and entering into responsibility" (Haraway, *Species* 36, 27). In practice, Haraway's

[19] Steve Baker, "What Does Becoming-Animal Look Like?" in *Representing Animals*, ed. Nigel Rothfels (Bloomington: Indiana University Press, 2002), 67–98, 80, 96, 95, 88, 89.
[20] Donna Haraway, *Primate Visions: Gender, Race, and Nature in the World of Modern Science* (New York: Routledge, 1989), 11.
[21] Donna Haraway, *When Species Meet* (Minneapolis: University of Minnesota Press, 2008), 42, 4, 35.

evidence and proving ground for this relationship is behavioral animal training—"the naturalcultural art, of training for sport with a dog" (Haraway, *Species,* 226).

Significantly, Haraway directly dismisses both Deleuze and Guattari's "becoming-animal" and Derrida's "animal that therefore I am," in both cases for their human-alienating implications. She finds that, though Deleuze and Guattari work, as she does, "to get beyond the Great Divide between humans and other critters to find the rich multiplicities and topologies of a heterogeneously and nonteleologically connected world," they symptomatically fail to achieve this aim in any genuine way because of their inability "to take earthly animals...seriously," because of their scorn, disdain, and even horror for the homely, ordinary, daily, affectional lives of animals (Haraway, *Species,* 27, 29, 30). Meanwhile, for Haraway, Derrida as well, though correct to reject "the facile and basically imperialist...move of claiming to see from the point of view of the other," stops too soon and fails to consider "an alternative form of engagement," residing instead too much on his side of what he himself characterizes as "the abyssal limit of the human."[22] Derrida thus "failed a simple obligation of companion species: he did not become curious about what the cat might actually be doing, feeling, thinking, or perhaps making available to him in looking back at him that morning" (Haraway, *Species,* 21, 20).

Haraway's criticism shows that she ultimately understands the post-structuralist view—in which the animal is thought in terms of aporia, self-difference, or antifoundational multiplicity—to be a human-alienating position, one that rejects any simple or direct forms of engagement, communication, or proximity between animal and human. And like Haraway, other recent Anglo-American cultural and literary critics have also invoked the continental tradition to support versions of this radically alien positioning of the animal. Cary Wolfe's *Animal Rites* (2003), for instance, leaning on Derrida's "animal that therefore I am," works from the grounding assertion of the abyssal rupture entailed by the other-than-human. Wolfe seeks to make this idea of radical animal alterity into the preeminent category of post-structuralist difference or heterogeneity by arguing that what "Derrida is struggling to say [is] that the animal difference is...not just any difference among others; it is, we might say, the most different difference, and therefore the most instructive." Wolfe's own struggle to bring this "posthumanist" understanding of the animal to bear upon questions of ethics leads him to emphasize the embeddedness of the "inhuman" in post-structuralist thinking in regard to the human, a move that almost brings the human-alienating position around full circle to the human-associated view. Citing Derrida especially, Wolfe claims that the animal "resides at the core of the human itself [as]...the 'trace'...that inhabits it," as "the outside

[22] Jacques Derrida, "The Animal That Therefore I Am (More to Follow)," *Critical Inquiry* 28 (2002): 369–418, 381.

that is always already inside," or the "non-power at the heart of power."[23] This near-full circle explains how Wolfe could begin a study designed to track the radical alterity of the animal with a strongly human-associated evocation of contemporary popular views (from *Time, Newsweek,* and *U.S. News and World Report*) of the breakdown of human-animal boundaries through accounts of experiments demonstrating animal subjectivity, cognition, altruism, and linguistic innovation. In the end, however, Wolfe's theoretical claims as he develops them in *Animal Rites* simply contradict these empirical, experiential, hands-on human-animal associations, which occupy a mode of understanding the animal that is ultimately incompatible with the philosophical discourse that generates the radical abyss of the post-structuralist animal-as-other.

As Wolfe's attention to Derrida indicates, some literary critics treat animal studies as an immediate successor to deconstruction by interpreting the critique of language and subjectivity through the lens of the human/animal difference, thus recreating post-structuralism as posthumanism. The 2009 *PMLA* issue on animal studies features several essays that echo these themes: that the animal embodies radical difference, that that difference is constitutive of the human, that we are always already radically inhuman, and that the idea of the animal challenges not only claims to humanity but also claims to agency and knowledge, including those assertions of moral certitude that defend the rights of animals.[24] The posthumanist view thus forces alterity and identity—the human-alienating and the human-associated positions that we have been pursuing from Descartes to Montesquieu—into one intensely aporetic depiction of the animal. And thus, like Wolfe, critics pursuing this perspective often express a strong allegiance to the human-associated position.

Not surprisingly, trainers, describing an immediate hands-on engagement with animals, have been the most direct advocates of the human-associated position. As we have seen, Haraway's "becoming with," in *When Species Meet,* directly recounts the experience of agility training. Vicki Hearne, an animal trainer and poet turned philosopher-theorist, had also drawn on her background as an animal trainer to propose a strongly antiskeptical and antialienating perspective. In fact, as the field of animal studies develops a canon, Hearne's *Adam's Task* (1987) has become recognized as the pioneering synthesis of moral philosophy, poetic impulse, and animal advocacy in the service of a strongly asserted human-associated argument. The core of Hearne's contribution is an engagement with language and communication. She takes up as an opening question

[23] Cary Wolfe, *Animal Rites: American Culture, the Discourse of Species, and Posthumanist Theory* (Chicago: University of Chicago Press, 2003), 67, 17, 72, 67, quoting Derrida.
[24] See *PMLA* 124 (2009): Susan McHugh, "Literary Animal Agents," 487–495; Una Chaudhuri, "Of All Nonsensical Things: Performance and Animal Life," 520–525; Rosi Braidotti, "Animals, Anomalies, and Inorganic Others," 526–521; Bruce Boehrer, "Animal Studies and the Deconstruction of Character," 542–547; Cary Wolfe, "Human, All Too Human: 'Animal Studies' and the Humanities," 564–575.

the anthropomorphic language of animal trainers, and moves on to her own operative category—the idea of inter-species "talking" or "conversation." Talking expresses her investment in the active participation and communication between trainer and animal. This is a form of communication that generates for Hearne a kind of knowledge— "knowledge of the loop of intention and openness that talk is, knowledge of and in language."[25] Hearne's "talking" evokes a respect for animal consciousness, intelligence, morality, courage, and even heroism, and leads to "transformations that are psychically miraculous," most especially the transformation "that takes the trainer and the animal out of the moral life and comforts of its patent goods into the life of art, a life of uncertain value but characterized by genuine risks and diamond-hard responses and unprecedented responsibilities" (245). Influenced by Cavell's ideas about doubt, language, and understanding, Hearne acknowledges the "problem of the other," but expresses this skepticism not as a problem of "knowing the other" but as a function of our own "unreadiness to be understood," "our making mysteries of ourselves with the aid of science and philosophy." Horses, for example, have a "capacity to feel our presence incomparably beyond our ability to feel theirs"; our "denial of our own knowability" by the horse, our "will to remain obscure" to the animal, express only our own failure to engage in the human-animal conversation of training.[26] This is a failure to grasp "true knowledge" (115).

Language is a core criterion, then, in these approaches to the dichotomy of the human-animal relationship, not only in cultural and critical theory but in the life sciences as well. Eileen Crist's *Images of Animals* (1999) argues that in behavioral thought, from natural science to ethology to sociobiology, "particular linguistic mediums" have played a powerful and formative role in "the creation of alternative visions of animals." In readings of selected texts, from Darwin to twentieth-century sociobiology, Crist distinguishes the "ordinary language of action and mind," often labeled as anthropomorphism, from the technical language of behavior. The first represents animals as subjects possessed of "knowledge, emotion, intention, thinking, and memory"; it "advances a powerful view of animal life as experientially meaningful, authored, and temporally cohesive and articulates a compelling argument for human-animal evolutionary continuity....[It offers] the understanding of animal life in semantic kinship with the human world." The second tends to remove "authorship from the animal world"; as a result "animals appear mindless...[and] the conceptual space for a tacit or explicit attribution of mentality drastically shrinks." This latter mode of discourse both reflects and also serves to construct the version

[25]Vicki Hearne, *Adam's Task: Calling Animals by Name* (New York: Knopf, 1987), 85.
[26] Ibid., 114–115. The third and fifth of these quoted passages are from a personal letter from Cavell, reproduced by Hearne.

of mind-body dualism that, Crist argues, has generated an "oppositional conception of the human and animal nature": an absolute distinction between action and behavior—the former being mindful, meaningful, and human, and the latter being unintentional, physiological, and animal.[27]

Even within the field of animal behavioral studies, then, some researchers advocate a rehabilitated anthropomorphism, a concern with continuities between animal and human mental capacities. In *Anthropomorphism, Anecdotes, and Animals*, a collection on the newly visible debate about the uses and abuses of anthropomorphism, Frans B. M. De Waal's foreword summarizes the dichotomy at hand:

> Students of animal behavior are faced with a choice between classifying animals as automatons or granting them volition and information-processing capacities. Whereas one school warns against assuming things we cannot prove, another school warns against leaving out what may be there....Inasmuch as descriptions [of volition and awareness] place animals closer to us than to machines, they adopt a language we customarily use for human action. Inevitably, these descriptions sound anthropomorphic.[28]

The authors of the book's introduction describe both the earlier engagement with and the renewed interest in animal consciousness, observing that "attitudes towards these approaches to understanding animals are changing within the scientific community" (3).

As we have seen, the imaginary Sir Oran Haut-ton, Baronet, is very far from this debate. His multiple meanings intersect and diverge unpredictably, comically, ironically, or satirically, making it impossible either to assign him entirely to the world of the other or to embrace him as a partner or fellow animal, and rendering irrelevant those categories of authenticity, immediacy, respect, and responsibility that have served to valorize one side or the other of the human-animal debate. The perspectives developed from the conflicting representations of the nonhuman animal in science, philosophy, and cultural and critical theory are not much help as we try to understand the fantasies of animal-kind presented in the literature of Sir Oran's era. Guided by the figure of Sir Oran, we might hypothesize that, unlike the animals given to us by theory, science, and philosophy—which are either absolutely alien or intimately familiar—the representations of animal-kind in the literary culture of this period offer a diverse range of formal, thematic, rhetorical, and generic innovations that resemble each other

---

[27] Eileen Crist, *Images of Animals: Anthropomorphism and Animal Mind* (Philadelphia: Temple University Press, 1999), 8, 204, 202, 203, 214.
[28] Frans B. M. De Waal, forward to Robert W. Mitchell, Nicholas S. Thompson, and H. Lyn Miles, eds., *Anthropomorphism, Anecdotes, and Animals* (Albany: State University of New York Press, 1997), xv.

not in their adherence to either a human-alienating or human-associated perspective, but in their dissonance—in their tendency to surprise, to invert, to challenge, or to experiment with expected modes of order and stable structures of meaning.[29] In this dissonance, Sir Oran and his eighteenth-century predecessors establish their own models for the imaginary animal—models that take a different tack from and shed new light on the opposition between anthropomorphism and alienation, and that provide a distinctive understanding of both the human-animal relationship and the animal's role in history.

Humans and Other Animals in Human History

Anthropological and archaeological approaches to animals have proposed an intimate, even constitutive, connection between human culture and the representation of animal-kind. In summarizing his argument that the metaphoric use of the "totemic" animal represents a complex embodiment of "ideas and relations conceived by speculative thought" rather than simply an arbitrary symbol or an indication of a potential food source, Lévi-Strauss produced a now widely cited aphorism: that animals are selected for human cultural activities "not because they are 'good to eat' but because they are 'good to think.'"[30] Thinking about animals is a uniquely human trait—a mode of imagining that seems to have emerged with the development of human culture. Steven Mithen, in his study of "the prehistory of human-animal interaction," produces a theory of the representation of animals that suggests the historical centrality of imaginary animal-kind to human evolution itself. For Mithen, the human-animal relationship—as a cultural phenomenon and as a conceptual problematic—is a core evolutionary event. He claims that humans have moved "beyond the predator, competitor and prey relationships that other animals experience into a whole new world of inter-species interactions that are unique to ourselves." For Mithen, "the course of our biological and cultural evolution is indeed intimately tied up with the emergence of those new inter-species relationships" that are grounded in the realm of representation:[31]

[29] Christine Kenyon-Jones argues in a similar way that literary representations of animals can "have an advantage over cultural history, anthropology, sociology and scientific disciplines" by offering "a space in which human creativity can experiment with different ideas about animals, without claiming for itself a specious (speciesist?) 'rightness' or 'correctness' about what is being done." She also notes "animals' capacity for consolidating, challenging and reforming human ideas and cultures." *Kindred Brutes: Animals in Romantic-Period Writing* (Aldershot, UK: Ashgate, 2001), 8–9.
[30] Claude Lévi-Strauss, *Totemism*, trans. Rodney Needham (1962; repr. Boston: Beacon Press, 1971), 89.
[31] Steven Mithen, "The Hunter-Gatherer Prehistory of Human Animal Interaction," *Anthrozoös* 12 (1999): 195–204, 195, 201.

The first modern humans…developed that diverse range of relationships with animals that we see in the modern world today. One of the key mental developments lying behind these new relationships seems to be that of anthropomorphizing animals. As long ago as 500,000 years ago, our human ancestors are likely to have evolved a theory of mind: interpreting the behavior of other human individuals by attributing to them beliefs and desires different to one's own.…This ability would have been essential for the development of more complex human societies.…After 50,000 years ago, it seems that this way of thinking was also applied to animal minds, one manifestation of what I have termed the emergence of "cognitive fluidity."…In this regard, by attributing animals with human-like minds, those animals were brought into the world of human culture and society. (126)

In other words, imaginary animal-kind has both created complex human society and also given animals themselves a role in human history—the potential to affect and alter human culture.

As in human prehistory, in human history thinking about nonhuman animals has been a generative activity, shaped by the conditions of the particular historical moment, but in turn informing the realm of human culture. An examination of distinctive fantasies of animal-kind thus engages both the cultural impact and the historical role of the animal. For eighteenth-century England, imaginary animals reflect a new historical experience and indicate a new mode of understanding, distinct from the concrete experiences and structures of thought characteristic of the medieval and early modern representations of the natural world. The assessment of the change in the mode of thought from the early modern to the modern period has been shaped by Foucault's account of the turn away from the "age of similitude" in the mid-seventeenth century.[32] William B. Ashworth has defined this cultural shift specifically from the perspectives of natural history and the representation of animals. What Ashworth calls "the emblematic world view" dominates the late-Renaissance perspective on the natural world and is evident in the humanist discourse of the Renaissance encyclopedists Conrad Gesner and Ulisse Aldrovandi. Theirs is "a discipline forged in the library with the bibliographic tools of the scholar," characterized by the collation of symbolic, metaphorical, and emblematic materials, whose goal is "to capture the entire web of associations that inextricably links human culture and the animal world."[33] The works of emblematic natural history are

[32] Michel Foucault, *The Order of Things: An Archaeology of the Human Sciences* (New York: Pantheon, 1970).
[33] William B. Ashworth Jr., "Emblematic Natural History of the Renaissance," in *The Cultures of Natural History*, ed. Nicholas Jardine, J. Anne Secord, and Emma C. Spary (Cambridge: Cambridge University Press, 1996), 17–37, 19, 35.

complex exegetical compilations of classical mythology, associative images, Aesopian symbolism, adages, devices, and emblems.

Ashworth argues that this approach to the representation of animals is transformed in the mid-seventeenth century by the appearance of the first documentation of new-world animals in natural histories—animals who had "no known similitudes" and no "emblematic significances" to be collated. When the representation of old-world animals was adapted to match the model of new-world descriptions, suddenly "the Old World animals lay naked to the observer's eye for the first time."[34] Meanwhile, even for the earlier encyclopedists the use of naturalistic images within their emblematic texts diverged fundamentally from the exclusively symbolic bestiary illustrations of the medieval period. Their interest in carefully naturalistic illustrations seems to have derived from the botanical images of medicinal books, where accurate representation was essential to the identification of particular plants. Combined with a new engagement with empirical thinking, and new efforts to test the truth of the associative and symbolic information gathered by the Renaissance natural historians, these impulses turned the project and discourse of natural history decisively away from an emblematic understanding, and the meanings and significances of animals took an entirely different direction.

This major shift in the understanding of the natural world is implicated in and contemporaneous with historical novelty—with the concrete new encounters between human and nonhuman beings that mark the eighteenth century as a decisive moment in the understanding and representation of animal-kind. Social and cultural historians of this period have accumulated evidence for this new engagement with the animal in a range of studies. Harriet Ritvo has focused on the "new human assertiveness" toward animals connected with the development of stock breeding, the rise of the life sciences, and the major taxonomic systems of the eighteenth century. She describes this period as indicating a "fundamental shift in the relationship between humans and their fellow creatures." Keith Thomas treats a range of themes that demonstrate the changes in attitude toward animals that take place in the period up to 1800 and that generate what he terms the "modern sensibility," including the rise of empiricism, the development of biological classification, the creation of the companion animal, the speculation about animal souls, the effects of urbanization, and the pursuit of humanitarianism. J. H. Plumb believes the new eighteenth-century practice of pet keeping to be a key factor in the "acceptance of modernity." Londa Schiebinger describes the "excitement and confusion" of eighteenth-century taxonomists as they sought to confer order on a natural world that was being strangely reshaped by the discovery of the hominoid

[34]William B. Ashworth Jr., "Natural History and the Emblematic World View," in *Reappraisals of the Scientific Revolution,* ed. David D. Lindberg and Robert S. Westman (Cambridge: Cambridge University Press, 1990), 303–332, 318, 319.

ape. Philip Armstrong focuses on the role of scientific experimentalism in generating the "radical" "shift in human-animal relations occurring in Europe in the eighteenth century"—a shift that is felt most directly in the "confusion of this boundary between wild anthropomorph and human." Ingrid H. Tague argues that eighteenth-century epitaphs and elegies for animals demonstrate the widespread practice of pet keeping in the period. And H. W. Janson's classic study of "ape lore" has demonstrated the impact on the modern imagination of the "discovery" of the hominoid ape, whose "formal entry…into the consciousness of Western civilisation" he dates to 1699.[35]

These and other studies suggest that the experience of nonhuman animals was dramatically reshaped by two major and related historical phenomena that coincided in this period: the discovery of the hominoid ape and the rise of widespread bourgeois pet keeping. In each case, animals entered the space and consciousness of human beings in a distinctively new way. The discovery of the hominoid ape grew out of the globalizing context of mercantile capitalism, through travel, trade, and exploration, and gave rise to an explosion of popular and scientific speculation about the relationship between humans and nonhuman animals that threw European thought into "turmoil," and that ultimately led to the development of theories of evolution (Thomas, 129). Contact with the hominoid ape thus worked in the realm of concept and cognition to raise problems of ontology and to disrupt accepted ideas of human identity or genealogy. At the same time, the cultural practice of pet keeping arose in the commercial, bourgeois society of eighteenth-century England, creating the companion animal as an antidote to the alienation and commodification of modern urban life. Humans have always had intimate connections with other animals, but the particular material practices and modes of interaction characteristic of the relationship with the pet are highly distinctive and historically specific. This period saw extensive experimentation with types of pets, the breeding and sale of pets, their adornment and taming, and their memorialization in literature and other arts. Thus intimacy with the pet pertained to the everyday experience of the life world and presented novel alternative structures of kinship and difference, affection and antithesis.

Together these two historical innovations in human-animal contact generated a vital imaginative power that fundamentally shaped the idea and the roles of nonhuman

---

[35] Harriet Ritvo, *The Animal Estate: The English and Other Creatures in the Victorian Age* (Cambridge, Mass.: Harvard University Press, 1987), 13, 2; Keith Thomas, *Man and the Natural World: A History of the Modern Sensibility* (New York: Pantheon, 1983); J. H. Plumb, "The Acceptance of Modernity," in *The Birth of a Consumer Society: The Commercialization of Eighteenth-Century England*, ed. Neil McKendrick, John Brewer, and J. H. Plumb (Bloomington: Indiana University Press, 1982); Londa Schiebinger, *Nature's Body: Gender in the Making of Modern Science* (Boston: Beacon Press, 1993), 80; Philip Armstrong, *What Animals Mean in the Fiction of Modernity* (New York: Routledge, 2008), 49, 55; Ingrid H. Tague, "Dead Pets: Satire and Sentiment in British Elegies and Epitaphs for Animals," *Eighteenth-Century Studies* 41 (2008): 289–306; and H. W. Janson, *Apes and Ape Lore in the Middle Ages and the Renaissance* (London: Warburg Institute, 1952), 336.

animals as they are represented in the literature of the modern period. Because they are tied to relatively sudden disruptions in established ways of understanding animal—and human—kind, the imaginary animals of this historical moment offer dissonant, alternative, or unconventional avenues for approaching literary form, human identity, genealogical continuity, relationships of hierarchy, and ideas of coherence, and raise larger questions about the nature of the human, the definition of love, the experience of diversity, and the possibility of transcendence. As Tague argues, "Eighteenth-century people used animals to think about the world and their place in it" (292). Writing about animals in this period brought some of the abstract ideas of contemporary philosophical and scientific speculation into the realm of everyday experience and found distinctive forms for the expression of these ideas. Thus Plumb finds that "quite humble activities [of human-animal contact] played their part in the acceptance of modernity and of science…[thus creating] one of the greatest revolutions in human life" (233). Indeed, the depiction of nonhuman animals in eighteenth-century literature generated more instances of unconventional ways of thinking than were available in the contemporaneous treatment of human difference. Native American, African, and Polynesian "princes" who visited London in the eighteenth century were accommodated as European aristocrats. Slaves were represented as sentimental objects, to create support for the popular antislavery movement. Africans were caricatured as "Hottentots" or apes. But dogs could revise norms of intimacy, monkeys could expose systems of violence, orangutan could become inappropriate heroes, and imaginary animals could cross over the boundary of the real into a realm of inter-species transcendence.

The chapters that follow pursue significant instances of these dissonances, showing that the aesthetic effects of animals and the kinds of conceptual or ontological thinking that they inspire are inseparable and systematically coordinated. The chapter entitled "Mirror Scene" pursues the motif of the indistinguishability of human and ape—which can be traced in writings from seventeenth-century travel narratives to *Frankenstein*—to suggest the ways in which imaginary animals posed disorienting ontological questions and deranged the core eighteenth-century concepts of human self-definition: the heritage of classical humanism and the new affective values of sensibility. The trope of the lady and the lapdog from Pope to Dickens is the subject of chapter 3, "Immoderate Love," which argues that the structures of inversion typical of that image produce a new understanding of intimacy, based on the alienating effects of reversal and dissonance rather than on norms of kinship and coherence. Chapter 4, "Violent Intimacy," shows that the image of the pet monkey connects the dramatic comedy of the early eighteenth century to Frances Burney's influential novel of manners, *Evelina*. The monkey generates questions about the eighteenth-century ideal of companionate marriage in a way that extends beyond social satire and beyond prescriptions for decorous female conduct, to portray the experience of gender difference as an alien, even violent struggle. And "Dog

Narrative," chapter 5, describes the sub-genre of dog-centered and dog-narrated fiction, invented in the eighteenth century and surviving through the twentieth. This chapter shows that ideas about canine behavior and character—its endemic itinerancy and its implication with the diversity of beings—provide ways of representing the aberrant or unconventional, of creating a fantasy of species transcendence, and of challenging conventions of novelistic realism.

These are some of the founding figures for the flood of animal literature that then follows Peacock's *Melincourt; or, Sir Oran Haut-ton.* They belong to the first phase of the rise of the animal in the modern literary imagination, and thus they express most clearly the disruptive forces of novelty and innovation. The emblematic Aesopian tradition, which, as we have seen, played such a significant role in late-Renaissance natural history, continues as an influential strain throughout the eighteenth century, initially through its neoclassical redactions by John Dryden and John Gay, and especially in its later adaptations for the juvenile press.[36] But as Keith Thomas says, "It was direct experience rather than classical tradition which did the most" to create the new views of animal-kind in the eighteenth century and to inspire their literary redactions (121). In large part, the fable tradition tends to hold this immediacy of experience, and the literary dissonance it produces, at a distance. Furthermore, as it develops in the course of the later eighteenth century, the animal fable begins to dissolve into natural history and realist description, blending materials from contemporary experience and observation with the symbolic depiction that made it a core component of the emblematic worldview. Louise E. Robbins has described the complex relationship between fables and natural history in this period, arguing that "nature continued to be a source for lessons, but in a different way than it had been in earlier periods." In Robbins's account, "the mingling of fable and natural history occurred in both directions," creating a "hybrid genre" that mixed scientific observation and moral meanings. By this means, moralizing was translated from the classical format of the Aesopian fable to the empirical context of the naturalists' descriptive writing. Thus, for Robbins, "Buffon was a master of the new fable."[37]

---

[36] Studies of the Aesopian tradition include Annabel M. Patterson, *Fables of Power: Aesopian Writing and Political History* (Durham: Duke University Press, 1991); Jayne Elizabeth Lewis, *The English Fable: Aesop and Literary Culture, 1651–1740* (Cambridge: Cambridge University Press, 1996); Mark Loveridge, *A History of Augustan Fable* (Cambridge: Cambridge University Press, 1998); Frank Palmeri, "The Autocritique of Fables," in *Humans and Other Animals in Eighteenth-Century British Culture*, ed. Frank Palmeri (Aldershot, UK: Ashgate, 2006), 83–100; Frank Palmeri, "The History of Fables and Cultural History in Eighteenth-Century England," in *Historical Boundaries, Narrative Forms: Essays on British Literature in the Long Eighteenth Century in Honor of Everett Zimmerman*, ed. Lorna Clymer and Robert Mayer (Newark: University of Delaware Press, 2007). Palmeri argues in "Autocritique" that certain critical fables "examine the form from within," and thus constitute another kind of divergence from emblematic representation (83).
[37] Louise E. Robbins, *Elephant Slaves and Pampered Parrots: Exotic Animals in Eighteenth-Century Paris* (Baltimore: Johns Hopkins University Press, 2002), 179, 181.

The imaginary animals generated by these new views of animal-kind are flexible and complex fantasies which, as Sir Oran has taught us, are best understood through a close analysis of the diverse images, themes, or formal structures that they generate within their particular texts, and through a perspective that attends to the potential for disruption of accepted ways of ordering or understanding that these structures may imply. Thus they mingle human-associated and human-alienating impulses, anthropomorphism and alterity, in a way that takes the question of the human-animal relationship in a different direction from that of the strict dichotomy that we have seen to be common in theoretical and scientific discourse. All these animals exist only in the realm of representation, but all are also mediated expressions of the new human contact with actual animals in this period of historical transition. Whether in literature, philosophy, or science, claims to an authentic rendering of the historical existences of "real" animal beings are obviously problematic, and assertions about respect and responsibility are highly contentious. The perspective provided by a critique of literary culture, on the other hand, finds a different way of assessing the presence of animals in history. First, it suggests a means of understanding imaginary animal-kind as emerging from a particular dimension of the historical contact between humans and other animals. And second, these imaginary animals can themselves be seen to participate in history by opening up distinctive opportunities for creativity, which in turn shape the human relationship with the world. The monster of Mary Shelley's *Frankenstein*, an imaginary being generated by the discovery of the hominoid ape, continues to exert an influence on the modern understanding of science, technology, and identity. And the itinerant dog narrator, a creation of the bourgeois phenomenon of pet keeping, still helps us imagine experiences ordinarily beyond our ken—the lives and deaths of the homeless, as well as the worlds beyond boundaries that all beings might share.

On a broader scale, the perspective of literary culture may also prove useful in suggesting approaches to other portrayals of animals in purportedly nonimaginative contexts. Of course, all discursive modes of delineating or understanding animals are powerfully mediated by the effects and forms of language. As we have seen for example, Eileen Crist's close readings of the "linguistic mediums" of behaviorism illustrate the ways in which the process of representation itself constructs particular visions of animals even in the fields of sociobiology and ethology. But more pervasively, absolutely every effort to gain access to animals "on their own terms" or to "the animal as other" raises the basic representational paradox that continues to challenge modern critical approaches to the animal: that all such efforts emanate from the realm of human language and culture. In his study of *What Animals Mean in the Fiction of Modernity* (2008), Philip Armstrong provides a summary acknowledgment of this problem: "Of course novelists, scientists and scholars can never actually access, let alone reproduce, what other animals mean on their own terms. Humans can only represent animals' experience through the mediation of cultural encoding, which inevitably involves a reshaping according to our own intentions, attitudes and preconceptions." Armstrong here summarizes some of the subtle remedies for the paradox of representation that have been proposed by modern critics: strategies of indirection that include a search for subtle "traces" or the more animal-based "tracks" left by actual animals within human texts, signs of destabilization and deconstruction of agency, or a kind of revulsion against the human that is said to propel the reader toward an inter-species sympathy (2, 3, 46–47). The application of these remedies has been limited to strenuous, local close reading, and thus their larger usefulness and relevance to a conceptualization of the human-animal relationship have been circumscribed. But the problem of representation, as understood in animal studies, does suggest a special relevance for imaginative literature, which this study seeks to exemplify. To the extent that literary texts openly lay claim to the realm of representation, foregrounding the medium and the processes of mediation and making those processes available to detailed analysis, imaginative literature may provide a template for assessing a wider range of discursive representations of animals, including those of ethics and philosophy, or biology and evolution. In other words, if we admit the whole world of imaginary animals into our thinking about the human-animal connection, we can develop a new vocabulary for understanding that connection.

And literature has a deeper relevance to other representations of animals as well. The interactions of humans and other animals—and the issues of justice and rights that have emerged from these interactions in our own period—are to at least some extent historically implicated with the imaginary representation of animal-kind. Since the eighteenth century, as we have seen, literary animals have inspired modes of thought that question conventional hierarchies, and they have projected such questions into the modern debate about the status of animals. It was in the period of Sir Oran Haut-ton that the range of political topics that have formed the basis of modern animal-rights discussions took shape: the animal-protection movement and the founding of the Society for the Prevention of Cruelty to Animals (1824), the vegetarian movement, the antivivisection movement, and the inspiration for the utilitarian defense of animals in Jeremy Bentham's famous query, "Can they *suffer?*"[38] These were followed by the first sustained argument for animal rights by Henry Salt in his *Animals' Rights Considered*

---

[38] Jeremy Bentham, *An Introduction to the Principles of Morals and Legislation*, 2nd ed. (1823; repr. Darien, Conn.: Hafner Publishing, 1948), 311n. On these political developments, see Thomas, *Man and the Natural World*, 143–191; Kenyon-Jones, *Kindred Brutes*; Gates, *Kindred Nature*; James Turner, *Reckoning with the Beast: Animals, Pain, and Humanity in the Victorian Mind* (Baltimore: Johns Hopkins University Press, 1980); and Kathryn Shevelow, *For the Love of Animals: The Rise of the Animal Protection Movement* (New York: Henry Holt, 2008).

in Relation to Social Progress (1892), and ultimately by the major modern works of Peter Singer, Tom Regan, Mary Midgley, Martha Nussbaum, and others.[39] Thus, though they exist only within the imagination, the animals of eighteenth-century literature possess an historical effectivity. From the realm of the human imagination, they can alter the world of all beings.

[39] Peter Singer, *Animal Liberation: Towards an End to Man's Inhumanity to Animals* (London: Jonathan Cape, 1976); Tom Regan, *The Case for Animal Rights* (Oxford: Basil Blackwell, 1985); Mary Midgley, *Animals and Why They Matter* (Harmondsworth, UK: Penguin, 1983); and Nussbaum, *Frontiers of Justice.*

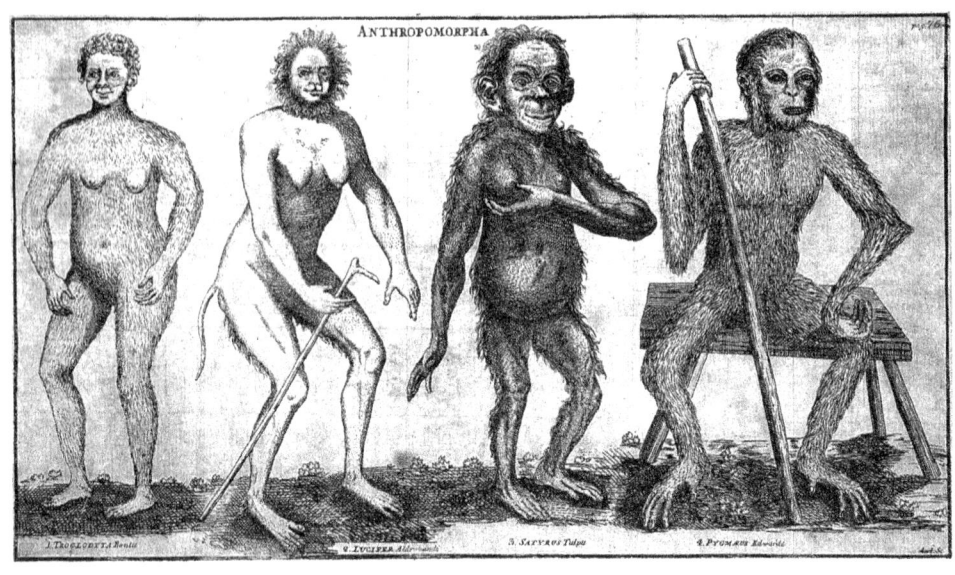

Figure 1. Carolus Linnaeus, from *Anthropomorpha* (1760). Courtesy of Wellcome Library, London.

2

MIRROR SCENE

The Orangutan, the Ancients, and the Cult of Sensibility

In a work of medicine and natural history written in Java and published in Amsterdam in 1658, the Dutch physician Jakob de Bondt (Jacob Bontius) used his account of what we now know to be the Bornean orangutan to recognize a human face in the representation of a nonhuman being:

> Goat-footed Satyrs, Sphinges, and frisky Fauns.
> Not even boys believe in those.
> But contemplate this wonderful Monster
> With a human face, so like human-kind not only
> In groaning, but also in wetting the face with weeping.[1]

A century later, George-Louis Leclerc, Comte de Buffon, the premiere naturalist of the age, in describing the hominoid ape, also finds himself looking in a mirror: "This orangoutang or pongo is only a brute, but a brute of a kind so singular, that man cannot behold it without contemplating himself" (1749).[2] Lemuel Gulliver, who has survived the

---

[1] Iacobi Bontii (Jacobus Bontius), *Medici civitatis Bataviæ Novæ in Iava ordinarii, historiæ naturalis & medicæ, Indiæ Orientalis*, 5:84 (continuously paginated). Bound in Willem Piso, *De Indiæ utriusque re naturali et medica* (Amsterdam: Ludovicum et Danielem Elzevirios., 1658). Bondt's text is separately paginated. The relevant passage is set in verse: "Hircipedes Satyros, Sphingas, Faunosque petulcos./Nec pueri credunt: tamen hoc mirabile Monstrum/Humana specta facie, tum moribus illi/Assimile in gemitu, tum fletibus ora rigando." Bondt's observations and writing date from 1626 to 1631, the period that he spent in Jakarta in the employ of the Dutch East India Company, where he died in 1631. Bondt is best known for his medical observations; those and his materials on natural history were published posthumously in the composite volume cited above, by Willem Piso in 1658. See Harold J. Cook, "Global Economies and Local Knowledge in the East Indies: Jacobus Bontius Learns the Facts of Nature," in *Colonial Botany: Science, Commerce, and Politics in the Early Modern World*, ed. Londa Schiebinger and Claudia Swan (Philadelphia: University of Pennsylvania Press, 2005), 100–118.

[2] Georges Louis Leclerc, Comte de Buffon, *Natural History, General and Particular* [*Histoire naturelle*], translated into English, 9 vols. (Edinburgh: William Creech, 1780–85), 8:41. Buffon's *Histoire des animaux* was published in 1749.

experience of recognizing the Yahoos as human beings like himself, resolves at the end of part 4 of Jonathan Swift's *Gulliver's Travels* (1726) to do just that: "[T]o behold my Figure often in a Glass, and thus if possible habituate my self by Time to tolerate the Sight of a human Creature."[3] And like Gulliver, the monstrous creature of Mary Shelley's *Frankenstein* (1816) finds startling self-knowledge in the contemplation of his own reflection: "How was I terrified when I viewed myself in a transparent pool! At first I started back, unable to believe that it was indeed I who was reflected in the mirror."[4] Gazing into the mirror held up for them by animal-kind, these speakers recognize in their own reflected faces the images of monster, orangutan, or Yahoo. Their wonder, their speculation, their mortification, or their "Shame, Confusion and Horror" (Swift, 261) indicate the intense and extensive impact of the "discovery" of the hominoid ape on the modern imagination.

In the English eighteenth century, the contours of this impact were set in place by the ambitious and influential anatomical study of a juvenile chimpanzee, *Orang-Outang, sive Homo Sylvestris: or, the Anatomy of a Pygmie*, published in 1699 by the well-known physician and member of the Royal Society, Edward Tyson. Tyson's title follows contemporary usage: *orangutan* and *pygmy* were two of the most commonly and indiscriminately used terms for the great apes until the latter part of the eighteenth century.[5] Tyson's *Anatomy of a Pygmie* represents, in the words of H. W. Janson, "the formal entry of the anthropoid ape into the consciousness of Western civilisation."[6] *The Anatomy of a Pygmie* created the human encounter with the great ape in this period, and for more than a century Tyson's text presided over this being's presence in the literary, philosophical, and scientific enterprises of the day. Tyson's book advances a technical argument about the anatomical proximity of chimpanzee and human, an argument that remains impressive in its detail and systematicity to modern anatomists. And in the course of demonstrating this proximity, *The Anatomy of a Pygmie* launches two powerful theses about the hominoid ape

---

His complete *Histoire naturelle* was published over a longer period (1749–1778). English translations of Buffon were available beginning in 1775. The wording here comes from the translation of 1780–1785, a widely read English version, with three editions before 1800.

[3] Jonathan Swift, *Gulliver's Travels*, ed. Christopher Fox (Boston: Bedford, 1995), 265.

[4] Mary Shelley, *Frankenstein* (New York: New American Library, 1965), 108.

[5] Today we recognize four kinds of humanoid ape: orangutan (Asia), chimpanzee (Africa), gibbon (Asia), and gorilla (Africa). The term *orangutan* appeared in 1641 and was used until the nineteenth century indiscriminately to refer to the great apes of both Africa and Asia. Other terms commonly used were *satyr* and *pygmy*—derived from the classical tradition—and *jocko* and *pongo*—derived from attempted African-language transliterations. The term *chimpanzee* first appeared in Europe in 1738, but it was only in the 1780s that this term came to be used to distinguish the African from the Asiatic great ape. The gibbon was first described by Buffon in the second half of the eighteenth century. *Gorilla* was the last term to be introduced, in 1847, and gorillas were the last of the great apes to be "discovered" and observed, though that "discovery" took place in the early nineteenth century. Londa Schiebinger provides a thumbnail account of these issues of nomenclature in *Nature's Body: Gender in the Making of Modern Science* (Boston: Beacon Press, 1993), 78–79. On the discovery of the gorilla, see Robert M. Yerkes and Ada W. Yerkes, *The Great Apes: A Study of Anthropoid Life* (New Haven, Conn.: Yale University Press, 1929), 27–35.

[6] H. W. Janson, *Apes and Ape Lore in the Middle Ages and the Renaissance* (London: Warburg Institute, 1952), 336.

that together shape the imaginative engagement with this being. Its first claim takes on the neoclassical tradition by presenting a fully elaborated accommodation of classical mythology to modern science, in which mythological beings are replaced by apes. Its second claim anticipates notions of natural sensibility by projecting, through extended accounts of ape behavior, this being's inherent modesty, sympathy, and benevolence. These theses thus operate through two of the most prominent cultural and aesthetic modes of the period—the neoclassical and the sentimental—inserting the hominoid ape into each of these systems as a defining example. In the mirror of animal-kind, as we shall see, both Socrates and the man of feeling are reflected as the great ape.

The Great Ape

The European encounter with the hominoid ape seems to develop suddenly at the turn of the eighteenth century. But the rapidity with which this being came to prominence in the human imagination can be understood largely in terms of a shift in the nature of the human conceptualization of animal-kind rather than as the result of a sudden change in the level of exposure. Great apes had been observed by Europeans in the past: possibly during antiquity in accounts of explorers of the coast of west Africa, and certainly since the early voyages of discovery; even earlier, in the thirteenth century, Marco Polo brought back a description of orangutan that he had learned of in Southeast Asia. But those representations invariably accommodated this being to questions of philological authority or zoological and geological classification: whether they should be identified as *satyri* or *pygmi,* and where they belonged in the contemporary schema of species of semihuman *monstra.* Thus, as Janson demonstrates, the zoologists of classical antiquity, the medieval period, and the Renaissance received reports of hominoid apes "with almost complete equanimity."[7] It was the rise of comparative anatomy in the late seventeenth century, the development and practice of techniques of dissection, and the establishment of the science of physiology based on direct observation that created a new conceptual environment for the human engagement with the hominoid ape. But significantly, and in a reciprocal way, these new empirical approaches were in turn shaped by the newly prominent status of the great ape in the human imagination. Indeed, the question of the differences or similarities between humans and apes itself became the foundational material of the rising discipline of anatomy. In Janson's words, "From now on every anatomist had to concern himself to some extent with the physical differences between men and apes" (335).

[7] Ibid., 327. Janson summarizes the early depictions of the great apes, 332–335.

Accounts of direct encounters with the great apes were few in this period, and these few together formed a core textual and graphic resource that was repeatedly retailed throughout the eighteenth century as the basis for ongoing speculation—taxonomic, imaginative, and ontological. As Londa Schiebinger has suggested in her important essay on "The Gendered Ape," "It is hard for us today to recapture the excitement and confusion of naturalists as they tried to order nature."[8] Among the earliest of these personal accounts is that of Andrew Battell, whose summary of his time in Africa, which was published in *Purchas His Pilgrimes* (1625), describes African hominoid apes (gorillas) whom he terms "monsters"; the larger, he claims, is designated "pongo" by the local peoples, and the lesser "engeco." Battell describes only the "pongo": "This *Pongo* is in all proportion like a man, but that he is more like a Giant in stature, than a man: for he is very tall, and hath a mans face, hollow eyed, with long haire upon his browes."[9] Two decades later, the Dutch physician and anatomist, Nicolaas Tulp, in his *Observationum medicarum libri tres* (1641), published a sketch of the first living hominoid ape known to have reached Europe, another chimpanzee, which Tulp designated an orangutan or an Indian satyr. Along with an illustration of a hirsute figure that accompanied Bondt's 1658 account of the "Monster with a human face" that we have already noted, and the illustrations in Tyson's *Anatomy of a Pygmie*, Tulp's drawing was frequently reproduced and revised in subsequent accounts and taxonomies. Tyson's chimpanzee, the subject of his *Anatomy of a Pygmie*, is reputed to be the first hominoid ape to reach England alive. This animal was taken in Angola in 1697 and injured on the voyage to England, dying from a resulting infection after a few months in London. Tyson was able to observe his "pygmy" alive on at least one occasion, and to obtain possession of the body for his dissection.[10]

In the course of the eighteenth century, reports of the great apes encountered both in Africa and in Asia increased in frequency and currency. In 1718 Daniel Beeckman's *Voyage to and from the Island of Borneo* describes the orangutan there, who "grow up to be six Foot high...walk upright, have longer Arms than Men, [and] tolerable good Faces

---

[8] Schiebinger, *Nature's Body*, 80. The following description of seventeenth- and eighteenth-century accounts of the great apes is indebted to and summarizes the work of: Janson, *Apes and Ape Lore*, 327–346; Yerkes and Yerkes, *The Great Apes*, 8–26; Olav Röhrer-Ertl, "Research History, Nomenclature, and Taxonomy of the Orang-utan," in *Orang-utan Biology*, ed. Jeffrey H. Schwartz (Oxford: Oxford University Press, 1988), 7–18; Schiebinger, *Nature's Body*, 75–114; and Julia Douthwaite, "Rewriting the Savage: The Extraordinary Fictions of the 'Wild Girl of Champagne,'" *Eighteenth-Century Studies* 28 (1994): 163–192. For a useful compilation and translation of some of the core texts and images in the early representations of the great apes, see C. D. O'Malley and H. W. Magoun, "Early Concepts of the Anthropomorpha," *Physis: Rivista di storia della scienza* 4 (1962): 39–63.
[9] Andrew Battell in Samuel Purchas, *Purchas His Pilgrimes*, 4 vols. (London: William Stansby, 1625), 2:982.
[10] For a detailed account of the dissection, see the authoritative biography of Tyson, M. F. Ashley Montagu's *Edward Tyson, M.D., F.R.S., 1650–1708, and the Rise of Human and Comparative Anatomy in England* (Philadelphia: American Philosophical Society, 1943), 225–307.

(handsomer I am sure than some *Hottentots* that I have seen)." The young orangutan that Beeckman took with him was "very nimble footed" and "stronger than any Man on the Ship," but "would sigh, sob, and cry" if treated harshly.[11] The next living hominoid ape seen in London was a female chimpanzee, brought from Angola in 1738. As we shall see from Thomas Boreman's account, this being created a visible stir, as she was celebrated for her modesty and her manners at the tea table. She was observed by the French engraver, Louis Gérard Scotin, who produced a copperplate engraving of her holding a teacup, an image that was widely disseminated at the time, and that became another staple resource for contemporary descriptions. William Smith in *A New Voyage to Guinea*, published in 1744, describes the chimpanzee of Sierra Leone as an animal with a "near Resemblance of a human Creature....Their Bodies, when full grown, are as big in Circumference as a middle-siz'd Man's. Their Legs much shorter, and their Feet longer, their Arms and Hands in Proportion....The Face, which is cover'd by a white Skin, is monstrously ugly, being all over wrinkled as with Old Age, the Teeth broad and very yellow....They never go upon all Four like Apes, but cry when vex'd or teas'd, just like Children."[12] And John Barbot reports his observation of apes in *A Description of the Coasts of North and South Guinea*, published in 1746.

Dutch and French travelers, naturalists, and anatomists in this period contributed from across the channel to accounts of the great apes, especially the orangutan. In 1705 Willem Bosman described smaller apes or monkeys in Guinea; and Gautier Schouten (1707) and François Leguat (1708) provided accounts of the orangutan of south Asia. Meanwhile the Dutch zoologists and anatomists continued their influence on the physical descriptions of the hominoid ape; in the last quarter of the century, several living animals were available in Holland for study and dissection. In 1778 the Dutch naturalist Arnout Vosmaer provided an account of a live orangutan, and between 1779 and 1792 Petrus Camper published several physiological studies based on his dissection of five orangutan, out of eight living individuals that he had obtained.

The eighteenth century saw the rise of biological and botanical taxonomy, and the major taxonomists of the age figured significantly in this complex imaginative engagement with the hominoid ape and the problem of that being's relationship to the human. Myth, invention, anecdote, redaction, synthesis, and textual collation, as much as empirical observation, underwrote the development of the major classificatory efforts of the age, when it came to the idea of the hominoid ape. Describing the work of Linnaeus, Julia Douthwaite observes of eighteenth-century taxonomy that it was "a science tinged with fiction, especially as regards the distinctions between apes and man" (178). Indeed, among the major taxonomists, only Buffon had actually observed the great ape directly.

[11] Daniel Beeckman, *A Voyage to and from the Island of Borneo* (London: T. Warner and J. Batley, 1718), 37–38.
[12] William Smith, *A New Voyage to Guinea* (London: John Nourse, 1744), 51–52.

John Ray, in his *Synopsis methodica animalium quadrupedum et serpentini generis* (1693), opened the field of taxonomy, providing for a group that he designated *Anthropomorpha*—those clawed animals (*unguiculata*) that are "nail bearing" or "anthropoid." Ray's *Anthropomorpha* included apes, but his scheme omitted human-kind, since the sacred nature of the *animal rationale* excluded the human from the early taxonomic systems. Even Tyson, who directly documented the parallel between human and ape, did not allow man to appear in his classification of the unguiculate animals (Montagu, *Edward Tyson*, 352).

But Linnaeus's taxonomies, as he and his students develop and revise them over the period from 1735 to 1788, bring ape and human into increasingly closer relationship with one another. From the outset, according to Linnaeus scholar Gunnar Broberg, "Linnaeus sees nature as a whole, united by the same life, and he finds no justification for setting man apart."[13] In Linnaeus's words: "I can discover scarcely any mark by which man can be distinguished from the apes....Neither in the face nor in the feet, nor in the upright gait, nor in any other aspect of his external structure does man differ from the apes."[14] In the first edition of his *Systema naturae* (1735), Linnaeus grouped humans (*Homo*) with apes (*Simia*) under the genus of *"Anthropomorpha,"* which he had borrowed from Ray. And in the tenth edition (1758) of this work, Linnaeus described as a second species of human a type of ape, *Homo troglodytes*—a nocturnal cave dweller with the capacity for speech, in which Linnaeus included Bondt's Bornean orangutan.[15] But for Linnaeus this was a theoretical species; despite his efforts, he never found an opportunity to observe such a being. Buffon, however, had had experience with a young chimpanzee, and himself kept an adult orang-utan. In his *Histoire naturelle* (1749–1778) he provided the most comprehensive attempt to classify the known species of apes. But even Buffon's work was based largely on a compilation of information extracted from Battell, Tulp, Tyson, and others.

Indeed, these attempts to describe the hominoid ape are characterized by a continuous cross-referencing, synopsizing, and textual collation that suggests that this being first engaged the human imagination through a complex and sustained form of intertextuality.[16] Threads of repeated ideas and impressions cross and connect these

---

[13] Gunnar Broberg, "*Homo sapiens*: Linnaeus's Classification of Man," in *Linnaeus: The Man and His Work*, ed. Tore Frängsmyr (Berkeley: University of California Press, 1983), 156–194, 165.

[14] Linnaeus, *Anthropomorpha*, 66. Cited in Schiebinger, "The Gendered Ape: Early Representations of Primates in Europe," in *A Question of Identity: Women, Science, and Literature*, ed. Marina Benjamin (New Brunswick, N.J.: Rutgers University Press, 1993), 123.

[15] For Linnaeus's classification of hominoid apes and humans, see Broberg, 156–194. For a compact summary of the development of Linnaeus's *Systema* from the first to the thirteenth edition, see Phillip Sloan, "The Gaze of Natural History," in *Inventing Human Science: Eighteenth-Century Domains*, ed. Christopher Fox, Roy Porter, and Robert Wokler (Berkeley: University of California Press, 1995), 112–151, esp. 122–123.

[16] This method of compilation and citation is characteristic of the major sixteenth-century emblematic natural histories (e.g., by Conrad Gesner and Ulisse Aldrovandi), in which the humanist tradition focuses its attention on the natural world. Tyson and the eighteenth-century natural historians and taxonomists all

accounts. Bondt, for instance, gets his story that orangutan do not speak because they do not want to be forced to work from Richard Jobson in *The Golden Trade* (1623), who reported that certain African apes are regarded as "a race and kind of people, who in regard they will not bee brought to worke, and live under subjection, refuse to speake."[17] This question of hominoid access to language becomes a central topic in later comparisons between the great apes and human-kind. Meanwhile, Bondt's description of the "great modesty" of his female satyr becomes a defining trait of the female chimpanzee, most notably highlighted in Boreman's and Scotin's representations of the individual whose behavior they personally observed in London in 1738. Bondt's illustration of the "monster with a human face" is similarly intertwined with other graphic images, past and future. This illustration—depicting a tall hirsute female with a mane encircling its face—is clearly copied from a sixteenth-century representation of a great ape by Conrad Gesner (*Historia animalium*, 1551), which is itself, in turn, a reproduction of an image Gesner found in Bernhard von Breydenbach's *Journey to the Holy Land* (1486), described there as a creature "of uncertain name." Janson has demonstrated that this latter creature is a redaction of representations of the sacred baboon by the ancient Egyptians. With the tail removed, and with the addition of bodily hair derived from Tulp's "Orang-outang" plate of 1641, it becomes Bondt's orangutan. As Janson observes, the image was to have "an extraordinary career" in the European imagination, becoming "a familiar feature in the zoological literature of the next two centuries."[18]

Buffon's own method of collation, in creating his descriptions of the hominoid ape, was astutely characterized by Étienne Geoffroy-Saint-Hilaire in a 1798 article debating the different species of great apes: "This animal [the orangutan], such as it is described in the immortal work of that celebrated author, is an imaginary being to which Buffon has assigned a form and characterising marks, by confounding, under the same name, and in the same description, six different species of apes described by travellers."[19] Buffon's relationship to Battell provides a telling example of this technique of synthesis

---

transmit, transform, and finally undercut the humanist methodology of their predecessors. This juxtaposition of methodologies captures the major shift in the representation of the significance of the natural world that takes place during this period. See William B. Ashworth Jr., "Emblematic Natural History of the Renaissance," in *Cultures of Natural History*, ed. Nicholas Jardine, J. Anne Secord, and Emma C. Spary (Cambridge: Cambridge University Press, 1996), 17–37.

[17] Richard Jobson, *The Golden Trade: or, A Discouery of the Riuer Gambra and the Golden Trade of the Aethiopians* (London: Nicholas Okes, 1623), 153.

[18] Janson, *Apes and Ape Lore*, 334. This genealogy of the Breydenbach baboon is based on Janson, 333–335. On the complex interrelationship of the early images of the great ape, including those of Tulp, Tyson, Bondt, Gesner, and Breydenbach, and noting the omnipresence of the walking stick, see also Robert Wokler, "Tyson and Buffon on the Orang-utan," *Studies on Voltaire and the Eighteenth Century* 155 (1976): 2301–2319, esp. 2301–2303.

[19] Étienne Geoffroy-Saint-Hilaire, "Observations on the Account of the Supposed Orang Outang of the East Indies," *Philosophical Magazine* (London, 1798), 341–342. Cited in Yerkes and Yerkes, *The Great Apes*, 25.

and revision. In the fourteenth volume of the *Histoire naturelle* (1766), Buffon redacts Battell's account of the pongo and engeco from *Purchas His Pilgrimes*. Buffon's chapter, entitled "Les orang-outangs ou le pongo et le jocko," is explained in his note on these names:

> Orang-outang nom de cet animal aux Indes orientales: Pongo nom de cet animal à Lowando Province de Congo. Jocko, Enjoco, nom de cet animal à Congo que nous avons adopté. *En* est l'article que nous avons retranché.

> [Orangutan—name of this animal from the east Indies; Pongo—name of this animal from Lowando in the Province of Congo. Jocko, Enjocko—name of this animal from Congo which we have adopted. *En* is the article, which we have omitted.]

By imagining the syllable *en* as an article in an African language, Buffon created from Battell's account a new term, *Jocko*, which was then widely promulgated in subsequent attempts to classify the great apes. We know that Buffon read Battell's account in a translation by Abbé Prévost, in his *Histoire général des voyages* (1748). The translation generated additional creativity. From Prévost's translation of Battell's original statement that the pongos "cannot speake, and have no understanding more than a beast," Buffon developed the claim "qu'il ne peut parler quoiqu'il ait plus d'entendement que les autres animaux" ("that they cannot speak, but they have more ability to understand than other animals"). And he reproduced Prévost's revision of Battell's account: where Purchas wrote, "He told me in conference with him, that one of these Pongos tooke a negro boy of his which lived a moneth with them," the French translation by Prévost becomes "un pongo lui enleva un petit negre qui passa un an entier dans la societé de ces animaux" [a pongo took with him a negro boy who spent an entire year in the company of these animals].[20]

Linnaeus, in his *Anthropomorpha* (published in 1760 under the authorship of his student, Christianus Emanuel Hoppius), performs the same kind of creative redaction, revision, and collation in composing his authoritative account of the four types of hominoid apes. The illustration on page 26 shows four differentiated full figures of ape-like or human-like beings in a row, numbered from left to right. The first, labeled *TROGLODYTA Boentii*, is directly derived from Bondt's 1658 illustration of his orangutan, but shorn of the copious, spiky bodily hair that Bondt had provided, and also of the full face-framing mane; its more human-like facial features perhaps show the

---

[20] For Buffon's relationship with the French translation of Battell, see Thomas H. Huxley, *Man's Place in Nature* (1863; Ann Arbor: University of Michigan Press, 1959), 24. For a summary of Buffon's synthesis and invention of the names for the orangutan, see Wokler, "Tyson and Buffon," 2310–2311.

influence of Tyson's very slightly revised reproduction of Bondt's orangutan illustration, published as figure 16 in his anatomical study, *The Anatomy of a Pygmie*. And as we have already seen, Bondt's illustration itself is a derivation of Breydenbach's ape, constructed from the sacred baboon of the ancient Egyptians. Linnaeus's second image, labeled *LUCIFER Aldrovandi*, has the same genealogy as his first, though it makes its way to the *Anthropomorpha* by a different route. This creature is a more-or-less immediate transcription of Breydenbach's ape and retains that image's tail, though in a shortened form. Thus in the array that Linnaeus presents it appears as a clearly differentiated being.

Linnaeus's third ape, *SATYRUS Tulpii*, is copied from Scotin's very popular engraving of the tea-drinking female chimpanzee, but omits the teacup that added the iconographic significance of modest manners to the image that was widely circulated in London at the time. And finally, Linnaeus's fourth ape, *PYGMAEUS Edwardi*, is a slightly revised redaction from a contemporary drawing contained in George Edwards's, *Gleanings of Natural History, Exhibiting Figures of Quadrupeds* (1758–1764). Linnaeus lightens the creature's skin coloring, and slightly alters the face to give it more human features. Significantly, Edwards's rendering itself is a composite. Robert M. Yerkes and Ada W. Yerkes, in their encyclopedic summary of the history of the European understanding of the great apes, suggest that Edwards "so skillfully mingled the structural characters of orang-outan, chimpanzee, and gibbon that one cannot more exactly name the figure than by the synonyms which the artist himself used" (Yerkes and Yerkes, 19): Edwards entitled this illustration "The Satier, Sauage, Wild-man, Pigmy, Orang-outang, Chimp-anzee &c."[21] Thus, the complexity of Linnaeus's effort to group and classify these beings is matched by a strikingly elaborate intertextuality. Indeed, Broberg characterizes Linnaeus's various conceptualizations of man-like beings as "a motley collection": "New myths were formed from the remnants of old ones, ancient traditions were mixed with more recent reports. It was often in this weird light that writers attempted to clarify the phenomenon of man" (177).[22]

In the eighteenth-century imagination, then, the hominoid ape is not a singular or a coherent individual. Though the discovery of the great ape in this period is directly linked to the vital ontological debates that have shaped modernity, the creature who loomed so large over this cultural and intellectual event was a "motley," composite being, stitched together from remnants of past traditions and awkwardly linking those precedents with contemporary anecdote and empirical observation. In the mirror

---

[21] George Edwards, *Gleanings of Natural History, Exhibiting Figures of Quadrupeds*, trans. E. Barker of J. Du Plessis, Glanures d'histoire naturelle (London, 1758–1764). Cited in Yerkes and Yerkes, *The Great Apes*, 19.

[22] For various accounts of Linnaeus's image of the four species, see Schiebinger, *Nature's Body*, 83; Huxley, *Man's Place in Nature*, 22; and Yerkes and Yerkes, *The Great Apes*, 20.

held up by animal-kind, human beings recognized themselves in a weird hominoid creation—a hairy reanimation of the beings of classical mythology, a naturally sensible, innately modest ape of feeling. These redactions of the hominoid ape enter the literary culture of the eighteenth century as rough drafts for an ongoing experiment in human identity.

The Anatomy of a Pygmie

Edward Tyson's *Orang-Outang, sive Homo Sylvestris: or, The Anatomy of a Pygmie* sets the agenda for the imaginative role of the great ape in the course of the eighteenth century and provides an encyclopedic summary of the currently available commentary on this being. The major items of this agenda, as we shall see, include the pygmy's size, his physical proximity to man, his sensitive nature, and his presence in classical literature, mythology, and history. At the outset, Tyson explains that he has used the designation "pygmy" because of the creature's small size, and because he believes

> the *Pygmies* of the Antients were a sort of *Apes*.... And if the *Pygmies* were only *Apes*, then in all probability our *Ape* may be a *Pygmie*; a sort of *Animal* so much resembling *Man*, that both the Antients and the Moderns have reputed it to be a *Puny Race* of Mankind, call'd to this day, *Homo Sylvestris*, The *Wild Man; Orang-Outang*, or a *Man* of the *Woods*; by the *Africans Quoias Morrou*; by others *Baris*, or *Barris*, and by the *Portuguese*, the *Salvage*.[23]

Strongly cognizant of the complexities resulting from these diffuse terms, sources, and observations regarding the great apes, Tyson acknowledges:

> I must confess, there is so great Confusion in the Description of this sort of Creature, which I find is a very large Family (there being numerous *Species* of them) that in Transcribing the Authors that have wrote about them, 'tis almost impossible but to make mistakes; from the want of their well distinguishing them. I shall endeavour therefore in my Account of this, so to discriminate it, that it may be easily known again, where-ever 'tis met with. (*Anatomy*, 1–2)

Indeed, Tyson's anatomical description is so precise and meticulous that it served for more than two centuries as a major resource for anatomists and remains accurate today.

---

[23] Edward Tyson, *Orang-Outang: sive Homo Sylvestris, or, The Anatomy of a Pygmie*, facsimile ed. (London: Dawsons, 1966), 1.

But despite its strong empiricist core, Tyson's text as a whole—in its collation of diverse accounts and especially in its claims to classical precedents—exemplifies the "motley" nature of the eighteenth-century representation of the hominoid ape.[24]

Bound together with the *Anatomy* is a separately paginated section entitled *A Philological Essay Concerning the Pygmies, the Cynocephali, the Satyrs and Sphinges of the Ancients;* and each of these four topics—pygmies, cynocephali, satyrs, and sphinxes—is treated in a separate essay. In this sense, then, though it is usually designated by the single title—*The Anatomy of a Pygmie*—Tyson's book is itself a composite work.[25] The central task of Tyson's main treatise is the detailed comparative anatomical examination of the chimpanzee:

> What I shall most of all aim at in the following Discourse, will be to give as particular an Account as I can, of the formation and structure of all the Parts of this wonderful *Animal;* and to make a *Comparative* Survey of them, with the same Parts in a *Humane Body*, as likewise in the *Ape* and *Monkey*-kind. For tho' I own it to be of the *Ape* kind, yet, as we shall observe, in the *Organization* of abundance of its Parts, it more approaches to the Structure of the same in *Men*: But where it differs from a *Man*, there it resembles plainly the Common *Ape*, more than any other *Animal*. (*Anatomy*, 2)

Tyson proceeds to describe, step by step, the results of his own dissection, and to juxtapose those details with reports about "*Ape* and *Monkey*-kind" derived from many other sources—including other contemporary anatomical observations, works of classical philosophy, and anecdotes from travelers and naturalists.

In this description of "*Ape* and *Monkey*-kind," Tyson conflates a variety of beings from the group that we would now designate as the Anthropoid suborder, which includes New World monkeys, Old World monkeys, and hominoid apes. Meanwhile, for the comparisons to human anatomy, Tyson draws on his own experience as a physician. He concludes with a graphically presented list, which provides forty-eight specific items where "[t]he Orang-Outang *or* Pygmie *more resembled a* Man, *than* Apes *and* Monkeys *do*," and thirty-four items where "[t]he Orang-Outang *or* Pygmie *differ'd from a* Man, *and resembled more the* Ape *and* Monkey-kind" (*Anatomy*, 92–95). Tyson's conclusion, then, confirms the extraordinary similarity that he has pursued throughout the anatomy and that

---

[24] For another reading of the "mixed-genre writing of social/natural science" in the period, through the coexistence of "empirical methodology and historico-anthropological narrative" in Tyson's study, see Susan Wiseman, "Monstrous Perfectibility: Ape-Human Transformations in Hobbes, Bulwer, Tyson," in *At the Borders of the Human: Beasts, Bodies, and Natural Philosophy in the Early Modern Period,* ed. Erica Fudge, Ruth Gilbert, and Susan Wiseman (Basingstoke, UK: Macmillan, 1999), 215–238, esp. 225, 219.

[25] Hereafter I will cite text from *The Anatomy of a Pygmie* proper as (*Anatomy* xx) and text from the essays as (*Philological Essay* xx).

he introduced in the first paragraph of the preface, where he described the pygmy as a "Creature so very remarkable...and so much resembling a Man." For Tyson, "there is no *Animal,* I have hitherto met with, or heard of, that so exactly resembles a *Man,* in the Structure of the *Inward Parts,* as our *Pygmie*" (*Anatomy,* 25). But the pygmy is definitely not a hybrid being. In Tyson's words: "[N]otwithstanding our *Pygmie* does so much resemble a *Man* in many of its Parts, more than any of the *Ape-kind,* or any other *Animal* in the World....Yet by no means do I look upon it as the Product of a *mixt* Generation; 'tis a *Brute-Animal sui generis,* and a particular *Species* of *Ape*" (*Anatomy,* 2). Thus, the existence of this "remarkable" being confirms Tyson's idea of an infinitely graduated chain of creation:

> This... *Gradation* can't but be taken notice of...and it would be the Perfection of *Natural History,* could it be attained, to enumerate and remark all the different *Species,* and their *Gradual Perfections* from one to another. Thus in the *Ape* and *Monkey*-kind, Aristotle's *Cebus* I look upon to be a degree above his *Cynocephalus;* and his *Pithecus* or *Ape* above his *Cebus,* and our *Pygmie* a higher degree above any of them, we yet know, and more resembling a *Man:* But at the same time I take him to be wholly a *Brute,* tho' in the formation of the Body, and in the *Sensitive,* or *Brutal* Soul, it may be, more resembling a Man, than any other *Animal;* so that in this *Chain* of the *Creation,* as an intermediate Link between an *Ape* and a *Man,* I would place our *Pygmie.* (*Anatomy,* 5)

In keeping with this proximity to the human, then, particularly in regard to the "*Sensitive,* or *Brutal* Soul," Tyson's text recounts several anecdotes that supply his pygmy with "soft, tender Passions" (*Anatomy,* 20). In fact, these appear in his opening pages, as a preamble to the dissection itself, which takes second place to the attempt to render the "soul" of the pygmy. Here Tyson provides a compendium of direct accounts of living beings of this species. He claims that these stories are designed to encourage the future study of this creature "which comes so near to a Man" (*Anatomy,* 22)—and they certainly did have that result in the decades to follow. In this text, however, the more immediate effect of these narratives is to provide the being whose "inward *Viscera*" (preface) will shortly be on display with an outward set of behaviors, a character, even an identity.[26] Tyson's sources do not agree in their assessment of this being's nature, and Tyson himself calls attention to the discrepancies among them in noting that "*Bontius* describes it with soft, tender Passions; *Tulpius* and *Dapper* make it Warlike and Fighting" (*Anatomy,* 20). But it is the representations of sensibility and modesty from Tyson's book

---

[26] Wiseman's reading of Tyson's *Anatomy* describes the tradition of ape description that Tyson draws upon here as "the ape imaginary"—a set of "mythic ideas" or "fantasies" that come to constitute the new understanding of the ape in the early modern period (Ibid., 216–225).

that capture the imagination of many subsequent readers. Tyson quotes at length from Bondt's account of the orangutan's modesty and human-like emotion:

> I saw several of both sexes walking erect, first that young female satyr (whose image I include here) with great modesty hiding her private parts...and also her face with her hands from unknown men, weeping profusely, groaning, and performing other human actions, so that you would say nothing human was lacking except speech. (*Anatomy*, 20)[27]

And he concludes this opening section with a page-long quotation from an English translation of the travels to China of the French Jesuit, Louis Daniel le Comte, whose stories also provide a view of the natural affections of the "Savage Man":

> [I]t cries exactly like a Child; the whole outward Action is so Humane, and the Passions so lively and significant, that dumb Men can scarce express better their Conceptions and Appetites. They do especially appear to be of a very kind Nature; and to shew their Affections to Persons they know and love, they embrace them, and kiss them with transports that surprise a Man. (*Anatomy*, 24)[28]

These narrative views of the pygmy's nature push him even further toward the human—in anticipation of the particular comparisons of the anatomical parts that follow—and provide him with an extended and discursive familiarity, in striking contrast to this text's alternative evocation of his strangeness, as "a Creature so very remarkable, and rare" (preface). In this sense, Tyson's pygmy is a composite not only in terms of the redaction and collation through which he is represented, but also in terms of his weird linking of the effects of strangeness with the affects of familiarity.[29] In this double role, the hominoid ape provides an opportunity for the recognition and contemplation of a particular mode of human identity.

[27] This is my translation of Tyson's Latin quotation from Bondt (with the aid of Walter Cohen). The Latin original is as follows: "Vidi ego aliquot utriusque sexus erecte incedentes, imprimis eam (cuius effigiem hic exhibeo) Satyram fœmellam tanta, verecundia ab ignotis sibi hominibus occulentem, tum quoque faciem manibus (liceat ita dicere) tegentem, ubertimque lacrymantem, gemitus cientem, & cæteros humanos actus exprimentem, ut nihil ei humani deesse diceres præter loquelam" (Bondt, 84). Note the allusion on Bondt's part to Terence's "Homo sum, humani nihil a me alienum puto," a well-known catchphrase of the cult of sensibility.
[28] Louis Daniel le Comte, *Nouveaux mémoires sur l'état présent de la Chine* (Amsterdam, 1697). The 1737 English translation is virtually identical to that quoted by Tyson. Lewis le Comte, *Memoirs and Remarks Geographical, Historical,...and Ecclesiastical, Made in Above Ten Years Travels through the Empire of China* (London: J. Hughs, 1737), 509–510.
[29] Wiseman provides another perspective, based on Tyson, of the "troubled way in which apes and humans were found comparable in a dynamic of similarity and difference" ("Monstrous Perfectibility," 217).

Tyson's engagement with classical mythology and history and their reception since ancient times also gives the pygmy this composite valence—familiar and strange at once. The four treatises on the ancients that are attached to *The Anatomy of a Pygmie* together make up about a third of Tyson's entire work. These essays use extensive comparative citation from classical authors and their immediate and more modern commentators to argue that many mythological figures—namely, the pygmies, the cynocephali, "the *Satyrs*, the *Fauni*, *Pan*, *Ægipan*, *Sylvanus*, *Silenus*, and the *Nymphæ*, as also the *Sphinges*"—were a species of great ape (preface). Tyson introduces his reasoning thus:

> This great [anatomical] Agreement, which I observed between [my pygmy] and a *Man*, put me upon considering, whether it might not afford the Occasion to the Ancients, of inventing the many Relations, which they have given us of several *sorts* of *Men*, which are no where to be met with but in their Writings. For I could not but think, there might be some Real Foundation for their *Mythology.*... *Homer's Geranomachia* therefore, or *Fight* of the *Cranes* and *Pygmies*, I have rendered a probable Story. *Aristotle's* assertion of the being of *Pygmies*, I have vindicated from the false Glosses of others. The conjectures of other Learned Men about them, I have examined: And...I think I have fully proved, that there were such *Animals* as the Ancients called *Pygmies*, *Cynocephali*, *Satyrs*, and *Sphinges*; and that they were only *Apes* and *Monkeys*. (*Anatomy*, preface)

For the first essay—*A Philological Essay Concerning the Pygmies of the Ancients*—the urtext of the pygmy is a passage from the *Iliad*—a heroic simile that describes the Trojans' advance to battle at the opening of the third book. In Pope's translation:

> So when inclement Winters vex the Plain
> With piercing Frosts, or thick-descending Rain,
> To warmer Seas the Cranes embody'd fly,
> With Noise, and Order, thro' the mid-way Sky;
> To Pygmy-Nations Wounds and Death they bring,
> And all the War descends upon the Wing.[30]

For Tyson, these pygmy nations resonate throughout classical literature, and his subsequent thirty-seven pages offer a fully annotated and cross-referenced summary of subsequent stories of pygmies—their manners, their government, their speech or language, their weapons, and their battles with the cranes. Tyson uses evidence derived from the

---

[30] Alexander Pope, *The Iliad of Homer*, ed. Maynard Mack (1715–1720; New Haven, Conn.: Yale University Press, 1967), 3: 5–10.

texts he cites here to refute doubts about the existence of pygmies and to reject their representation as small human beings rather than apes.

The essays on the cynocephali, satyrs, and sphinxes that follow adopt the same methodology in abbreviated form. For instance, Tyson's elaborate intertextuality is evident in his reliance on Herodotus, Pliny, and their commentators in the *Philological Essay Concerning the Satyrs of the Ancients:*

> I am apt to think that *Pan, Ægipan, Silvanus* and *Silenus*, were all the same [i.e., apes]; as were the *Satyri* and the *Fauni*....But 'tis sufficient to my business, if I make it appear...that the *Satyrs* were not *Men*, nor *Demi-Gods*, nor *Dæmons*, but only Brutes of the *Monkey-kind*; which is plain enough even from the Ancients....For *Herodotus* tells us, and he is apt enough oftetimes to be over-credulous, [a quotation in Greek from Herodotus appears here, followed by its translation] for they are neither Men, nor have they such Feet. [Two additional quotations in Latin from Solinus and Mela appear here]...*Pliny* gives us a larger description of them. [A quotation in Latin from Pliny appears here, followed by its translation.] You may here perceive they have something of the shape of Men, but can't speak, they are hairy, they go sometimes upon all four, sometimes erect, they have Dogs Teeth, they are wild mischievous Animals. But *Ælian* is a little more express. [A quotation in Latin from Ælian appears here, followed by its translation.] *Ælian* here tells us that they have Tails like Horses, therefore they must be of the *Monkey* or *Baboon* kind. And *Pausanias*, who made it his Business to enquire more particularly about them, informs us they have such Tails, but can't speak, but are very Lascivious and Lustful, as they are observed to be this day. [A quotation in Greek from Pausanias appears here, followed by a quotation of the Latin translation of Pausanias by Conrad Gesner.] It appears therefore plainly that the *Satyrs* have Tails. But that there might not the least Scruple remain what sort of Animals these *Satyrs* were, I shall produce a passage out of *Philostorgius*, which is very express, and comes fully up to our Business: For he tells us [a quotation in Greek appears here] i.e. *That a Satyr is a sort of Ape with a red face, swift of motion, and having a Tail....* By what has been said, I think it fully appears that there were such *Animals* as the Ancients called *Satyrs*; and that they were a sort of *Monkeys* or *Apes* with Tails. (50–52)

Tyson's extensive engagement with and quotation from classical texts in this section of his book thus has the effect of re-creating a classical past in which his rare and remarkable pygmy is an almost ubiquitous presence. This technical anatomical study, then, which, looking forward, is recognized as a pioneering work in the development of modern physiology and empiricist methodology, here presents itself as a vindication of ancient learning, and introduces a new neoclassicism of the great ape—another weird mirror image of human-kind, this time reflecting classical humanist identity with a different face.

Martinus Scriblerus and "Pygmæan" Genealogy

In the history of the life sciences, Tyson's *Anatomy of a Pygmie* is understood to have been "an epoch-making event" that had a profound impact on the methodology and practice of comparative anatomy and on the study of physiology, as well as on the development of those systems of thought that led to the rise of the theory of evolution.[31] And in the imaginative literature of the period, Tyson's pygmy generated a strain of creative speculation that pursued certain key images and concerns—size, proximity to human-kind, sentiment, and classicism—and that quickly took on a life of its own. Tyson's biographer, M. F. Ashley Montagu, has suggested that "there is considerable evidence that [Tyson's] *Orang-Outang* was widely read among the learned both at home and abroad."[32] This influence is present both in the periodical press and in the major literary works and authors of the first part of the eighteenth century.

Significantly, Tyson's book is redacted in compact form and popular format in Richard Blackmore's *Lay-Monastery* (1714), a collection of the periodical essays that Blackmore had published during the months of November 1713 to February 1714 under the title of *The Lay-Monk.* Number 5, for Wednesday, November 25, 1713, begins with an encomium to the "regular and beautiful Subordination" of the scale of being, and then proceeds to a thumbnail summary of Tyson's *Anatomy of a Pygmie.*[33] Blackmore's first example of the proximity of species—the similarity between the lion and the cat—is directly derived from Tyson's opening pages, which explain the anatomical resemblance of animals belonging to the same family by means of an allusion to his simultaneous dissection of a lion and a cat (Tyson, *Anatomy*, 2). Blackmore goes on to paraphrase Tyson's account of the orangutan, describing this being as having "the nearest Resemblance to human

---

[31] Montagu has argued that "Tyson's demonstration of the fact that man stood as the natural successor to the ape in the transition and gradation of animal forms in Nature was really an epoch-making event, and there can be little question that both directly and indirectly it exercised a profound influence upon the intellectual development of the eighteenth century" (*Edward Tyson*, 392). For the argument that Tyson shaped the Enlightenment debate about the nature of man, in particular through his influence on Buffon, see Wokler, "Tyson and Buffon."

[32] Montagu, "Tyson's *Orang-Outang, Sive Homo Sylvestris* and Swift's *Gulliver's Travels*," *PMLA* 59 (1944): 84–89, esp. 84–85. For a broader account of the literary influence of Tyson's work in England, see Franck Tinland, *L'homme sauvage: Homo ferus et homo sylvestris de l'animal à l'homme* (Paris: Payot, 1968), 111–119.

[33] Richard Blackmore, *The Lay-Monastery* (London: Sam. Keimer, 1714), 28.

Nature" of all the apes, pointing in particular to "the Structure of his Body, his Ability to walk upright…his Organs of Speech, his ready Apprehension, and his gentle and tender passions" (30). The rest of the essay is taken up with a summary of Tyson's claims about classical mythology:

> There is the highest Probability, that the *Fauni*, and the *Dryades*, the *Satyr* and the *Sphinx*, *Sylvanus*, *Silennus*, and *Pan* himself, and all the rest of their sacred Elfs, and woodland Divinities, as well as the Nymphs, the Fairy-like Goddesses of the Lakes and Rivers…were nothing else than some of these Manlike Inhabitants of the Wood….And as this inferior Order of Deities were probably only Apes and Monkeys, dignify'd with divine Titles; so a Race of Men, call'd *Pygmies*, in whom the Frame of human Bodies is abridg'd, and express'd in Miniature, seem to owe their imaginary Being to the same Original. *Homer*, having describ'd the Shouts and Clamours of the *Trojan* Army falling on the *Greeks*, from the Noise made by the *Cranes* ready to engage their Enemies, in an elegant Figure calls their Foes…*Pygmæan Men*. (31)

Blackmore's essay presents the argument of *The Anatomy of a Pygmie* for a popular audience, omitting Tyson's technical anatomical analysis and his elaborate textual apparatus and quotation, but retaining and highlighting the key items of size, proximity to the human, "tender passions," and classical precedent.

At the same time that Blackmore's popularization was published in the periodical press, Tyson's book was being re-created in a very different form by that vitally engaged modern persona, Martinus Scriblerus. Scriblerus is the invention of the literary club established by Alexander Pope, Jonathan Swift, John Arbuthnot, John Gay, Thomas Parnell, and Robert Harley (subsequently Earl of Oxford). The Scriblerians met only briefly during a few months of 1713 and 1714, but the club produced a collaborative group of works in which the imaginary Martinus Scriblerus was used variously as a means to parody modern taste, literature, scholarship, and science. Though Scriblerus's most famous work, *Peri Bathous*, a parody of contemporary aesthetic theory, was published in 1728 under Pope's authorship, most of the Scriblerian materials were not printed until they were assembled for the 1741 edition of Pope's collected works. One of their initial compositions, however, was a parody of Tyson's *Anatomy of a Pygmie* by Pope and Arbuthnot—*An Essay of the Learned Martinus Scriblerus, Concerning the Origine of Sciences*.[34] As a physician and fellow member of the Royal Society, Arbuthnot was certainly acquainted with Tyson and his anatomical treatise. But

---

[34] For the date of composition and authorship, see Montagu, "Tyson's *Orang-Outang*," 86.

his and Pope's parody is directed at Tyson's new neoclassicism, and only implicitly at his scientific claims; it suggests the contemporary impact of Tyson's imaginative revision of classical humanism, which is expressed in the character of Scriblerus. *Concerning the Origine of Sciences* gives full and uninhibited expression to the weird notion of a classical past populated by "*Apes* and *Monkeys*" that emerges from Tyson's contemplation of the chimpanzee.

Toward the end of the essay, in fact, Scriblerus explicitly advertises his connection to Tyson by naming Tyson's pygmy as "the last of this great line" of apes that the text has traced from ancient times. Tyson's pygmy is designated as

> Oran Outang the great, the last of this line; whose unhappy chance it was to fall into the hands of Europeans. Oran Outang, whose value was not known to us, for he was a mute philosopher: Oran Outang, by whose dissection the learned Dr. Tyson has added a confirmation to this system, from the resemblance between the Homo Sylvestris and our humane body, in those organs by which the rational soul is exerted.[35]

But before arriving at this encomium, the text has led the reader through a much more wonderful genealogy. Scriblerus writes "from the Deserts of Æthiopia" in order to search out the source of human arts and sciences (263). He discovers that "nor Troy nor Thebes were the first of Empires; we have mention…of an earlier warlike people call'd the Pygmæans," who must be the source of all learning. Though their empire was lost—to "flocks of monstrous birds"—they are crucially in evidence, as Scriblerus's treatise demonstrates, in the unfolding of classical history (264). The following pages imitate Tyson in presenting an annotated summary of classical texts, which are interpreted in support of the claim for the influence of these "Pygmæans." First, Scriblerus shows, they civilized Egypt and India. Diodorus met them ("a sort of little Satyrs") in Ethiopia, and their "leader Pan accompanied him in his expedition for the civilizing of mankind" (264). They then went with Bacchus to India, in the person of Silenus, who had a tail and who settled a colony of tailed progeny there. In India they originated the ascetic philosophical order of gymnosophists, who "imitated, with all the exactness imaginable, the manners and customs of their masters. They are said to dwell in the thickest woods, to go naked, to suffer their bodies to be over-run with hair, and their nails to grow to a prodigious length. Plutarch says 'they ate what they could get in the fields, their drink was water, and their bed made of leaves or moss'" (265).

---

[35] Alexander Pope, *The Works of Mr. Alexander Pope, in Prose.* 2 vols. (London: J. and P. Knapton, C. Bathurst, and R. Dodsley, 1741), 2: 269.

Meanwhile, through Orpheus's arrival from Egypt, these Pygmæans carried arts and learning to Greece. Orpheus brought "some of this wonderful species along with him," and their presence evidently accounts for the legend "of the beasts following the musick of Orpheus," which thus has a simple literal explanation. In addition, Aesop, who was "short, deform'd, and almost savage" and who wrote about beasts, was therefore certainly descended from "these *sylvestres Homines.*" As was an even more revered figure of antiquity: Socrates, as we know, "was of an uncommon birth from the rest of men .... [and he] had a countenance confessing the line he sprung from, being bald, flat-nos'd, with prominent eyes, and a downward look." And of course his Pygmæan genealogy is confirmed by the fact that "he turned certain fables of Aesop into verse, probably out of his respect to beasts in general, and love to his family [of apes] in particular" (266).

In Italy, Scriblerus uncovers another Pygmæan at the founding moment of the Roman republic; "Such was he [Lucius Junius Brutus] who coming out of the woods in hatred to tyranny, encourag'd the Roman army to proceed against the [Etruscans], who would have restore'd Tarquin." And it is in Italy, around the time of Aristotle, Scriblerus says, that these beings "began to be silent," due to the increase in the "number, vanity and folly of human philosophers...by which men's heads became too much puzzled to receive the wisdom of these ancient Sylvans." "From this period, if we ever hear of their giving answers, it is only when caught, bound, and constrain'd, in like manner as was that ancient Grecian prophet, Proteus" (267). And we find traces of these beings even in the present day, according to Scriblerus, notably in Tyson's "Oran Outang the great." Scriblerus ends with a twist that turns to the question of human identity:

> This account, which is entirely my own, I am proud to imagine has traced knowledge from a fountain correspondent to several opinions of the Ancients, tho' hitherto undiscover'd both by them and the moderns. And now, what shall I say to mankind in the thought of this great discovery? What, but that they should abate of their Pride, and consider that the authors of our knowledge are among beasts. That these, who were our elder brothers, by a day in the creation, whose kingdom like that in the scheme of Plato was govern'd by philosophers, who flourish'd with learning in Æthiopia and India, are now undistinguish'd from, and known only by the same appellation as...the monkey! (269)

For Pope and Arbuthnot, Tyson's "discovery" that classical mythology and history were populated by monkeys merges with the *Anatomy's* demonstration of the proximity of human and ape "in the formation of the Body, and in the *Sensitive,* or *Brutal* Soul." The conclusion of *Concerning the Origine of Sciences* suggests that Pope and Arbuthnot perceive

Tyson's text to be thus undercutting or confusing any notions of the privileged position of human-kind. It is for this reason that Scriblerus, as parodic spokesman for Tyson, can recognize Socrates as an ape, while he criticizes human pride as based on the achievements of a monkey.[36]

Gulliver's Travels and the Hominoid Ape

Scriblerus's essay serves as a bridge between Tyson's treatise and Swift's *Gulliver's Travels*, allowing us to see the ways in which Swift's text, too, takes up the central agenda items generated by *The Anatomy of a Pygmie*—especially the obsession with size and the concern with the proximity of human and nonhuman. In regard to the latter, we have already noted the parallels between Gulliver's mirror scene—where he resolves "to behold my Figure often in a Glass"—and those other moments of recognition in which human-kind encounters, in its own reflection, the image of the great ape. The Yahoo is a vividly realized representation of the hominoid ape, drawn widely and closely from travelers' descriptions of these beings encountered in Africa and Asia, and reflecting the new contemporary imaginative engagement with this species of animal-kind. Jobson's description of the chimpanzee in *The Golden Trade* is a vivid account with a wide contemporary resonance, and provides a touchstone for comparison with the fourth book of *Gulliver's Travels*:

> In the rear comes vp a great quantity of the biggest sort,…and in this manner doe they march along: they are very bold, and as we passe in the riuer, when we come neare their troupes, they will get vp into the trees, and stand in gaze upon vs, and in a kind of collericke humour the great ones will shake the trees, and with his hands clatter the boughes in that fashion, as it doth exceed the strength of man, to doe the like, barking, and making a noyse at us, as if they were much offended, and in this manner, many times they will follow vs along;…when we are a shore and meete with these troupes, on a sudden the great ones will come forward, and seeme to grin in our faces; but offer vp a gunne, and away they packe. (152–153)[37]

---

[36] Wiseman suggests that Scriblerus's essay might be regarded as "semi-serious," indicating that "the text seems fascinated by the possibility that the ape-human divide is mutable" ("Monstrous Perfectibility," 229).

[37] Thomas Boreman provides another version of this scene: "I have both read and heard Travellers relate, that when they have pass'd thro' the Woods, where the Apes frequent, these unlucky Creatures have kept them Company for a great while together, by leaping from Bough to Bough, and from Tree to Tree; sometimes they would nimbly descend one Tree, and, crossing the Pathway just before them, as quickly ascend another; at other times they wou'd drop on a Sudden from a higher to a lower Branch, just, as it were, upon the Passengers Heads, and appear so daring and bold, as if they meant to attack them, all the while screaming, and making such a frightful hideous Noise, as was enough to terrify a Company of Travelers, much more a single one. But

Gulliver's first experience with the Yahoos includes the same grinning, pursuing, noise-making, and tree climbing:

> I met one of these Creatures full in my Way, and coming up directly to me. The ugly Monster, when he saw me, distorted several Ways every Feature of his Visage....But I drew my Hanger....[H]e drew back, and roared so loud that a herd of at least forty came flocking about me from the next Field, howling and making odious Faces; but I ran to the Body of a Tree, and leaning my Back against it, kept them off, by waving my Hanger. Several of this cursed Brood getting hold of the Branches behind, leaped up into the Tree, from whence they began to discharge their Excrements on my Head. (207–208)

Swift also reproduces in his Yahoos many other details of orangutan descriptions—including an account of the nails or claws, their frequent bipedalism, their nimble climbing and great agility, their lack of tails, their hanging breasts (for females), and in particular the amount and location of their bodily and facial hair (207). The central contemporary resource for all of these vividly represented and varied details, as we have seen, is Tyson's encyclopedic compendium of quotation and anecdote in *The Anatomy of a Pygmie*. Indeed, for the English eighteenth century, Tyson's pygmy is the empirical record, and Swift's Yahoo the canonical literary expression, of the discovery of the great ape.

But many of the details of Swift's Yahoos' appearance and behavior are also extracted from accounts of the "savage man" or the "Hottentot." Buffon's description of man in a state of nature in his *Natural History* illustrates the underlying logic of this connection in contemporary thought:

> To form a proper judgment between them, a savage man and an ape should be viewed together; for we have no just idea of man in a pure state of nature. The head covered with bristly hairs, or with curled wool; the face partly hid by a long beard, and still longer hairs in the front, which surround his eyes, and make them appear sunk in his head, like those of the brutes; the lips thick and projecting, the nose flat, the aspect wild or stupid; the ears, body, and limbs are covered with hair; the nails long, thick, and crooked;...the breasts of the female long and flabby, and the skin of her belly hanging down to her knees....This sketch, drawn from a savage Hottentot, is still a flattering portrait, for there is as great a distance between a man in a pure state of nature and a Hottentot,

they were always observ'd to turn their Backs and run away, whenever a Man attack'd them." *A Description of Some Curious and Uncommon Creatures* (London: Richard Ware and Thomas Boreman, 1739). 26–27.

as there is between a Hottentot and us. But if we wish to compare the human species with that of the ape, we must add to it the affinities of organization, the agreements of temperament,…and then consider, supposing them not of the same species, how difficult it is to discover the interval by which they are separated.[38]

Again, we can find all these details in Swift's Yahoos: the "flat and broad" countenance, with "the Nose depressed, the Lips large, and the Mouth wide" (212), the "thick hair, some frizzled and others lank," the "beards like goats," the "strong extended claws," and the "dugs [of the females hanging] between their fore-feet, and often [reaching] to the ground as they walked" (207, 212). Further parallels are evident between the accounts of the Hottentot's typical behaviors and Swift's description of the Yahoos' activities: for example, their eating of carrion, their lack of civil government, their offensive smell, and their treachery.[39] Of course Buffon himself draws on contemporary images of the great ape here to invent his idea of the savage man, as did other eighteenth-century travelers and protoethnographers; this description explicitly equates the savage man and the ape, insisting that they "should be viewed together" in comparison to the European ("us") and the Hottentot, and even refusing in the end to distinguish them. Swift's Yahoo is a composite of Hottentot and hominoid ape, but both of those models are themselves collated beings—the Hottentot mingling contemporary accounts of human and ape, and the ape itself, as we have seen, representing a complex intertextual creation.

The double genealogy of the Yahoo displays the confusion or ambivalence generated in this period by the idea of the proximity between human- and animal-kind. Buffon's speculative analogy—ape is to Hottentot as Hottentot is to European—is symptomatic of this confusion and typical of contemporary discourse on this topic. Blackmore's popularization of Tyson presents the same relativistic reasoning in its opening pages, in summarizing Tyson's claim for the orangutan's "Resemblance to human Nature":

[S]o the Ape or Monkey, that bears the greatest Similitude to Man, is the next Order of Animals below him. Nor is the Disagreement between the basest Individuals of our Species and the Ape or Monkey so Great, but that were the latter endow'd with the Faculty of Speech, they might perhaps as justly claim the Rank and Dignity of the human Race, as the Salvage *Hotentot*, or stupid Native of *Nova Zembla*. (29)

---

[38] Buffon, *Barr's Buffon: Buffon's Natural History* (London: H. D. Symonds, 1797), 9: 136–137. In this late edition the relativist comparison is developed slightly more fully than in the 1780–1785 Edinburgh edition.
[39] For a full account of the Yahoos' connection to contemporary descriptions of Africans, see Laura Brown, *Ends of Empire: Women and Ideology in Early Eighteenth-Century English Literature* (Ithaca, N.Y.: Cornell University Press, 1993), 188–196.

This time, however, the ape and the Hottentot occupy the same place in relation to the European. These relativist analogies symptomatically give the ape an ambiguous flexibility in relation to the hierarchy at hand. Buffon can only suggest "how difficult it is to discover the interval" by which the ape can be distinguished from the savage man. Blackmore indicates that this being "might perhaps" be indistinguishable from the savage man, from the Hottentot, or even from the "Dignity of the human Race" (Europeans)—a dignity that this passage suggests may not even be applicable to the "Salvage *Hottentot*, or stupid Native of *Nova Zembla*." The hominoid ape is thus a potential shifter within these relativist comparisons, gaining or losing status in the hierarchy depending on the particular perspective. This is the movement represented in the fourth voyage of *Gulliver's Travels*, as the Yahoos shift from ape to human, as Gulliver shifts from human to Yahoo, and as human-kind itself finds its dignity, and even its identity, redefined.

Swift's Houyhnhnms and Gulliver's identification with them replicate this movement. As R. S. Crane has shown, the Houyhnhnm/Yahoo relationship is an obvious, ironic reversal of the conventional pairing of rational man and irrational horse in the widely read logic textbooks of the day: "homo est animal rationale," but "equus est animal hinnibile."[40] In Swift's text, then, the Houyhnhnms, laying claim to that quality that exclusively defines human being, shift from animal to human. And at the same time, Gulliver, in his absurd imitation of the Houyhnhnms, shifts from human to animal:

> I fell to imitate their Gait and Gesture, which is now grown into a Habit, and my Friends often tell me in a blunt Way, that *I trot like a Horse*; which, however, I take for a great Compliment: Neither shall I disown, that in speaking I am apt to fall into the Voice and manner of the *Houyhnhnms*, and hear my self ridiculed on that Account without the least Mortification. (252)

In both cases—horse to human and human to horse—the reciprocal movement between animal and human produces a disturbing ambivalence, an echo of that same confusion that we have located in the new proximity of human and hominoid ape.[41]

An extension of this symptomatic relativism is evident in *Gulliver's Travels*'s engagement with the issue of size—in the form of the "*Puny* diminutive *Race* of *Mankind*"—that preoccupies Tyson's *Anatomy of a Pygmie* (*Anatomy*, 1). The Lilliputians' connection to

---

[40] R. S. Crane, "The Houyhnhnms, the Yahoos, and the History of Ideas," in *Reason and the Imagination: Studies in the History of Ideas, 1600–1800*, ed. J. A. Mazzeo (New York: Columbia University Press, 1962), 231–253, 245, 248.

[41] Philip Armstrong describes this same dynamic in the context of the Cartesian debates, concluding that "neither Yahoos nor Houyhnhnms should be considered as portraits of the human, ideal or otherwise." Philip Armstrong, *What Animals Mean in the Fiction of Modernity* (New York: Routledge, 2008), 11.

Tyson's text can most readily be tracked through the persona of Scriblerus. Around the time that Scriblerus's *Concerning the Origine of Sciences* was written, Pope, Swift, and Arbuthnot composed the Scriblerian biography, the *Memoirs of the Extraordinary Life, Works, and Discoveries of Martinus Scriblerus.*[42] This work concludes with a chapter (probably by Swift) *"containing some hint of* [Scriblerus's] *travels,"* which provides an advance notice for *Gulliver's Travels.* We learn that "it was in the year 1699 that Martin set out on his *Travels....* [I]n his first Voyage he was carry'd by a prosperous Storm, to a Discovery of the Remains of the ancient *Pygmæan* Empire.... In his second, he was as happily shipwreck'd on the Land of the *Giants....* In his third Voyage, he discover'd a whole Kingdom of *Philosophers....* And... in his fourth Voyage he discovers a Vein of Melancholy proceeding almost to a Disgust with his Species" (67–70). Scriblerus's and Tyson's Pygmæans develop into Swift's Lilliputians, and the date designated for Scriblerus's travels signals their link to Tyson—1699 was the publication date of *The Anatomy of a Pygmie.*

Tyson's compilation of classical pygmy anecdotes also provides material for the activities of Swift's Lilliputians. Here, again, Tyson's method of quotation and encyclopedic summary is a rich resource for the imaginative treatment of issues of size and questions of relativism. Tyson cites a story of an attack on Hercules by "the *Pygmies...in Philostratus*":

> Having found *Hercules* napping...[the Pygmies] mustered up all their Forces against him. One *Phalanx* (he tells us) assaulted his left hand; but against his right hand, that being the stronger, two *Phalanges* were appointed. The Archers and Slingers besieged his feet, admiring the hugeness of his Thighs: But against his Head, as the Arsenal, they raised Batteries, the King himself taking his Post there. They set fire to his Hair, put Reaping-hooks in his Eyes; and that he might not breath, clapp'd Doors to his Mouth and Nostrils; but all the Execution that they could do, was only to awake him. (*Philological Essay*, 29)

In the voyage to Lilliput, a similar siege is launched against Gulliver as he too lies sleeping in the grass:

> When I awaked, it was just Day-light. I attempted to rise, but was not able to stir: For as I happened to lie on my Back, I found my Arms and Legs were strongly fastened on each Side to the Ground; and my Hair, which was long and thick, tied down in the same Manner.... At length, struggling to get loose, I had the Fortune to break the Strings, and wrench out the Pegs that fastened my left Arm to the Ground.... But the Creatures ran off...before I could seize them;

[42] The *Memoirs* was first published along with *Concerning the Origine of Sciences* in Pope's volume 2 of his collected prose works, *The Works of Mr. Alexander Pope, in Prose.*

whereupon there was a great Shout…when in an Instant I felt above an Hundred Arrows discharged on my left Hand, which pricked me like so many Needles; and besides, they shot another Flight into the Air, as we do Bombs in *Europe;* whereof many, I suppose, fell on my Body, (though I felt them not) and some on my Face, which I immediately covered with my left Hand. When this Shower of Arrows was over, I fell a groaning with Grief and Pain; and then striving again to get loose, they discharged another Volly larger than the first; and some of them attempted with Spears to stick me in the Sides; but, by good Luck, I had on me a Buff Jerkin, which they could not pierce. (41–42)

And the image of the *"Puny* diminutive" people piercing Hercules's eyes is reproduced later on in *Gulliver's Travels,* in the story of the plans for Gulliver's punishment by the Lilliputian Council, when "very sharp pointed Arrows" are to be discharged "into the Balls of [his] Eyes" (83).

Furthermore, in recounting Gulliver's return from Lilliput, Swift's text pays special attention to an unusual detail: the Lilliputians' diminutive sheep. Tyson too highlights the tiny livestock that accompany classical descriptions of the Pygmies. He quotes, translates, and compares commentary on a passage from Aristotle that observes that "both they and the Horses…are a small kind" (*Philological Essay,* 15), returning again to this issue of animal size in a quote from Strabo, who, Tyson says, records that in certain parts of Africa "generally the Beasts are of a less size than ordinary; and this he thinks might give rise to the Story of the *Pygmies*" (*Philological Essay,* 35). Tyson cites other sources that describe the Pygmies who "attend the *King of India*" and "are good *Archers*": "Their Sheep are like Lambs; and their Oxen and Asses scarce as big as Rams; and their Horses and Mules, and all their other Cattle not bigger" (*Philological Essay,* 9). These classical images of tiny livestock take on an expanded and even fetishized imaginative life in *Gulliver's Travels.* Upon his rescue, Gulliver "put my Cows and Sheep into my Coat-Pockets, and got on board with all my little Cargo of Provisions." To prove his tale to the captain, he "took my black Cattle and Sheep out of my Pocket, which, after great Astonishment, clearly convinced him of my Veracity." He notes that on board ship he "had only one Misfortune, that the Rats…carried away one of my Sheep; I found her Bones in a Hole, picked clean from the Flesh" (88). The good news is that

the rest of my Cattle I got safe on Shore, and set them a grazing in a Bowling-Green at *Greenwich,* where the fineness of the Grass made them feed very heartily.…I made a considerable Profit by shewing my Cattle to many Persons of Quality, and others; And before I began my second Voyage, I sold them for six Hundred Pounds. Since my last Return, I find the Breed is considerably increased, especially the Sheep; which I hope will prove much to the Advantage of the Woollen Manufacture, by the Fineness of the Fleeces. (88–89)

As we have seen, comparative size gives Tyson the grounds for remaking the classical humanist tradition in the image of the great ape. In *Gulliver's Travels*, the question of size, and in particular the marvel of something's or someone's unusual size, gives rise to extended speculation on those relativist structures of thought that are generated by the discovery of this being, and that we have seen in Buffon's and Blackmore's comparisons of humans, apes, and Hottentots. In the fourth voyage, this relativism is implicit in the contemplation of the hominoid ape and the Hottentot together, in the form of the Yahoo. But in the first two voyages it is directly expressed through the relationship among Gulliver, the Lilliputians, and the Brobdingnagians. In Brobdingnag Gulliver reflects on the fact that he must appear "as inconsiderable in this Nation, as one single *Lilliputian* would be among us." At this point he provides a version of the familiar relativist analogy:

> Undoubtedly Philosophers are in the Right when they tell us, that nothing is great or little otherwise than by Comparison: It might have pleased Fortune to let the *Lilliputians* find some Nation, where the People were as diminutive with respect to them, as they were to me. And who knows but that even this prodigious Race of Mortals might be equally overmatched in some distant Part of the World, whereof we have yet no Discovery? (94–95)

The Lilliputians are to a more diminutive nation as Gulliver is to the Lilliputians, and as a more "prodigious Race" would be to the Brobdingnagians. Like Buffon's rhetoric of relativity—"as great a distance between a man in a pure state of nature and a Hottentot, as...between a Hottentot and us"—this passage projects an infinite regress with the human being—Gulliver or "us"—at its heart.

Swift enacts this relativist trope throughout the second voyage, in scenes where Gulliver reflects on the Brobdingnagians in terms of the Lilliputians, and vice versa. For instance, in noting the coarse appearance of the Brobdingnagians' skin, Gulliver observes that "when I was at *Lilliput*, the Complexions of those diminutive People appeared to me the fairest in the World," whereas his own face was "a very shocking sight" to his Lilliputian friend (99). And in regard to the "offensive Smell" of the gigantic Maids of Honour, he recalls that "an intimate Friend of mine in *Lilliput* took the Freedom in a warm Day, when I had used a good deal of Exercise, to complain of a strong Smell about me....I suppose his Faculty of Smelling was as nice with regard to me, as mine was to that of this People" (120). In the broader context, this preoccupation with comparison is a key issue in contemporary scientific thought, as we have already seen in the instance of Tyson's influential comparative anatomy. The prominent status of comparison in *Gulliver's Travels* indicates the implication of Swift's text in the major themes of the development of the life sciences. In the course of the eighteenth century, comparison becomes not only the primary aim of the science of anatomy but also the dominant methodology in the study of human culture and development, and of the differences between men and women.[43]

Swift's *Gulliver's Travels* is thus deeply engaged with the contemplation of the great ape, the speculation about this being's proximity to human-kind, the relativist structures of thought that issued from that speculation, and the implications of this "Monster with a human face" for human identity. Like Scriblerus in his discovery of the human debt to the monkey, which teaches human-kind "that they should abate of their Pride," Gulliver too finds a lesson in his own discovery of his resemblance to the Yahoos: "[B]ut, when I behold a Lump of Deformity, and Diseases both in Body and Mind, smitten with *Pride*, it immediately breaks all the Measures of my Patience" (266). Here in his own conclusion, Swift echoes the conclusion to Pope and Arbuthnot's parody of *The Anatomy of a Pygmie*. In this sense Gulliver, like Scriblerus, occupies the place of the "epoch-making" figure of Edward Tyson, anatomizing the hominoid ape for a wondering, speculating, mortified, or horrified human-kind.

The Affectionate and Melancholic Ape

The other vital mode of speculation put into play by Tyson's *Anatomy of a Pygmie* is the projection of sentimental values on the figure of the great ape. Tyson's summaries of accounts of the orangutan's modesty and affection indicate the tendency—increasing through the eighteenth century—to imagine the hominoid ape through the lens of sensibility. The London populace itself was involved in this exercise during the five-month period in 1738 when a young chimpanzee, recently arrived from Guinea, was put on display in the city. She could be viewed for a shilling at Randall's Coffee House, and she immediately became a regular topic in the periodical press. She evidently received many visitors, including some of the city's most distinguished figures as well as aristocrats and foreign dignitaries. She "sat for her Picture," done on copperplate by Scotin, which was

---

[43] For an annotated summary of these topics of comparison, see Christopher Fox, "Introduction: How to Prepare a Noble Savage; The Spectacle of Human Science," in *Inventing Human Science*, 1–30, esp. 14–15. For the subsequent history of comparative anatomy, see William Coleman, *Georges Cuvier, Zoologist: A Study in the History of Evolution Theory* (Cambridge, Mass.: Harvard University Press, 1964), 60–67.

in great demand throughout London over the next several months. The announcement of her arrival prepares the way for the accounts of her sensitivity and affection, which are evident in subsequent anecdotes describing her nature:

> A most surprising Creature is brought over in the *Speaker*, just arrived from *Carolina*, that was taken in a Wood at *Guinea*; it is a Female about four Foot high, shaped in every Part like a Woman excepting its Head, which nearly resembles the Ape: She walks upright naturally, sits down to her food, which is chiefly Greens, and feeds herself with her Hands as a human Creature. She is very fond of a Boy on board, and is observed always sorrowful at his Absence. She is cloathed with a thin Silk Vestment, and shows a great Discontent at the opening her Gown to discover her Sex.[44]

Later periodical accounts especially focus on her sitting at the table, decorously drinking tea, and eating "in so decent a manner." In one anecdote this being's affectionate nature is tested, when a mother sets her baby before her. She immediately put aside "a Cup of Tea...and an Apple," and "with both Hands clasped round the Child's Neck, embraced and kissed it, to the great Surprize of all the Gentlemen and Ladies then in Company."[45] She was autopsied at her death, and described as "perfectly of a human Specie."[46]

 The fame—and natural sensibility—of this chimpanzee visitor was probably most effectively promoted by Thomas Boreman, in a volume supplementary to his very successful work for a juvenile audience, *A Description of Three Hundred Animals*, originally co-published with Richard Ware and Thomas Game in 1730. *Three Hundred Animals* was a pioneering work of popular natural history, extraordinarily widely read and influential well beyond the children's market. The book went through thirty-eight editions by the end of the nineteenth century, and is credited with influencing Buffon's major natural history volumes.[47] The popularity of *Three Hundred Animals* prompted Boreman to print a supplement entitled *A Description of Some Curious and Uncommon Creatures* (1739), which includes as its first section a twenty-one page redaction of Tyson's *Anatomy of a Pygmie*, supported by extended (unacknowledged) extracts from Blackmore's essay on Tyson

[44] *The London Magazine, and Monthly Chronologer*, September 1738, 7: 464–465.
[45] *The Daily Post*, October 26, 1738. Cited in G. S. Rousseau, "Madame Chimpanzee," in *Enlightenment Crossings: Pre- and Post-Modern Discourses Anthropological* (Manchester: Manchester University Press, 1991), 198–209, this quote 201. See Rousseau for further details about "Madame Chimpanzee's" time in London.
[46] Cited in Rousseau, "Madame Chimpanzee," 203.
[47] For the influence of Boreman's popularizing natural history, see Harriet Ritvo, "Learning from Animals: Natural History for Children in the Eighteenth and Nineteenth Centuries," *Children's Literature* 13 (1985): 72–93. See also the *Oxford Dictionary of National Biography*, s.v. "Boreman, Thomas" (Oxford University Press, 2008), http://www.oup.com/oxforddnb.

in the *Lay-Monastery*, and followed by a second section, "An Account of the Female Chimpanzee," which describes the events of 1738. The latter essay extracts and compiles popular reports of the chimpanzee's manners and sensibility, setting out for a large audience a summary account of her character that is grounded in the authority of Tyson's scientific credentials. In fact, in the first section summarizing Tyson, Boreman provides a direct connection between Tyson's pygmy and the female chimpanzee, in terms of their natural sensibility. He observes that Tyson's pygmy

> was as gentle and loving to Man that could be: Those that he knew a Ship-board he would come and embrace with the greatest Tenderness, opening their Bosoms, and clasping his Hands about them....The Female *Chimpanzee* shew'd the like Affections to those Persons it was used to, particularly to a Boy, whom it would never suffer to go out of its sight; but would cry, and express the greatest Uneasiness till he return'd; and for the sake of pleasing and diverting it, they were obliged to keep him 'till the Creature died. (1–2)

In the next section, Boreman continues to emphasize this natural affection, describing the female chimpanzee as possessing "great affability beyond any other kind of Brute Animal" and being "extremely loving" (22, 23). He repeats the anecdote of the boy whom "she could not bare he shou'd go out of her Sight," adding that she "was very pretty Company at the Tea-table, behav'd with Modesty and good Manners, and gave great Satisfaction to the Ladies who were pleas'd to honour her with their Visits" (23–24).

Thus, the idea of the natural sensibility of the hominoid ape, which we have seen so effectively promulgated and then popularized by Tyson, Blackmore, and Boreman, is not a new notion by the time the Scottish philosopher James Burnet, Lord Monboddo, produces his argument that the orangutan is "a barbarous nation [of our species], which has not yet learned the use of speech" in the second edition of his treatise *Of the Origin and Progress of Language* (second edition, 1774).[48] Though Monboddo's views of the great ape are often described as idiosyncratic, in fact they represent yet another redaction and collation of prior anecdotes and observations, extending the resources and the agenda provided by Tyson and highlighting the idea of this being's sensibility. The extended treatment of the orangutan in volume one of the second edition of Monboddo's treatise is based on a reading of Tyson and a reflection on prior representations of this

---

[48] James Burnet, Lord Monboddo, *Of the Origin and Progress of Language*, 2nd ed. (Edinburgh, 1774; repr. New York: Garland, 1970), 1:270, 311. Although by the time of Monboddo's writing other differentiated terminology for the great apes is more available, Monboddo uses the term *orangutan* to refer broadly to the anthropoid ape. The beings whom he is chiefly describing are the African chimpanzee and gorilla.

being.[49] Here Monboddo seeks to prove that "[l]anguage is not natural to man" by demonstrating that "the Orang Outangs are men" who have not yet acquired the art of speech (v, 347).[50] Chapters 4 and 5 of book 2 in this volume support this claim, following the model of compilation and redaction that we have seen in representations of the hominoid ape throughout the eighteenth century by stitching together various reports of now-familiar accounts of this being's proximity to human-kind: the similar appearance, the parallel anatomies, the natural human-like behaviors, including manners of eating, drinking, and sitting at table, and the ready acquisition of certain human skills.[51]

But at the core of Monboddo's demonstration of the humanity of the orangutan is the idea of natural sensibility. Monboddo posits three rules "for ascertaining the identity of the species": the similarity of "the outward form"; the correspondence of the "inward configuration," or anatomy; and the resemblance "of the inward principle, which directs the motions and actions of the animal, and is the source of all its sentiments, inclinations, and affections" (337). The first two criteria Monboddo establishes through citations from Tyson and Buffon. He pursues the third—the idea of the "conformity…of the natural habits and dispositions of the mind" (338)—through the collation of a familiar repertory of anecdotes and observations, which, taken together, demonstrate that

> the Orang Outang is an animal of the human form, inside as well as outside: That he has the human intelligence, as much as can be expected in an animal living without civility or arts: That he has a disposition of mind, mild, docile, and humane: That he has the sentiments and affections peculiar to our species, such as the sense of modesty, of honour, and of justice; and likewise an attachment of love and friendship to one individual, so strong in some instances, that one friend will not survive the other. (289–290)

[49] Between the two editions, Monboddo received commentary on the topic of the orangutan and drafted an essay entitled "Of the Orang-Outang, and Whether He Be of the Human Species" (dating from 1733–1744). This essay was incorporated into the second edition and resulted in substantial changes. See Robert Wokler, "Apes and Races in the Scottish Enlightenment: Monboddo and Kames on the Nature of Man," in *Philosophy and Science in the Scottish Enlightenment*, ed. Peter Jones, (Edinburgh: John Donald Publishers, 1988), 145–168, 158.

[50] For a compact summary of the eighteenth-century debate about the relevance of language to the definition of the human, see Wokler, "Tyson and Buffon." For a full summary of Monboddo's argument here, see Wokler, "Apes and Race," 148–152. Monboddo's ideas about language are closely related to Rousseau's.

[51] For a summary of Monboddo's chapters on the great ape, the relationship of his ideas to those of Rousseau and Hobbes, and his significance in the rise of evolutionary thought in England, see Arthur O. Lovejoy, "Rousseau and Monboddo," *Modern Philology* 30 (1933): 275–296. Lovejoy notes Monboddo's focus on the natural benevolence of the orangutan (285). Wokler's account of Rousseau's understanding of savage man as "truly an orangutan" provides an important perspective on Monboddo. "Perfectible Apes in Decadent Cultures: Rousseau's Anthropology Revisited," *Daedalus* 107 (1978): 107–134, 117.

On modesty, Monboddo cites, among others, Bondt and Buffon, presenting the familiar scene of the female orangutan "conceal[ing] with their hand, those parts, which modesty forbids to shew" (272, 279, 291). On melancholy he relies again on Bondt for images of weeping and groaning, and on a more recent traveler, "Mr Maillet…who has collected a great many curious facts concerning the varieties of our species," who wrote that the orangutan he saw in New Guinea "were very melancholy, gentle and peaceable" (302–303). On the orangutan's "sweet temper," he cites Buffon's description of "one of the small kind, who…was grave and composed,…[and] behaved, in every respect, like a man" (280). On honor and justice, Monboddo produces a letter from a traveler in Africa describing instances in which these beings, exposed to crowds or insult, "take it so much to heart, that they languish and die" (287); an additional anecdote describes the "husband" of a female orangutan who had been killed: "He seized the negro [responsible] and [dragged] him out of the house, to the place where his wife lay dead…to shew him what he had done" (288). And on affection, Monboddo presents the testimony of "a gentleman who was an eye-witness of it": "An Orang Outang, which was on board his ship, conceived such an affection for the cook, that when, upon some occasion, he left the ship, to go ashore, the gentleman saw the Orang Outang shed tears in great abundance" (343–345).

This collation of images supporting the proximity of orangutan and human leads to the same relativist analogy that we have traced in Swift, Buffon, and Blackmore:

> If…the Orang Outang be not a man, then those philosophers of Europe, who, about the time of the discovery of America, maintained, that the inhabitants of that part of the world were not men, reasoned well; for, certainly, the Americans had not then, nor have they yet, learned all the arts of which their nature is capable. But I think the Pope, by his bull, decided the controversy well, when he gave it in favour of the humanity of the poor Americans: And for the same reason, we ought to decide, that the Orang Outangs are men. And, indeed, it appears to me, that they are not so much inferior to the Americans in civility and cultivation, as some nations of America were to us, when we first discovered that country. (347–348)[52]

Again, the hominoid ape generates a relativist schema—showing where the orangutan stand in relation to the Americans, and the Americans relative to Europeans—in which the hierarchies of beings are highlighted and problematized, and in which the flexible

[52] Here Monboddo refers to the 1537 papal bull of Pope Paul III that recognized Indians and all other indigenous peoples as humans, rather than brutes, and therefore protected from exploitation.

phrase "not so much" even suggests the potential for equivalency. Elsewhere, this text's images of equivalency generate another recognition scene, which recalls Bondt's "wonder" and Buffon's contemplation of himself:

> Is it then a wonder, that this man of nature, the Orang Outang, should be so different from us? Or, is it not rather a wonder, that we should find in him any of our own features? Yet the fact truly is, that the man is easily distinguishable in him; nor are there any differences betwixt him and us, but what may be accounted for in so satisfactory a manner, that it would be extraordinary and unnatural, if they were not to be found. (356)

This is, in essence, another mirror scene, in which Monboddo, contemplating the image of the orangutan that he has created from collation and synopsis, "easily" distinguishes his "own features" in that "wonderful Monster with a human face"—Bondt's description of the Bornean orangutan.

And significantly, Monboddo's contemplation of the proximity of the orangutan and the human culminates in a similar kind of critique of human pride that we have seen both in Blackmore's popular summary of Tyson and at the conclusion of Swift's *Gulliver's Travels:*

> That my facts and arguments are so convincing as to leave no doubt of the humanity of the Orang Outang, I will not take upon me to say; but thus much I will venture to affirm, that I have said enough to make the philosopher consider it as problematical, and a subject deserving to be inquired into. For, as to the vulgar, I can never expect that they should acknowledge any relation to those inhabitants of the woods of Angola; but that they should continue, thro' a false pride, to think highly derogatory from human nature, what the philosopher, on the contrary, will think the greatest praise of man, that, from the savage state, in which the Orang Outang lives, he should, by his own sagacity and industry, have arrived at the state in which we now see him. (360–361)

Monboddo and Gulliver both criticize human-kind for the refusal to recognize their proximity to the hominoid ape, though for Monboddo that recognition represents "the greatest praise of man," while for Gulliver it indicates the failure to grasp the "Lump of Deformity, and Diseases both in Body and Mind" that defines human nature (266). The mirror held up by animal-kind has radically divergent implications for those human viewers who recognize their faces within it—from nobility to depravity, and from praise to despair.

Frankenstein's Orangutan Protagonist

Depravity and nobility are conjoined in the monster of Mary Shelley's *Frankenstein*, in a way that indicates the common imaginative experience of proximity with the great ape that generates both of these divergent implications. Shelley's monster is extensively indebted to the eighteenth-century creation of the hominoid ape as we have traced it from Tyson and Swift through Monboddo. Though these ideas, as we have seen, were widely available in the major publications of Buffon and Boreman, Mary Shelley might also have encountered works on the hominoid ape through Percy Shelley, who was deeply engaged with the figure of the orangutan, likely influenced at least indirectly by Tyson, and probably an appreciative reader of Monboddo (Montagu, 416).[53] Critics have long been attentive to *Frankenstein*'s debt to Rousseau's idea of the natural man, expressed in his *Second Discourse* (1754). In a note to that essay, Rousseau himself suggests that the orangutan might be a primitive race of men, citing Andrew Battell's description from *Purchas His Pilgrimes*. But Rousseau's awareness of the prior tradition of accounts of the hominoid ape, and the scope of his treatment of this topic, are very limited in comparison to the extensive awareness of this body of material that Mary Shelley's novel demonstrates.

The physical appearance of Frankenstein's monster is built from the basic constituents of several collated descriptions of the great ape, from Tyson to Monboddo. The monster's size, strength, swiftness, agility, hair, eyes, face, and eating habits match up closely with passages from the contemporary literature that we have reviewed. For instance, Monboddo quotes a letter describing "this wonderful and frightful production of nature...[as] from 7 to 9 feet high...thick in proportion, and amazingly strong" (281). Many accounts, among them those included in Boreman's and Tyson's texts, testify to this being's speed and agility; they recount him "leaping from Bough to Bough, and from Tree to Tree" (Boreman, 27), and "endued with extraordinary strength, and...so swift of Foot, that they have much ado to out-run him" (Tyson, *Anatomy*, 24). Smith describes this being's face as "broad and flat, without any other Hair but the Eyebrows,...the Mouth wide, and the Lips thin. The Face, which is cover'd by a white Skin, is monstrously ugly, being all over wrinkled as with Old Age, the Teeth broad and very yellow" (Smith, 51–52). And Monboddo quotes another description of this being's face, with "a large wide mouth, almost from ear to ear,...eyebrows and forehead like ours, and good regular teeth like ours; makes comical grimaces with its face, and in its face is most like to the most ugly old mulattoe woman you ever saw, but uglier" (283–284). In

---

[53] Closely tied to the connection with the orangutan is the correspondence between Shelley's monster and the idea of the natural man, especially through the influence of Rousseau, which has been described in Paul Cantor, *Creature and Creator: Myth-making and English Romanticism* (Cambridge: Cambridge University Press, 1984), 120–124, and closely analyzed in David Marshall, *The Surprising Effects of Sympathy: Marivaux, Diderot, Rousseau, and Mary Shelley* (Chicago: University of Chicago Press, 1988), 178–227.

Tyson's own physical description, "the Hair...was of a Coal-black colour, and strait; and...down the sides of the Face 'twas very hairy," and in Tyson's redacted accounts, he "hath a Man's Face, hollow-eyed, with long Hair upon his brows," "his Eyes sunk in his Head, a stern Countenance" (Tyson, *Anatomy*, 8, 22–24). Numerous accounts from Tyson onward note that "they feed upon Fruits that they find in the woods, and upon Nuts; for they eat no kind of Flesh" (Tyson, *Anatomy*, 22).[54]

Shelley's monster is likewise "a being of a gigantic stature, that is to say, about eight feet in height, and proportionably large," "yet uncouth and distorted" (52, 207). He is "more agile than [man]," and has "more than mortal speed," as we see him "hanging among the rocks of the nearly perpendicular ascent of Mount Salève," or "scaling the overhanging" cliffs nearby (115, 192, 74). His face is surrounded by "long locks of ragged hair," and this "hair was of a lustrous black, and flowing; his teeth of a pearly whiteness; but these luxuriances only formed a more horrid contrast with his watery eyes, that seemed almost of the same colour as the dun-white sockets in which they were set, his shrivelled complexion and straight black lips" (207, 56). As he looks upon Frankenstein, "a grin wrinkled his cheeks" (57). Walton testifies to his ugliness: "Never did I behold a vision so horrible as his face, of such loathsome yet appalling hideousness" (207).[55] And Shelley also takes care to specify that the monster's food "is not that of man; I do not destroy the lamb and the kid to glut my appetite; acorns and berries afford me sufficient nourishment" (139).[56]

A striking figure from the last scene of the novel makes a vivid parallel to one of Monboddo's retailed anecdotes. In coming upon the monster hanging over Frankenstein's corpse in his shipboard cabin, Walton focuses on a single image—"one vast hand was extended, in colour and apparent texture like that of a mummy" (207). A very similar hand, in Monboddo's text, forms an extended section of the reprinted letter from the Bristol merchant, summarizing his son's experience of seeing "the hand of one of

[54] This is from Battell's account in *Purchas His Pilgrimes* (2: 982) and seems to be the source of the notion that these beings are vegetarians.
[55] In his appendix to a collection of essays on *Frankenstein*, U. C. Knoepflmacher compares Shelley's physical description of the monster to William Smith's 1744 description of the mandrill, and suggests additional parallels with *Purchas His Pilgrimes* and other travel literature. Knoepflmacher is observing a relationship between Shelley's novel and T. H. Huxley's representation of the great ape in *Man's Place in Nature* (1863), arguing that "both Shelley and Huxley force their readers into coming 'face to face' with alien and deformed features that they must recognize in themselves." I believe that Shelley's connection with representations of the great ape, and with Huxley's mirror scene—"brought face to face with these blurred copies of himself, the least thoughtful of men is conscious of a certain shock"—is more direct than Knoepflmacher suggests. *The Endurance of Frankenstein: Essays on Mary Shelley's Novel*, ed. George Levine and Knoepflmacher (Berkeley: University of California Press, 1974), 317–326, esp. 323.
[56] Cantor observes the precedent for the monster's consumption of fruit and nuts in Rousseau (*Creature and Creator*, 121), and Marshall more extensively describes the basis of this idea in contemporary travel literature, details that he argues Shelley received through her reading of Rousseau's accounts of travels (*Surprising Effects of Sympathy*, 184).

them, cut off about four inches above the joint of the wrist. It was dried and withered; yet, in that state, its fingers were as big as three of his, or bigger than his wrist, rather longer than the proportion of ours; and the part where cut off, in that wrinkled state, bigger than the biggest part of his arm" (282).

A more specific debt to Monboddo is evident in the language-learning section of *Frankenstein.* The first volume of Monboddo's treatise is centrally concerned with the relationship of language to the definition of man. Here Monboddo seeks to define language as an art of civil society rather than a feature "essential to man's nature" (297), first by demonstrating that there exist "Men living in the Brutish State" who lack arts, civility, and "the faculty of speech" (236, 241); next by arguing that the orangutan is of the same species as man, "though he have not the use of speech" (298); and finally by suggesting that therefore "the Orang Outang could be taught to speak" (299). Thus Monboddo's claims about language address the question, "What is man?" (313), and they engage extensively in descriptions about how the art of language might be acquired. He takes care to emphasize that language is an "artificial…operation," to refute the notion that "a mother without the use of speech" would easily and naturally create a language in rearing her child, and to demonstrate the effort, repetition, and "great labor" required in learning language (293, 294, 303).[57]

We see all of this enacted—the effort, the repetition, and the notion of language as a "science"—in the monster's experience with the De Laceys as he observes them through the chink in the wall of their humble cottage:

> By degrees I made a discovery of still greater moment. I found that these people possessed a method of communicating their experience and feelings to one another by articulate sounds. I perceived that the words they spoke sometimes produced pleasure or pain, smiles or sadness, in the minds and countenances of the hearers. This was indeed a godlike science, and I ardently desired to become acquainted with it. I was baffled in every attempt I made for this purpose.…By great application, however, and after having remained during the space of several revolutions of the moon in my hovel, I discovered the names that were given to some of the most familiar objects of discourse.…I cannot describe the delight I felt when I learned the ideas appropriated to each of these sounds and was able to pronounce them. (106–107)

But although language is clearly a learned art, the monster's sensibility, like the orangutan's, is innate. He responds naturally and immediately to the De Laceys: "The gentle

---

[57] Marshall shows that Shelley's account of language learning follows Rousseau on the origin of language (*Surprising Effects of Sympathy*, 184–185).

manners and beauty of the cottagers greatly endeared them to me; when they were un-happy, I felt depressed; when they rejoiced, I sympathized in their joys" (107). His emotions overflow in "tears of sorrow and delight" (113), and in his final scene with the De Lacey's blind grandfather, he plays the role of the overwrought man of feeling and "sank on the chair and sobbed aloud" (129). Even Frankenstein admits that "his tale and the feelings he now expressed proved him to be a creature of fine sensations" (139).[58]

From the perspective of the discovery of the hominoid ape, then, Shelley's monster can be seen as a weird collation of the accounts and images that created this being in the eighteenth-century imagination. Indeed, in terms of this distinctive matter of the creation of an orangutan protagonist, *Frankenstein* should be seen as a companion text to the contemporaneous *Melincourt; or, Sir Oran Haut-ton* (1818) by Percy Shelley's intimate friend, Thomas Love Peacock. Both texts are clearly built on the tradition founded by *The Anatomy of a Pygmie*. Like Tyson, Frankenstein is an anatomist, and his activities in "successfully collecting and arranging my materials" and assembling them to form his "new species" (52) parallel Shelley's selection and synthesis of the materials of contemporary anecdote and empirical observation, as she follows the model of Tyson, Buffon, Monboddo, and others in assembling a vividly realized composite being who challenges the distinctiveness of the human.[59] Even the ambiguity of the novel's evaluation of the monster—as a depraved demon or a "creature of refined sensations"—lines up with the divergent traditions generated by the argument for the proximity of human and hominoid ape, from Swift's "Shame, Confusion and Horror" to Monboddo's "greatest praise of man." Thus Victor Frankenstein's scene of self-reflection—when he sees the monster as "my own spirit let loose from the grave and forced to destroy all that was dear to me" (74)—links his recognition of himself as a "Monster with a human face" with those experiments in human identity that we have tracked from Tyson's *Anatomy of a Pygmie*.[60]

The mirror scene with which this chapter began is the figurative manifestation of these ongoing experiments, giving imaginative expression to the ontological questions

---

[58] On the allusion to Rousseau's natural man in the monster's capacity for compassion and original goodness, see James O'Rourke, "'Nothing More Unnatural': Mary Shelley's Revision of Rousseau," *ELH* 56 (1989): 543–569, esp. 549–552.

[59] Maureen Noelle McLane describes the intermediate status of the monster and the relationship of this status to the category of the human. "The thing originally intended to be a 'human being' becomes in fact a threat to 'human nature,' as Victor sees it. The monster is not decisively human; nor, as his eventual fluency and rationality suggest, is he decisively not human. Victor inadvertently engineers not a human being but the monstrous critique of the very category." "Literate Species: Populations, 'Humanities,' and Frankenstein," *ELH* 63 (1996) 959–988, 964. And Philip Armstrong argues that the theories of animation that produce Frankenstein's monster involve the recognition that "the human is not clearly separable from the animal." *What Animals Mean in the Fiction of Modernity* (New York: Routledge, 2008), 73.

[60] Marshall's reading of the thematization of ideas of recognition and identification in the novel extend and complicate my observation (*Surprising Effects of Sympathy*, 202–204).

generated by the human discovery of the hominoid ape in the eighteenth century. We have seen how Tyson's text directs these questions toward core contemporary projects of human self-definition: the founding tradition of classical humanism and the affective model of natural sensibility. Simultaneously human and nonhuman, familiar and singular, this "wonderful Monster with a human face" makes it possible to understand the authority of the ancients or the ideal of the man of feeling differently, to rewrite classical mythology with a population of chimpanzees, or to conceive fundamental values of modesty, honor, justice, sentiment, and affection through their manifestation in an orangutan. *Frankenstein* extends the compass of this ontological project by involving those questions raised by the mirror scene with the most undecidable components of modernity: the issue of human-kind's relation to animals and the natural world; the dangers of unchecked scientific or technological development; the violent tensions endemic to cultural difference; and the uncertainties surrounding claims and acts of kinship, family, and paternity or maternity. Tracking the images and ideas inspired by the great ape from the time of Tyson's first anatomization to Shelley's rich unfolding helps us discover the power of this being to influence the parameters of literary discourse, and suggests the participation of animal-kind in shaping the imaginative experience of modernity.

Figure 2. Gustav Courbet, "Nude with Dog" (1861). Photo credit: Réunion des Musées Nationaux/Art Resource, NY.

3

IMMODERATE LOVE
The Lady and the Lapdog

This chapter examines the imaginative experience inspired by a particular, striking, and now pervasive kind of intimacy—the inter-species intimacy engineered by the rise of modern pet keeping. In early eighteenth-century literature, this novel connection between humans and nonhuman animals is almost exclusively represented through a specific, gendered image: that of the lady and the lapdog. Indeed, this image is the inaugural event for the literary representation of pet keeping in England. The companion animal, in its diverse roles and relationships, becomes a significant figure in English literature by the nineteenth century. But in the prior period the image of the lady and the lapdog stands virtually alone in expressing the new cultural obsession with the household pet. Early eighteenth-century literary culture thus sees the initial establishment of this first trope of inter-species connection and strongly influences its subsequent elaboration in the very different literary modes that follow. This particular depiction of pet keeping inspires a literary form that expresses the encounter with difference through a rhetoric of sudden inversion—in which ideas of alterity are instantly transformed into experiences of intimacy. The paradigm of sudden inversion links pet keeping with the representation of other encounters experienced by Europeans at this crucial moment in the expansion of their culture across the globe, and with other attempts to engage unfamiliar beings through the activity of the imagination. And it suggests a special role for gender in the imaginative involvement with animal-kind, since women are constitutive both of this distinctive, domestic representation of human-animal conjunction and of other, global inter-species connections.

We can see the formal dynamic at stake here most clearly in a text from the end of our period of focus, in the young Elizabeth Barrett's poetic expression of love for her spaniel Flush in a sonnet entitled "Flush or Faunus," included in a collection published in 1850. Looking back to what we have seen in chapter 2 of the eighteenth-century struggles to situate the newly discovered hominoid ape in relation to a shifting understanding of the human, we can identify Barrett Browning's reference to Faunus as a signal of that ongoing ontological problem. As we observed in Edward Tyson's writings and their redactions, the classical semideities—the fauns, satyrs, nymphs, and Pan himself—were drawn directly into the debate about the definition of the human, since they were understood to be the classical record of the appearance of the great ape. And looking forward to the dog narrative of the twentieth century, which we will explore in chapter 5, we can find a redaction of Barrett Browning's poetic experiment with the representation of inter-species connection in Virginia Woolf's *Flush: A Biography* (1933), a story of change, travel, and reinvention from a dog's perspective, connecting his life to his mistress's relationship with Robert Browning. Inter-species intimacies often substitute for human ones in precisely this way in the representation of pet keeping in the eighteenth century as well, as we shall see. Barrett Browning's poem has multiple, intersecting connections with the experience of animal-kind in the eighteenth century and beyond. Its distinctive images and structures provide a specific formal perspective on that experience.

As we shall see, "Flush or Faunus" draws on an extended tradition of connection between dogs and women in its construction of a surprising moment of love between the lady and the lapdog:

> You see this dog; it was but yesterday
> I mused forgetful of his presence here,
> Till thought on thought drew downward tear on tear:
> When from the pillow where wet-cheeked I lay,
> A head as hairy as Faunus thrust its way
> Right sudden against my face, two golden-clear
> Great eyes astonished mine, a drooping ear
> Did flap me on either cheek to dry the spray!
> I started first as some Arcadian
> Amazed by goatly god in twilight grove:
> But as the bearded vision closelier ran
> My tears off, I knew Flush, and rose above
> Surprise and sadness,—thanking the true PAN
> Who by low creatures leads to heights of love.[1]

The opening gesture—"you see this dog"—places Flush at a comfortable and familiar distance in the composition of the scene of the poem; we might even visualize him in

---

[1] Elizabeth Barrett Browning, "Flush or Faunus," *Poetical Works of Elizabeth Barrett Browning* (Boston: Houghton Mifflin, 1974), 196.

a domestic setting, lying at the hearth. And it also locates him, as a nonhuman being, at a distance from the speaker and reader as they are joined by their common human connection with one another. Thus, at the outset, alterity is both naturalized and unexamined. This opening gesture also works to establish a contrast between the distant and familiar dog, on the one hand, and the immediately following representation of that nonhuman being's intimate, surprising engagement with the woman, on the other. Suddenly, the animal's head appears on the speaker's pillow, as the setting becomes a bedside and the account becomes retrospective.

At this point in the poem, distance is transformed to proximity and familiarity to strangeness through a formal reversal that, as we shall see, is characteristic of the figure of the lady and the lapdog. The distant, familiar dog appears as a strange, "hairy" or "goatly," "bearded" being at the speaker's pillow, and the speaker at first fails even to connect him with the dog of the poem's opening lines. Rhetorically, this is an intensely felt and surprising moment, marked by the words "sudden," "against," "thrust," "started," and "amazed," which replaces the ordinary or naturalized distance of the opening with a striking alterity produced by the intimate contact between human and animal and leading directly to the experience of "heights of love." The intimacy is signaled by the tear that Flush wipes away from the speaker's face with his drooping ears; the alterity by the insistent hairiness of this nonhuman being; and the channel of connection by the gaze of the nonhuman "golden-clear great eyes" that joins the lapdog and the lady. The surprise and even the intimacy in this case is also sexual, indicated by the evocation of the classical god Pan as well as by the bedside setting, and climaxing in the concluding discovery of a love that is itself defined by the transformation of "low" to "heights," a reversal of the normal hierarchy of human- and animal-kind. As we shall see, this rich structure of inversion, and the constellation of images that brings it about, is a rehearsal of a long-established fantasy of a connection between dogs and women. Barrett Browning's poem is paradigmatic of a particular imaginative experience—an experience that has a link to contemporary culture, a sustained literary history, a correlation with gender, and a role in the larger contemporary problematic of the representation of human-animal encounters.

The Cultural Fantasy of the Canine Pet

The image of the lady and the lapdog arises as a widespread literary trope at the same time as companion animals become widely evident in the bourgeois household. I have already suggested that the human relationship with nonhuman animals is profoundly reshaped in the eighteenth century, and that pet keeping is one of the central cultural signs of and means to that reshaping. As Keith Thomas has shown, the rise of certain "privileged species" to a relationship of special proximity with human beings in the early modern period reveals deep shifts in human-kind's perception of the natural world and indicates the "narrowing gap" between human and animal that then defines some of the fundamental claims and debates of the modern era. Thomas describes the foundations of pet keeping—including domestic intimacy, the use of proper names, the sense of companionship, the growing idea of animal intelligence, new notions of animal character, the belief in animal souls, the new demarcation of domestic space, and the material practices involved in the breeding and maintenance of pets—and demonstrates the progression of this historical phenomenon to the point of "obsession" in the eighteenth century.[2] Through an examination of epitaphs and elegies for animals, Ingrid H. Tague shows that "pet keeping first developed as a widespread phenomenon [during the eighteenth century, in a period that also] saw the rapid growth of literary works dealing with pets."[3] And J. H. Plumb argues that this new engagement with pets within the bourgeois household is one of the means by which "quite humble men and women, innocent of philosophical theory, [were led to accept] perhaps unconsciously, the modernity of their world."[4]

The pet plays a complex cultural role in this period: as commodity, companion, paragon, proxy, and even kin. The practice of pet keeping was initially an urban phenomenon and served as a response to modern alienation and commodification by creating a being who could generate a sense of connection and meaning in a world of things.[5] In this era of dramatic increases in consumption, pets were increasingly visible as a sign of prosperity and widely bred and sold for profit. New practices of selective breeding, developed at first for livestock, were exploited to produce more desirable types of ornamental fish, canaries, and pigeons, while exotic pets like parrots and monkeys were coveted possessions (Plumb, 318–322).[6] And the eager pursuit of potential household pets resulted in the inclusion of nondomesticated species, including ferrets, squirrels, rabbits, and mice.

But, then as now, cats and dogs were the animals most readily embraced as companions for human beings, and in this period both were frequently associated with the

[2] Keith Thomas, *Man and the Natural World: A History of the Modern Sensibility* (New York: Pantheon, 1983), 92–142, 117.

[3] Ingrid H. Tague, "Dead Pets: Satire and Sentiment in British Elegies and Epitaphs for Animals," *Eighteenth-Century Studies* 41 (2008): 289–306, 291.

[4] J. H. Plumb, "The Acceptance of Modernity," in *The Birth of a Consumer Society: The Commercialization of Eighteenth-Century England*, ed. Neil McKendrick, John Brewer, and Plumb (Bloomington: Indiana University Press, 1982), 316–334, 316.

[5] See Kathleen Kete, *The Beast in the Boudoir: Petkeeping in Nineteenth-Century Paris* (Berkeley: University of California Press, 1994), 38.

[6] On the history and spread of parrot keeping, see also Edward J. Boosey, *Parrots, Cockatoos and Macaws* (Silver Springs, Md.: Denlinger's, 1956), chapter 1: "Parrot-keeping in the Past."

cultural practices of women. Domestic cats, who were especially appreciated for their character and affection, are frequently mentioned in the eighteenth century. Though the male tradition has several famous instances of cat companionship, including Horace Walpole's Selima, Samuel Johnson's Hodge, and Christopher Smart's Jeoffrey, Margaret Doody shows that Anna Seward's poem on her own cat Selima's death, "An Old Cat's Dying Soliloquy," is representative of a strong interest in animals that marks eighteenth-century women's poetry. According to Doody, Seward's cat "proves capable of loyalty and affection, her virtues thus making her implicitly worthy of cat heaven—or of human heaven too" in a concluding assertion that demonstrates the connection between the culture of pet keeping and the contemporary debate about animal souls. Doody's perspective on the ways that women poets of the eighteenth century "defiantly adopt the sensibility of animals" suggests the special connection between women and imaginary animal-kind in this period.[7] The earliest literary depictions of companion animals associated these beings primarily with female pet keepers, and many women writers themselves shared this assumption.

Dogs, of course, were the most visible and ubiquitous companion animal. Many factors contributed to the increasing appreciation of this particular nonhuman being's potential for household intimacy with human-kind in the course of the early modern period. Early on, among the aristocracy, the mastiffs who protected the estate and the hounds who made up the hunting pack were privileged creatures. Small dogs were cultivated as personal companions by aristocratic women in the medieval period, with the fashion for toy spaniels most prominent in the early sixteenth century, and for pugs in the seventeenth. At the end of the seventeenth century, Charles II refined the toy spaniel, introducing the King Charles spaniel in his court in London. This attachment to canine companions spread widely among the English bourgeoisie in the eighteenth century, when pugs and toy spaniels were widely kept in the household and depicted as eating at table, arrayed in jeweled collars, attended by physicians, sleeping in human beds, riding in carriages, and sitting for portraits (Thomas, 117). These practices were accompanied by a rapidly developing new conception of animal character, including an array of strongly positive assumptions about the intelligence, loyalty, affection, gratitude, and courage of the canine being that was rapidly becoming understood as "man's best friend." Indeed, as pet keeping became pervasive, animals were sometimes cited as exemplary models for human behavior, preferable to humans themselves: dogs might be seen as more loyal or more sympathetic than humans, and a canine companion might take the place of a suitor, husband, father, or daughter. Dogs thus became the center

---

[7] Margaret Doody, "Sensuousness in the Poetry of Eighteenth-Century Women Poets," in *Women's Poetry in the Enlightenment: The Making of a Canon, 1730–1820,* ed. Isobel Armstrong and Virginia Blain (New York: St. Martin's Press, 1999), 3–32, 18, 20.

of an influential cultural fantasy about the potential proximity of human- and animal-kind.

As pet keeping inspired new ways of thinking about and representing animals, concurrent historical events engaged the eighteenth-century imagination in other experiences of alterity. Pet keeping arose as a major cultural phenomenon during the period that marks the first age of British imperial expansion; the establishment and growth of the slave trade; and a widespread popular enthusiasm for global projects involving the control of territories and, along with this impulse, the accumulation of information about the geography, the botany, and the nonhuman and human inhabitants of the world. As we shall see, the image of the lady and the lapdog can be understood in relation to this larger, global context, as an imaginative experiment that reaches beyond the domestic, inter-species proximity of the fashionable woman and her pug. In this period, the lady and the lapdog is an especially resonant figure, in relation to the larger contemporary concern with the European encounter with the world.

Imaginary Lapdogs and Poetic Form

Significantly, the representation of the canine pet finds its first widely prevalent literary expression through a gendered image. We can find an early version of the lady and the lapdog in the General Prologue of Chaucer's *Canterbury Tales*, where the Prioress dotes upon her "smale houndes," feeding them with special "rosted flessh" and milk, and weeping at their injuries.[8] Chaucer's satire here makes reference to the practice of pet keeping in English convents, which Keith Thomas identifies as an early instance of this cultural phenomenon (110). Lapdogs are also mentioned in seventeenth-century poetry, notably in the misogynist tradition of the 1680s and 1690s.[9] Markman Ellis notes the early role of lapdogs as a "misogynist trope of female venereal concupiscence, repeatedly described as one of the *artes amatoriae* of the modern woman by libertine writers."[10] This heritage clearly shapes the sexual signification that continues to attend the figure and influences its particular gendered referent: woman-kind.

---

[8] Geoffrey Chaucer, General Prologue, *The Canterbury Tales*, ed. Albert C. Baugh (New York: Appleton-Century-Crofts, 1963), 144–149.
[9] See, for instance, Robert Gould, *Love Given O're: or, a Satyr against the Pride, Lust, and Inconstancy, &c. of Woman* (1682), repr. in *Satires on Women*, Augustan Reprint Society (Los Angeles: William Andrews Clark Memorial Library, 1976).
[10] Markman Ellis, "Suffering Things: Lapdogs, Slaves, and Counter-Sensibility," in *The Secret Life of Things: Animals, Objects, and It-Narratives in Eighteenth-Century England*, ed. Mark Blackwell (Lewisburg, Pa.: Bucknell University Press, 2007), 92–116, 97. For other studies of the role of lapdogs in antifemale satire in this period, see Ingrid H. Tague, "Dead Pets" and Theresa Braunschneider, "The Lady and the Lapdog: Mixed Ethnicity in

But the prominence of this image increases significantly and its literary prevalence is substantially expanded in the subsequent period. As we shall see, the figure of the lady and the lapdog—with its particular repertory of images and attendant formal dynamics—becomes a staple trope of the antifemale verse satire of the first half of the eighteenth century.

In this period, then, at the time of the rapid rise in the keeping of companion animals, the figure of the lady and the lapdog develops its distinctive profile. The literary representation of lapdogs occurs mainly in poetry, though dramatic social comedy includes references to pet keeping by women as well. As Tague has observed, many of the lapdog poems are elegies and epitaphs, in which mockery and satire are the dominant modes. But more significantly, these portrayals of inter-species connection follow and develop a common scenario. They typically invoke a set of allied images of female sexuality: the woman's bed, the breast, the nap, the lap, sometimes the gaze, and especially the kiss. And formally this depiction of the lady and the lapdog is configured through structures of dissonance, reversal, and sudden inversion—structures that are indebted to the tradition of neoclassical satire, but that place that heritage in a new, inter-species construct.[11]

In a satiric letter "To a Lady on the Death of her Lapdog and Squirrel in One Day" included in a collection published in 1710, a "person of quality" highlights the special privilege of the lady's lapdog: "[L]ittle *Dory*...had the charmingest Creature in the World for his Bedfellow."[12] All through the first half of the eighteenth century, verses on the lady and the lapdog focus on this theme of bedside intimacy. Typical rhyme words—*nap* and *lap*; *miss*, *bliss*, and *kiss*; or *lies* and *thighs*—give a series of verbal anchors for the ideas of sexual connection. Jonathan Smedley, in his verses "On the Death of a Lap-Dog" (1723), provides a typical sample:

> To him her softest things she'd say:
> Oft on her downy Breast he lay;
> And oft he took a gentle Nap,
> Upon her Sleep-inticing Lap.[13]

A couplet from Edward Stephens's poem "On the Death of Delia's Lap-Dog" (1747) illustrates another of these verbal pairs: "Pompey, Companion dear to Miss,/Full oft'

Constantinople, Fashionable Pets in Britain," in *Humans and Other Animals in Eighteenth-Century British Culture*, ed. Frank Palmeri (Aldershot, UK: Ashgate, 2006), 31–48.
[11] Braunschneider canvases some of this satiric material in "The Lady and the Lapdog."
[12] Letter 16, in *Serious and Comical Essays* (London: J. King, 1710), 180.
[13] Jonathan Smedley, *Poems on Several Occasions* (London, 1723), 122.

was honour'd with a Kiss",[14] as does Henry Carey's complaint to the lady in "The Rival Lap-Dog" (1713):

> Corinna, pray tell me,
> When thus you repel me,
> When humbly I sue for a Kiss,
> Why *Deny*, at pleasure,
> May kiss without measure,
> And surfeit himself with the Bliss?[15]

And these canine parodies of love lyric can also involve the Petrarchan discourse of the gaze, which accompanies the kiss and extends the physical link between the lady and the lapdog into the incorporeal realm. For example, Isaac Thompson's "The Lap-Dog" (1731) adds an evocation of the animal's eyes:

> Securely on her Lap it lies,
> Or freely gazes on her Eyes;
> To touch her Breast, may share the Bliss,
> And unreprov'd, may snatch a Kiss.[16]

The "bliss" mentioned here evokes a sexual connection that some poems explore more directly. "An Epitaph upon My Lady M———'s Lapdog" presents the "bedfellow" idea in warmer language:

> Beneath this Stone, ah woful Case!
> Poor little *Doxy* lies,
> Who once possess'd a warmer Place
> Between his Lady's T———hs.[17]

Indeed, the lapdog seems to be both an inappropriate or perverse sexual partner for the woman, and also a metonym for female sexuality—a dynamic that places the animal simultaneously within and outside the realm of the human, or—from another perspective—places the woman both within and outside the realm of the animal. John Gay's interesting poem "The Mad Dog" (1730) takes on this problem directly, seeking to provide an explanation for the relationship between the dog and the sexualized woman.

---

[14] Edward Stephens, *Miscellaneous Poems* (Cirencester: Tho. Hill, 1747), 25.
[15] Henry Carey, *Poems on Several Occasions* (London: J. Kent; A. Boulter, and J. Brown, 1713), 25.
[16] Isaac Thompson, *A Collection of Poems* (Newcastle upon Tyne, 1731), 94.
[17] Mr. "Bavius," *The Grub-Street Miscellany* (London: J. Wilford, 1731), 45.

The libidinous female subject of the poem describes to her confessor her obsession with "Love's soft Extasy":

> She tells him now with meekest Voice,
> That she had never err'd by Choice;
> Nor was there known a Virgin chaster,
> 'Till ruin'd by a sad Disaster.
>
> That she a Fav'rite Lap-dog had,
> Which (as she strok'd and kis'd) grew mad,
> And on her Lip a Wound indenting,
> First set her youthful Blood fermenting.[18]

Gay's comic etiology proposes that the "disease" of female sexuality originates in human-animal affection—the interaction of stroking and kissing that links the lapdog and the lady—and that it is transmitted by the inter-species "kiss." In other words, female nature is ironically produced by the violent contact between the realm of the human and that of the nonhuman; in this reversal, the woman is defined by the animal, who is also her antithesis.

As we have seen in Carey's "Rival Lap-Dog," these poems—all presented in the voice of a male onlooker—express the envy that the potential human partner feels for the nonhuman being positioned at the lady's breast or between her thighs. For instance "On a Lap-Dog" (1721) by Thomas Brown addresses the dog with this exclamation: "[A]h! could'st thou know/How thou dost my Envy raise." As the dog lies in "that Lap," the speaker suggests an "Exchange" between human and animal, a reversal of "Place" and "Station" which, if granted, will entitle the lapdog to a uniquely human privilege: "[A]n Epitaph upon thy Grave."[19] Here, the speaker wishes himself into the animal's place—and the animal into the human's—in a way that highlights an inversion of the implicit hierarchy that ranks human above animal. Thompson's "The Lap-Dog" goes further and extends the hierarchy inversion into a gender inversion, by describing a magic substitution of the male lover for a female pet:

> Give me a Spell, a potent Charm,
> To turn myself to MINNY's form!
> In sportful Dance, and wanton Play
> On *Silvia's* Lap I'll spend the Day. (94)

[18] John Gay, *The Mad Dog* (London: A. Moore, 1730), title page, 7.
[19] Thomas Brown, *The Fifth Volume of the Works of Mr. Thomas Brown* (London: Sam. Briscoe, 1721), 333.

And John Hewitt's "Upon *Cælia's* having a little Dog in her Lap" (1727) expresses a clear preference—to be a "four-footed" being rather than a man:

> 'Tis four-footed *Cloe*, your Smiles can engage,
> Whilst a Shape that is human must bear with your Rage,
> Since, thus, my Addresses by *Cælia's* refused,
> Pray, who wou'd be Man? when a Dog's so well us'd?[20]

These last two examples go beyond envy, and beyond ironic reversal, in presenting a comic fantasy of species transposition arising from the idea of canine-human affection.

All of these effects are played out at length in a long poem in Hudibrastics published in 1730 entitled *The Rival Lapdog and the Tale.* The "Little Rival to the Great" is a King Charles spaniel "of *antient Stock,*" whose "monst'rous" act is to supplant his lord in his lady's bed. We learn that "he was *Courtly-bred*" and that "*Court-Company* he always kept,/ With *Lords* he din'd,—with Ladies slept."[21] He takes "*sawcy Freedoms*" (8) with his lady's belongings and her clothes, but beyond that he is seen to "towze Her, with his Paw," while the lady in turn "*was proud to have her dear Dog rude,/ As rude with Her, as e'er He cou'd*" (36). The poem ends with a sustained inter-species love scene:

> ... *Breast to Breast,* incorporate
> Almost,—He lay like *Dog in State;*
>
> .   .   .   .
>
> *Fair-Lady,* all in Raptures, to
> Be so *caress'd* by *such a Beau;*
> *She hugg'd, and kiss'd, and cry'd, and clung,*
> *And He return'd all with his Tongue;*
> Put *Lady-Fair* quite out of Breath,
> And buss't her, *e'en a'most* to Death;
> *Sir Lick Lips* was so *tir'd* too,
> He fell a sleep while *One* tell's *Two.* (39)

Here we can find the full repertory of lapdog imagery: the bed, the breast, and the caress, combined with raptures, kissing, crying, and climaxing with the licking tongue. The moral of the tale condemns women's passion for pet keeping:

> ... [M]ust *the great Affairs of State,*
> Be forc't for *Dogs,* or *Cats,* to *wait?*

---

[20] John Hewitt, *Miscellanies in Prose and Verse* (Bristol: Penn, 1727), 29.
[21] [Stephen Fox?], *The Rival Lapdog and the Tale* (London: W. Smith and G. Greg, 1730), 7.

> What *Mortal* can *with Patience see't?*
> For *some* are's fond of *Cat* and *Kitten,*
> As *other Ladys* are *Dog-smitten;*
> And that's *a Vice, too rampant grown.* (44)

But its message can finally be compactly summarized in a phrase: "Ne'er dote on *Dogs*" (55).

The Rival Lapdog's critique of intimacy between women and their dogs is signified rhetorically through a characteristic inversion; the text generates a series of Hudibrastic incongruities through its representation of the animal's connection with the human. Thus, the end rhymes might comically juxtapose *cur* and *sir*—"This may be thought *strange* of a *Curr,*/But not of *this fine Dog,* (good Sir)" (31), or call attention to the reversal in status entailed by the dog's proximity to the fine lady—"His Tast, *too, was of Quality,*/ *With Lady-Fair He'd always lie*" (9). As with Thompson's magic substitution or Hewitt's fantasy of transposition, *The Rival Lapdog*'s ironic end rhymes express surprising or deflating convergences between the dog and the human—conjunctions that are also evident, though in a different rhetorical device, in the canonical antifemale satire of the period, Alexander Pope's *Rape of the Lock* (1717).

Pope's use of lapdogs shows the relevance of animal-kind to the most complex ironies of Augustan satire. Though his appearance in this text is brief, Belinda's lapdog, Shock, along with the poem's broader references to the practice of women's pet keeping, create effects that are closely related to those of *The Rival Lapdog. The Rape of the Lock* opens with the familiar inter-species bedfellow scene, which, as we have seen, becomes the locus classicus of the figure of the lady and the lapdog in the poetry of this period. The first canto begins as the sun peeps through the curtains at the lapdog and the lady. The lapdog is the earlier riser: "Lapdogs give themselves the rowzing Shake," but *"Belinda* still her downy Pillow prest." Belinda sleeps for another hundred lines until *"Shock,* who thought she slept too long,/ Leapt up, and wak'd his Mistress with his Tongue."[22] We have already found the tongue to be a vivid signal of inter-species intimacy in the contemporary lapdog poetry, of course. Here, the canine-woman connection is further developed as a parallel to the crisis of the plot: when the baron cuts Belinda's lock, "Not louder Shrieks to pitying Heav'n are cast,/ When Husbands or when Lap-Dogs breathe their last" (3.156–157). And Thalestris incites Belinda's fury by describing the dire consequences of the loss of Belinda's hair in these famous words: "Sooner let Earth, Air, Sea to Chaos fall,/ Men, Monkies, Lap-Dogs, Parrots, perish all!" (4.119–120).

In these verses, Pope's characteristic zeugma, the signature rhetorical device of this poem, develops around the surprising conjunction of human and animal, generating

---

[22] Alexander Pope, *The Rape of the Lock,* in *Poetry and Prose of Alexander Pope,* ed. Aubrey Williams (Boston: Houghton Mifflin, 1969). 1.15, 115–120.

couplet incongruities much like those of *The Rival Lapdog*. In the first pair of lines, husbands and lapdogs are joined by "breathe their last"; in the second, men and lapdogs are linked by the predicate "perish all!" This repeated juxtaposition serves a general satiric end—to criticize the fashionable female for her proximity to her lapdog in preference to her husband, and, in short, to express *The Rival Lapdog*'s moral: "Ne'er dote on Dogs." But the deeper formal structures of these works are even more significant than their explicit morals for our understanding of the long-term impact of the figure of the lady and the lapdog. Like the Hudibrastic rhymes of the later poem, the yoking of Pope's couplets here forces disparate ideas into proximity. The resulting collision of ordinarily separated beings, kinds, or positions unbalances assumptions about difference and kinship, hierarchy and equality, creating the possibilities for new alliances and frameworks—possibilities that carry forward into future imaginative engagements between woman and animal-kind.

Imagining the lapdog through the mode of antifemale satire—the dominant literary context for the representation of this companion animal in the period—imprints the figure of the lady and the lapdog with the inversions of satiric form. In addition, the focus on the female is generated through the dual opportunities of social practice and literary tradition. The contemporary assumption that women have a special affinity with animals and the related tendency to portray the newly prominent culture of pet keeping as a specifically female activity find a ready locus in eighteenth-century satire in part because this neoclassical mode itself draws deeply upon the image of the woman, through the influence of Juvenalian misogyny. Women and especially female sexuality are familiar topics of critique for the Augustans. But the idea of affection for an imaginary animal, emanating from the historical rise of pet keeping, adds a distinctive problematic to the structures of inversion that express this critique. The figure of the lady and the lapdog reconceives the Augustan and Juvenalian attack on female sexuality as an inter-species experiment—an experiment that introduces a new and different realm of potential intimacy to the modern imagination. Now the fantasy is not limited to the exposure of female sexual excess, as in the famous exploits of the "imperial whore" of Dryden's Juvenal, who leaves her husband's bed for the brothel where "expectingly she lies,/With heaving breasts, and with desiring eyes."[23] For these lapdog poems, the familiar ironic reversals call up larger questions generated by the portrayal of inter-species connection—questions about the absolute antithesis of beings, about the definition of the human by the animal, about the substitutability of animal for human, about the challenge to hierarchy and privilege, or even about the potential for these

[23] John Dryden, "The Sixth Satire of Juvenal," in *The Poetical Works of John Dryden*, ed. George R. Noyes (1693; Cambridge: Riverside Press, 1950), 176–177.

reversals themselves to lead to "heights of love." Within this particular satiric tradition, then, the representations of animals provide seeds for what is to become a rich formal and thematic contemplation of such questions. These poems create a literary practice that gathers imaginative depth and significance in the course of the eighteenth century and beyond.

Perversions of Kin and Kind

As the literary representation of pet keeping develops in the second half of the eighteenth century and the first half of the nineteenth, the male human figure enters the picture in a new way. In the romantic period, dogs come to be seen as companions to solitary male characters—wanderers, hunters, shepherds, hikers, and poets especially. And in the literature of this period, relationships between men and dogs explore notions of canine loyalty and devotion in contrast to human versions of such traits, maintaining the social satire from the figure of the lady and the lapdog but investing the inter-species connection with sentiment. Thus, Eliza Reeves's "An Epistle to a Friend, with a Setting Dog" (1780) very typically compares the purity of a dog's loyalty to the self-interest of a human's:

> Such pure attachment, without guile or art;
> Such faith, a satire on the human heart,
> Which int'rest warps from Friendship's sacred line,
> To tread the paths of treacherous design.[24]

Thus the literary treatment of the companion animal undergoes a decided shift in valence from the early eighteenth to the nineteenth century. As Tague has described it, as the period goes on, "Pets were used less to point up human follies than to demonstrate human virtues, including the virtue of experiencing a special bond with animals" (290). But, significantly, the structures of sudden inversion that derive from Augustan satire and that provide the figure of the lady and the lapdog with its distinctive impact continue to inform that depiction of animal-kind, even as that figure is integrated into narratives of sensibility.

We can witness this integration in process in the statement of advice about female conduct by a well-known philanthropist of the mid-eighteenth century, Jonas Hanway.

---

[24] Eliza Reeves, *Poems on Various Subjects* (London: C. Dilley, 1780), 69.

In his "Remarks upon Lapdogs" (1757), Hanway provides a complex approach that indicates the shift in attitude toward female pet keeping that occurred in the course of the eighteenth century:

> I think a woman of sense may entertain some *degree* of affection for a *brute*; I do not mean a human *brute*, but a *dog*; for instance, which is a faithful animal....The great fault seems to lie in the *degree* of esteem in which we place such objects; and the manner in which we express our humanity towards them....But to the honour of *lap-dogs*, this is not their case! When under *proper discipline*, how *greatly* are they instrumental to the *felicity* of fine ladies! and how happy are these to find an object to amuse their idle moments, and perchance to preserve themselves from the *danger* which always attends having *nothing to do*.[25]

Hanway's injunctions regarding women's behavior in relation to their dogs do not follow the rules of the satiric poetry of the period—"Ne'er dote on *Dogs*"—but rather advocate pet keeping, painting an attractive picture of inter-species contact by describing the "felicity" and "happiness" generated by inter-species "affection." Indeed, the lapdog even serves, according to Hanway, as a means to regulate female behavior and to preserve female character by keeping women from a "danger" that alludes directly to female sexuality. In Hanway's version, the figure of the lady and the lapdog points in the opposite direction from that of the satiric poetry—it signals the preservation of female virtue rather than the problematic expression or awakening of female sexuality.

But Hanway's account takes a turn that demonstrates the continuity between this later, sentimental image of affection between women and their lapdogs and the idea of sudden inversion that we have seen emphasized in the earlier satiric tradition:

> But, alas! the *best* things may be abused, and the kind intentions of providence perverted! Thus we may sometimes see a fine lady, act as if she thought the *dog*, which happens to be under her precious care, was incomparably of more value, in her eyes, than a *human* creature, which is under the care of any other person, or peradventure, under no care at all. From hence we may conclude, that an immoderate love of a brute animal, tho' it may not destroy a charitable disposition, must weaken the force of it. Where "the *milk* of human kindness," where the choicest powers of humanity prevail most, there most care ought to be taken to find the *proper object* of them, lest this disposition, excellent and admirable in itself, should

[25] Jonas Hanway, "Remarks upon Lapdogs," in *A Journal of Eight Days Journey*, 2nd ed. (London: H. Woodfall and C. Henderson, 1757), 1.104–105.

degenerate into a foolish and absurd tenderness, or an undistinguishing regard for the *noblest* and *vilest* of GOD's creatures. (105)

Hanway is performing a balancing act here, since on the one hand he wishes to privilege the relationship between the lady and the lapdog as an "excellent and admirable" disposition; as a manifestation of the "best" and "choicest" of human powers, namely, that of sympathy. But on the other hand, pet keeping is said to represent a misdirection of charity, a "perversion" of the "intentions of providence," a leveling of accepted hierarchies of "noble" and "vile," and an "immoderate love." This idea of "immoderate love" evokes that very sexualization which, in Hanway's earlier appreciation of the lapdog, pet keeping is said to forestall. Indeed, the idea of a sexualized affection appears at this point in Hanway's discourse through the same rhetoric that we have seen to be typical of satiric poetry: Hanway criticizes "the *kissing* of a dog" as "absurd and ridiculous" (107) and insists that "a man of taste and sentiment … will be *shock'd* to see a lady ravishing a *dog* with her caresses; and the more distinguished she is for her personal charms, the more shocking she will appear" (107). The "kissing" and "ravishing," the "caresses," the "tenderness," and the "immoderate love" that the text vividly specifies here are not compatible with Hanway's initial understanding of lapdogs as an antidote to the "dangers" of female sexuality. Far from it. In those opening paragraphs, the inter-species relationship is a tame and safe connection that promotes a socially accepted, even morally exemplary, norm of female conduct. But at the very point when a woman's love for her dog comes to be promoted as a signal of the human virtue of charity, it also becomes shocking and immoderate. Ironically, seeing the figure of the lady and the lapdog as an exemplary image of natural sympathy entails the representation of that connection between human- and animal-kind as a perversion of the "intentions of providence," a challenge to relations of hierarchy, and an experience that stands outside the realm of the "proper." Here, then, the inversions and reversals that we have seen to be central to the developing scenario of the lady and the lapdog become implicated with ideas of the normal.

The impropriety or abnormality of this inter-species intimacy can be expressed in terms of a perversion of kinship connections as well. For instance, in Susan Ferrier's *Marriage* (1818), the fashionable female's preference for her lapdog over her daughter substitutes an inter-species affection for a familial one. Mary, the sentimental protagonist of the novel, is newly introduced to her long-lost mother, Lady Juliana, and also to Lady Juliana's lapdog:

> "Your style of dress is very obsolete, my dear," said [Lady Juliana], as she contrasted the effect of her own figure and her daughter's in a large mirror; "… I shall desire my woman to order some things for you; … Apropos, you will find it dull here by yourself, won't you? I shall leave you my darling Blanche for a companion,"

kissing a little French lap-dog, as she laid it in Mary's lap; "only you must be very careful of her, and coax her, and be very, very good to her; for I would not have my sweetest Blanche vexed, not for the world!" And, with another long and tender salute to her dog, and a "Good bye, my dear!" to her daughter, she quitted her to display her charms to a brilliant drawing-room, leaving Mary to solace herself in her solitary chamber with the whines of a discontented lap-dog.[26]

This scene presents a compact invocation of the figure of the lady and the lapdog, including the familiar image of kissing and the rhetoric of tenderness that signals this inter-species intimacy. But this is a misdirected mother's kiss, bestowed on the dog instead of the child. The mother's heartless obliviousness to her child is contrasted with her affection for the lapdog, and the misdirection of her kiss marks the immoderate love that in this passage is represented as outside the bounds of a normal, familial intimacy—a transgression of the relationships of kin as well as kind.

Ironically, by transgressing the boundary of kind, the idea of intimacy with the lapdog helped to extend the compass of natural sympathy beyond the European. In a central scene from Sarah Scott's sentimental novel, *The History of Sir George Ellison* (1766), the male protagonist's fashionable wife demonstrates an incongruous inter-species connection, much like that of Lady Juliana with her lapdog. As Mrs. Ellison and her husband walk through their Jamaican plantation, discussing the treatment of their slaves, their discussion is interrupted by the lady's lapdog:

> [Mrs. Ellison] was turning the conversation to another subject, when a favourite lap-dog, seeing her approach the house, in its eagerness to meet her jumped out of the window where it was standing; the height was too great to permit the poor cur to give this mark of affection with impunity; they soon perceived that it had broken its leg, and was in a good deal of pain; this drew a shower of tears from Mrs. Ellison's eyes, who, turning to her husband, said, "You will laugh at me for my weakness; but I cannot help it."[27]

The lady in this scene is driven by some unnamed compulsion—"I cannot help it"—to an inter-species connection that both she and her husband regard as problematic. The "shower of tears" that she bestows on the lapdog is a natural sentiment, and her husband, like Hanway, applauds this as an indication of her virtue, if not as a signal of

---

[26] Susan Ferrier, *Marriage* (London: John Murray, 1818), 158–159.
[27] Sarah Scott, *The History of Sir George Ellison*, ed. Betty Rizzo (Lexington: University Press of Kentucky, 1996), 13. Markman Ellis has also read this passage closely in an important essay and book chapter, "Suffering Things" and *The Politics of Sensibility: Race, Gender and Commerce in the Sentimental Novel* (Cambridge: Cambridge University Press, 1996), 96–98.

her sexual self-control: "You will one day know me better than to think I can laugh at any one for a token of sensibility; to see any creature suffer is an affecting sight; and it gives me pleasure to observe you can feel for the poor little animal, whose love for you occasioned his accident" (13). But, like Lady Juliana's kiss, Mrs. Ellison's sympathy is misdirected. The appropriate recipient is identified in her husband's plea that she attend to "the sufferings…of her fellow creatures," namely, the mistreated slaves on their Jamaican plantation. Mrs. Ellison's compulsion of love for her lapdog, though a natural effusion of sentiment, leads her to leap over the boundaries of kind. Mr. Ellison's reference to the Africans, her "fellow creatures," calls attention to this violation of the boundary between species, at the same time as it encourages her sympathy for beings of her own kind. As in Hanway's essay, the lady's attachment to the lapdog in this episode of Scott's novel is both an exemplary model of human virtue and a perversion of that virtue.

Dickens's Inter-Species Embrace

Charles Dickens's fiction is a core resource for the representation of the canine pet, and Dickens finds a signal use for the figure of the lady and the lapdog in three of his major novels: *Little Dorrit* (1857), *Dombey and Son* (1848), and *David Copperfield* (1850). Dickens's dogs provide a perspective on both the continuity and the transformation of this figure from its eighteenth-century versions. The images and effects that accompany Dickens's dogs emerge directly from the earlier satiric tradition, except, interestingly, for these animals' size. Though they behave like Pope's Shock, *Little Dorrit's* and *Dombey and Son's* canine pets are not lapdogs, but giants. The lady-and-the-lapdog figure in *Little Dorrit* appears in a local scene and serves to uncover the lady's affections. This exchange is set at the Meagles's country estate, where Minnie Meagles's two suitors arrive together for a visit to the family. Minnie's romantic attachment to Henry Gowan becomes evident to Gowan's rival, the novel's male protagonist, Arthur Clennam. Gowan appears with his giant Newfoundland dog, and Minnie's connection with him is telegraphed in her evident affection for the animal, rendered through the jealous consciousness of Arthur Clennam: "How she caressed the dog, and how the dog knew her! How expressive that heightened color in her face, that fluttered manner, her downcast eyes, her irresolute happiness!…The dog had put his great paws on her arm and laid his head against her dear bosom. She had laughed and welcomed them, and made far too much of the dog, far, far, too much."[28] Here we see in compact form the caress, the female bosom, the strange inter-species embrace, and the "far, far, too much" that indicate the familiar

---

[28] Charles Dickens, *Little Dorrit*, ed. Harvey Peter Sucksmith (Oxford: Clarendon Press, 1979), 198.

connection of immoderate love. From Clennam's point of view, the lady's intimacy with the dog is a both a testimony to Minnie's natural sentiment and a signal of impropriety, and both of these effects are pursued within the novel, as Minnie's true virtue is confirmed, while her marriage to Gowan—the dog's master—leads her to ruin.

The question of the transgression of the boundaries of kin is directly relevant to Florence Dombey's relationship with Diogenes, another "great hoarse shaggy dog," whose size is a means of underlining his comic alterity, and whose name alludes to the Cynic philosopher who argued that animals are superior to humans.[29] Florence is given the dog on her brother's death, and her intimate connection with him is presented as a direct substitute for her cruel alienation from her father. In the scene in which Diogenes is introduced, we see the same contrast between ordinary distance and immoderate intimacy that is characteristic of the representation of the lady and the lapdog elsewhere in this period. At his first appearance, Diogenes is a comical and familiar object of human amusement, a "poor cur," or "that dog" of familiar parlance: "Diogenes was as unlike a lady's dog as dog might be;...as ridiculous a dog as one would meet with on a summer's day; a blundering, ill-favoured, clumsy, bullet-headed dog, continually acting on a wrong idea that there was an enemy in the neighbourhood, whom it was meritorious to bark at" (212). In fact, Diogenes' first act is to scare off Florence's friend, Mr. Toots:

> [He] suddenly took it into his head to bay Mr. Toots, and to make short runs at him with his mouth open. Not exactly seeing his way to the end of these demonstrations,... Mr. Toots, with chuckles, lapsed out at the door: by which, after looking in again two or three times without any object at all, and being on each occasion greeted with a fresh run from Diogenes, he finally took himself off and got away. (213)

This baying and barking and comical cavorting is followed by a very different encounter, a connection between dog and woman that includes all of the now-familiar elements of the trope: a strange, hairy face; an alien gaze; an intimate embrace; a falling tear; a bedside encounter; an immoderate love; and a transgression of the boundaries both of kin and kind, as follows:

> Though [Diogenes] was far from good-tempered, and certainly was not clever, and had hair all over his eyes, and a comic nose, and an inconsistent tail, and a gruff voice; he was dearer to Florence...than the most valuable and beautiful

---

[29] Charles Dickens, *Dombey and Son*, ed. Alan Horsman (Oxford: Oxford University Press, 1966), 156. For the Cynics' regard for animals, see Richard Sorabji, *Animal Minds and Human Morals: The Origins of the Western Debate* (Ithaca, N.Y.: Cornell University Press, 1993), 160.

of his kind.… "Come, then, Di! Dear Di! Make friends with your new mistress. Let us love each other, Di!" said Florence, fondling his shaggy head. And Di, the rough and gruff, as if his hairy hide were pervious to the tear that dropped upon it, and his dog's heart melted as it fell, put his nose up to her face, and swore fidelity.…He…rose up on his hind legs, with his awkward fore paws on her shoulders, licked her face and hands, nestled his great head against her heart, and wagged his tail till he was tired. Finally, Diogenes coiled himself up at her feet, and went to sleep. (212–213)

In this dynamic of comic distance and alien intimacy, Diogenes, like so many of his imaginary canine predecessors, takes the place of a missing human and familial contact. Florence, and Dickens, see Diogenes as a substitute for Florence's cruel father. She calls on her dog to "love me for his sake!" Dickens concludes the painful account of Mr. Dombey's rejection of Florence with another bedside representation of the lady and the lapdog:

Diogenes already loved her for her own [sake], and didn't care how much he showed it. So he made himself vastly ridiculous by performing a variety of uncouth bounces in the ante-chamber, and concluded, when poor Florence was at last asleep,…by scratching open her bedroom door: rolling up his bed into a pillow: lying down on the boards, at the full length of his tether, with his head towards her: and looking lazily at her, upside down, out of the tops of his eyes, until from winking and winking he fell asleep himself, and dreamed, with gruff barks, of his enemy. (217).

The strange bedside gaze here is the channel that joins Florence and Diogenes, marking their intimacy. Again, this connection between a woman and an animal substitutes for the natural, familial intimacy that should subsist between father and daughter, in the same way that the connection between Lady Juliana and her lapdog takes the place of the love that should naturally join mother and child. The transgression of the boundaries of kin and kind, and the reversals and inversions rehearsed in this passage, lead directly to an alternative realm of affection, proposed in Florence's words "let us love each other."

David Copperfield's Jip is a true lapdog, and his interaction with David's child-wife, Dora, is built on the familiar prototype and alludes directly to its satiric heritage. During David's courtship of Dora, Jip elicits the envy of the displaced human lover, and Dora's treatment of the dog reproduces the language of immoderate love, with its caresses, its erotic "punishments," and its licking tongue. In David's words:

He was mortally jealous of me, and persisted in barking at me. She took him up in her arms—oh my goodness!—and caressed him, but he insisted upon barking still. He wouldn't let me touch him, when I tried; and then she beat him. It increased my sufferings greatly to see the pats she gave him for punishment on the bridge of his blunt nose, while he winked his eyes, and licked her hand, and still growled within himself like a little double-bass. At length he was quiet—well he might be with her dimpled chin upon his head!—and we walked away to look at a greenhouse.[30]

When David announces his straitened circumstances to Dora and encourages her "perseverance and strength of character," the solution is kissing the lapdog:

> "But I haven't got any strength at all," said Dora, shaking her curls. "Have I, Jip? Oh, do kiss Jip, and be agreeable!"
>
> It was impossible to resist kissing Jip, when she held him up to me for that purpose, putting her own bright, rosy little mouth into kissing form, as she directed the operation, which she insisted should be performed symmetrically, on the centre of his nose. I did as she bade me—rewarding myself afterwards for my obedience—and she charmed me out of my graver character for I don't know how long. (609–610)

Jip's special intimacy with Dora is emphasized at the time of her decline and death, and the representation of their relationship has the same structure as Diogenes' connection with Florence Dombey—a dynamic of distance and intimacy, in which the lapdog's proximity to the lady is contrasted with his comic distance from those around her, including her husband, and is seen as a substitute for a natural or normal human connection. Jip, like Diogenes, attacks innocent bystanders, in this case David's aunt, Dora's nurse, with an energy that contrasts with his intimacy with his mistress, and that resembles Diogenes' comical attacks on Mr. Toots:

> Dora had helped him up on the sofa; where he really was defying my aunt to such a furious extent, that he couldn't keep straight, but barked himself sideways. The more my aunt looked at him, the more he reproached her; for, she had lately taken to spectacles, and for some inscrutable reason he considered the glasses personal.
>
> Dora made him lie down by her, with a good deal of persuasion; and when he was quiet, drew one of his long ears through and through her hand, repeating, thoughtfully, "Even little Jip! Oh, poor fellow!" (789–790)

The sofa is Dora's invalid bed, where the canine companion, with his long ears, takes an intimate place in relation to the lady, in contrast to the comical distance from

---

[30] Charles Dickens, *David Copperfield* (Oxford: Oxford University Press, 1999), 444.

human-kind with which he begins the encounter. Jip had also barked at David when he first courted Dora, a behavior that especially endears him to her, as she says: "I couldn't be such friends with any other dog but Jip; because [another dog] wouldn't have known me before I was married, and wouldn't have barked at Doady when he first came to our house. I couldn't care for any other dog but Jip, I am afraid, aunt" (790). Jip's special relationship with Dora, based on their intimacy "before [she] was married," and his attacks on her husband-to-be, can be compared to Belinda's relationship with Shock, who wakes his mistress with his tongue as a substitute for the human lover she dreams of.

For the innocent Dora, or Florence Dombey, however, the sexual innuendo is difficult to apply. Though these scenes include the same inter-species embrace that we can track back even to *The Rival Lapdog*, the suggestion of an awakening or excessive or perverse female sexuality does not illuminate either of those characters or belong to the imaginative experience generated by their texts. On the other hand, the idea of an alternative realm of affection created through this inter-species embrace certainly emerges as an experiment in the definition of love in Dickens's novels. Adding these sentimental female characters to our survey of the appearances of the lady and the lapdog helps us see that the significance of such experiments with the idea of inter-species love is not limited to the early eighteenth-century satire on sexual excess. Immoderate love—or heights of love—evokes a broader idea, relevant to all these occasions of inter-species affection, whatever their local role; an idea of a realm outside the bounds of the normal, which emerges from the relationships of inversion and reversal that characterize this imaginative encounter with animal-kind.

Immoderate Love

The lady and the lapdog has a powerful literary resonance. The range of examples that we have surveyed suggests that this figure, even when it appears in very different texts and modes of discourse and across a period of a century and a half, carries a lasting imaginative vitality. The "bedfellow" setting, the female breast, the tenderness, the caress, the embrace, the kiss, the tear, and, in short, the heights of love, express the intimacy of the human-animal connection. The nonhuman gaze marks the channel of contact. The hairy or supersized being, the immoderate or unnatural attraction, and the misdirected or substituted affection signal its shocking, surprising, or sudden alterity. Brought together in one imaginative moment, these effects collide. And the result of their collision is the sudden inversion that we have tracked from satiric poetry—those structures of discordance, antithesis, magical substitution, hierarchy reversal, or species transposition that define the figure of the lady and the lapdog.

Why such resonance? Most immediately, as we have already seen, the lady and the lapdog provides an occasion to explore ideas of human-animal intimacy generated by the rise of pet keeping. Is the animal a force within or a being external to the human? Do animals regulate or liberate human behavior? Can humans become or substitute for animals, and vice versa? Does love define or transcend species?[31] But in addition, this inter-species fantasy and the questions it contemplates have a broader purview. The cultural phenomenon of pet keeping and the female connection with animals were closely related to the generalized humanitarian movements of this era. What Keith Thomas describes as "that growing concern about the treatment of animals which was one of the most distinctive features of late-eighteenth-century English middle-class culture" (144) found resonances in the new philanthropy.[32] Hanway's essay illustrates this connection clearly, as he evokes, in connection with the beloved lapdog, the idea of "a *human* creature, which [may be]…under no care at all." Furthermore, as Markman Ellis has demonstrated, lapdogs served as a common point of reference in contemporary discussions of sympathy toward African slaves. Ellis argues that "the campaigns against slavery and animal cruelty [were] intertwined in the public imagination" in this period: "Just as the abolitionists sought to reposition Africans as thinking and feeling people, the animal-cruelty campaigners sought to refigure the cultural construction of brute creation, showing them to be not things but animals possessed with feeling and thus endowed with certain rights" ("Suffering Things," 106–107). We have seen this association illustrated in Mr. Ellison's reproof to his wife for her failure to apply the same sympathy to her "fellow creatures" as to her lapdog (13).[33] This broader relevance suggests that the questions raised by the figure of the lady and the lapdog intersect actively with a wider engagement with the connection between women and animals—an engagement that persists and develops over the course of this period. Ladies and lapdogs inform ideas about humanity or charity, as well as the understanding of sympathy or love, as those ideas are construed in relation to notions of kin and kind. In this respect, the lady and the lapdog is a particular instance of a collective imaginative project.

Meanwhile, the issues of sexuality that we have seen to be endemic to this particular human-animal conjunction find a strange echo in contemporary representations of inter-species miscegenation—in the frequent and widely accepted stories of apes

---

[31] Ellis also explores the deep problematization of the lapdog, describing "the intensity of the struggle over the meanings of the lapdog in the mid-eighteenth century" ("Suffering Things," 99).

[32] For a sustained account of the rise of "compassion for the brute creation," see Thomas, *Man and the Natural World*, 143–192.

[33] Ellis has treated this text in detail in "Suffering Things" and *The Politics of Sensibility*. See also Laura Brown, *Fables of Modernity: Literature and Culture in the English Eighteenth Century* (Ithaca, N.Y.: Cornell University Press, 2001), 254–256.

engaging in sexual intercourse with women.[34] These stories arise, of course, from the extraordinary shifts in the definition of the human in relation to the hominoid ape—shifts that we saw in chapter 2 to be deeply resonant in the eighteenth-century imagination. The image of apes raping women appears in Edward Long's *History of Jamaica* (1774), in a sustained summary of seventeenth and eighteenth-century natural historians' and travelers' accounts of the hominoid ape in Africa:

> So far as [apes] are hitherto discovered to Europeans, it appears that they herd in a kind of society together, and build huts suitable to their climate; that, when tamed and properly instructed, they have been brought to perform a variety of menial domestic services; that they conceive a Passion for the Negroe women, and hence must be supposed to covet their embraces from a natural impulse of desire, such as inclines one animal towards another of the same species, or which has a conformity in the organs of generation.[35]

These apes "endeavour to surprize and carry off Negroe women into their woody retreats, in order to enjoy them" (360). And, Long supposes, "I do not think that an oran-outang husband would be any dishonour to an Hottentot female" (364). James Burnet, Lord Monboddo, recites the same stories—that "these Orang Outangs...carry away young negroe girls, and keep them for their pleasure: And, [one traveler] says, he knew one negroe girl that had been with them three years."[36]

Famously, the bathing scene from the fourth voyage of Jonathan Swift's *Gulliver's Travels* redacts this familiar ape-rape myth. Here, as we have seen in chapter 2, the Yahoos are Swift's composite version of the hominoid ape, with their "thick hair" and "beards like goats," and Gulliver the vulnerable rape victim:

> Being one day abroad with my protector the sorrel nag, and the weather exceeding hot, I entreated him to let me bathe in a river that was near. He consented, and I immediately stripped myself stark naked, and went down softly into the stream. It happened that a young female yahoo, standing behind a bank, saw the whole proceeding, and inflamed by desire...came running with all speed, and leaped into the water within five yards of the place where I bathed. I was never in my life so terribly frighted....She embraced me after a most fulsome manner; I roared as loud as I could and the nag came galloping towards me, whereupon she quitted her grasp, with the utmost reluctancy, and leaped upon the opposite bank, where

[34] For a summary of the ape-rape myth, see H. W. Janson, *Apes and Ape Lore in the Middle Ages and the Renaissance* (London: Warburg Institute, 1952), 261–286, and Brown, *Fables of Modernity*, 236–245.

[35] Edward Long, *The History of Jamaica*, 3 vols. (London: T. Lowndes, 1774), 2:364.

[36] James Burnet, Lord Monboddo, *Of the Origin and Progress of Language*, 2nd ed. (Edinburgh, 1774; repr. New York: Garland, 1970), 1: 277–278.

she stood gazing and howling all the time I was putting on my clothes.... [N]ow I could no longer deny that I was a real yahoo in every limb and feature, since the females had a natural propensity to me as one of their own species.[37]

In this image of inter-species sexual contact, where the hairy, alien being embraces the human, Swift is clearly experimenting with the established miscegenation fantasy by proposing, in the event, that these alien creatures are, surprisingly, of the same species as the human.

These anecdotes of ape-rape can be used to suggest the degenerate nature of non-European—especially African—peoples, as Long's account clearly does. Or they can implicitly support the protoevolutionist idea of continuity from nonhuman to human-being, as is the case with Monboddo's interpretation of these stories. But in either instance, this fantasy has the same shape and many of the same components as that of the lady and the lapdog—an image structured around the representation of a sudden movement of intimacy across a divide of alterity; a moment of connection between a woman and an alien, hairy nonhuman being; an immoderate love; and a violation of the ordinary norms of kin and kind. In Barrett Browning's words:

> A head as hairy as Faunus thrust its way
> Right sudden against my face,
>
> .   .   .   .
> ...the bearded vision...
>
> .   .   .   .
> ...the true PAN
> ...leads to heights of love.

Stripped to their imaginative core, this inter-species love sonnet and the eighteenth-century miscegenation anecdote represent the same unexpected historical experience of human-animal contact. And furthermore, in thanking "the true PAN" who presides over this moment in which the normal human-animal hierarchy is so fundamentally chal-lenged, Barrett Browning's poem reaches back to the turn of the eighteenth century and to Edward Tyson's influential connection of the orangutan with the semideities of clas-sical mythology—with the fauns, the satyrs, Silenus, and with Pan himself, a connection evident in the poem's title, "Flush or Faunus." We examined this connection at length in chapter 2, where we saw its centrality to the ontological questions generated by the new

---

[37] Jonathan Swift, *Gulliver's Travels and Other Writings*, ed. Louis A. Landa (Boston: Houghton Mifflin, 1960), 207, 215. For a reading of Gulliver's bathing scene in the context of the rape myth, see Brown, *Fables of Modernity*, 240–242.

experience of animal-kind. And we saw it highlighted in chapter 1, in Thomas Love Peacock's complex characterization of his ape hero in *Melincourt; or, Sir Oran Haut-ton* (1818).[38]

Of course we know that Flush is not Barrett Browning's figure for Tyson's *homo sylvestris* or for Long's ape that rapes African women, and that Florence Dombey is not Dickens's redaction of the so-called Hottentot female caught in the embrace of the "rough and gruff," "hairy" beast as "he...rose up on his hind legs, with his...fore paws on her shoulders." But the deep formal resemblance among these texts helps us grasp the richness and the speculativeness of the figure of the lady and the lapdog. In its earlier satiric versions, as we have seen, this figure gathers a fund of images, forms, and effects whose ironies shape a distinctive, destabilizing approach to inter-species connection. These effects carry forward, transferring that array of questions about identities, hierarchies, and stabilities to successive sentimental and affective literary forms, and thus reproducing, through those processes of destabilization, some of the most troubling dimensions of the modern experience of alterity. In this way, this feminized, domestic trope of inter-species household intimacy comes to mirror one of this era's most powerful global images of the encounter with alterity.

In both the miscegenation anecdote and the representation of women's pet keeping, the experience of difference takes the same form. Like the Yahoo in Swift's rape scene or the Hottentot in Long's history, Flush, Diogenes, and the "Rival Lapdog" are portrayed as most alien, most disturbing, or most perverse at the point of their closest contact with the human. But the representations of this sudden encounter in the realms of race and culture produce no positive innovations. In the case of the lady and the lapdog, however, this collision propels the account of human-animal connection outside the bounds of the normal and creates the opportunity for a new and vital imaginative framework in which ideas about kinship and species difference, hierarchy and privilege, or antithesis and affection are fundamentally revised. "Immoderate love" emerges as the surprising fulfillment of this revision. The product of astonished difference, this new notion of love is based on alterity rather than identity, and on a structure of dissonance, reversal, and inversion rather than of sameness or coherence. The literary figure of the lady and the lapdog, in its long reach from social satire to sentiment and from the bedside setting to the habitats of Africa, makes the historical engagement with animal-kind into an imaginative experience that is "good to think."[39]

---

[38] Pan has many meanings, most of them consonant with the humanist interpretations of the classical tradition. In this context, Barrett Browning's "true Pan" is usually seen as a Christ figure. For instance, Patricia Merivale reads this sonnet as a contrast between Flush, a "goatish and terrifying" pseudo-Pan, and the representation of Christianity in the "true Pan" who replaces him in the poem's conclusion. Patricia Merivale, *Pan the Goat-God: His Myth in Modern Times* (Cambridge, Mass.: Harvard University Press, 1969), 82.

[39] Claude Lévi-Strauss, *Totemism*, trans. Rodney Needham (1962; repr. Boston: Beacon Press, 1971), 89.

Figure 3. William Hogarth, from "The Harlot's Progress" (1732).

4

VIOLENT INTIMACY

The Monkey and the Marriage Plot

Animal-kind appears at the periphery of imaginative representations of marriage in the eighteenth century. A close look at one of these peripheral moments suggests that imaginary animals can even undercut the represented stability of human institutions. As we have seen in the previous chapter, the portrayal of the lapdog's rivalry with the husband or human lover in the early eighteenth century begins to impinge on the ideal of married intimacy by generating an alternative fantasy of inter-species love. But a different animal inspires a more direct attack on the conventional notion of love and marriage as the ultimate goal of virtuous female conduct: the pet monkey. In fact, the monkey is the missing link between satiric treatments of marriage in the early eighteenth-century dramatic comedy of manners, on the one hand, and one of the major canonical idealizations of marriage in the domestic novel of the latter part of the century, on the other. In its last pages, Frances Burney's conduct novel, *Evelina; or, The History of a Young Lady's Entrance into the World* (1778), suddenly introduces a new non-human character—a fully dressed monkey—whose appearance enables us to explore the relevance of animal-kind to the marriage plot as well as some of the particular ties between literary culture and contemporary engagements with problems of ontology.

Evelina has been a key text in the critical understanding of the novel of manners, because this work seems to bring together those aspects of the genre that are most significant to its impact, innovations, tensions, and influence. Burney's first novel demonstrates the nature of the relationship between narrative form and contemporary culture in this period, because it joins the discourse of the influential social-conduct manuals of the second half of the eighteenth century with the fictional world of the novel of manners. From another perspective, this work provides a range of paradigms of plot, character, and rhetoric that influence the subsequent development of realist fiction, and that, for example, Jane Austen's works systematically adapt and transform. In terms of the history of the novel, *Evelina* links eighteenth-century domestic fiction with the nineteenth-century social novel, the epistolary forms of Samuel Richardson with the complex voices of nineteenth-century realist narration. Meanwhile, *Evelina* suggests the tensions implicit in the patriarchal resolution of the novel of manners, tensions that shape the female narrative tradition for over a century to follow.[1] *Evelina*'s monkey, then, belongs to a complex and influential work in which the ideal of companionate marriage is provided with a fully imagined narrative form. Identifying the significance of the monkey in this text places that animal being at a key moment in the fictional treatment of marriage, and thus can help us understand the relevance of the ontological questions of this period to the institution of marriage, as well as the particular function of animal-kind in generating that relevance.

Evelina's entrance into the world has a paradigmatic shape, which closely follows the conventional plot structure of the novel of manners. Suddenly thrust into society, Evelina must negotiate the complexities of social interaction as an unattached female, without the benefit of an experienced adviser. She immediately encounters a male world made up of a spectrum of potential suitors that seems to constitute a microcosm of society—Sir Clement Willoughby, the rake; Mr. Lovel, the fop; and Lord Orville, the "best of men." Within this carefully delineated social realm, Evelina commits a series of errors of conduct, which indicate both her innocence and, at some points, her natural moral superiority to rigid behavioral norms. Her ideal marriage partner, Lord Orville, is distinguished from the other suitors by his appreciation of Evelina's natural virtue, but their union is impeded by her accumulating social trials as her entrance into the world unfolds. The conclusion of the action resolves Evelina's errors of conduct by aligning her natural virtue with social decorum, while it simultaneously unites her in marriage with her ideal partner. This union, which at last supplies Evelina with appropriate male supervision, is matched by her corollary discovery of her long-lost aristocratic father, Sir John Belmont, in a reiteration of her conclusive subordination to patriarchy and her accommodation to social norms.

The marriage does not come off without a hitch, however. Lord Orville proposes; Sir John Belmont blesses his daughter; and the official marriage is subsequently confirmed in the first line of Evelina's brief, last letter—"All is over."[2] But Lord Orville's

---

[1] See, for example, Kristina Straub, *Fanny Burney and Feminine Strategy* (Lexington: University of Kentucky Press, 1987); Margaret Doody, *Frances Burney: The Life in the Works* (Cambridge: Cambridge University Press, 1988); Julia Epstein, *The Iron Pen: Frances Burney and the Politics of Women's Writing* (Madison: University of Wisconsin Press, 1989); Irene Tucker, "Writing Home: *Evelina*, the Epistolary Novel and the Paradox of Propriety," *ELH* 60 (1993): 419–439; Audrey Bilger, *Laughing Feminism: Subversive Comedy in Frances Burney, Maria Edgeworth, and Jane Austen* (Detroit: Wayne State University Press, 1998); and Susan Greenfield, *Mothering Daughters: Novels and the Politics of Family Romance, Frances Burney to Jane Austen* (Detroit: Wayne State University Press, 2002).

[2] Frances Burney, *Evelina*, ed. Stewart J. Cooke (New York: W. W. Norton, 1998), 336. Subsequent references to *Evelina* are to this edition.

proposal is separated from the marriage ceremony by a shocking, violent, and formally anomalous event. Captain Mirvan, whose carnivalesque activities have supplied satiric interest at several points in the course of the action, suddenly arrives on the scene unannounced, to encounter Mr. Lovel, a character directly derived from the fop of the Restoration comedy of manners. Though Lovel is prominent in the opening movement of the plot where Evelina's social world is mapped out, he plays only the slightest role in the second half of the novel, as Evelina's errors of conduct are modulated and her natural virtue takes precedence. But at the very end of the story, as the marriage plot reaches its denouement, Lovel briefly occupies center stage, as the object of a prank directed by Captain Mirvan in which Lovel is paired with a new character, a monkey "full dressed, and extravagantly *à-la-mode*" (331).

Captain Mirvan has the monkey brought in before the company in the drawing room of their fashionable hostess, Mrs. Beaumont, as an attack on Lovel's affectation of dress and manner. The representation of this nonhuman being's interaction with the humans in the room moves between proximity and distance, in a dynamic structure that is significant for our understanding of the relevance of this strange scene. First, Captain Mirvan provides a strong assertion of affinity: he tells the company that "the little gentleman" he is about to introduce is so like Mr. Lovel that he could have been his "twin-brother." As soon as the monkey appears, however, this professed affinity turns into aversion, as Lady Louisa deems the nonhuman visitor a "monster," and the other guests respond with various demonstrations of shock or surprise:

> The dismay of the company was almost general. Poor Mr. Lovel seemed thunderstruck with indignation and surprise; Lady Louisa began a scream, which for some time was incessant; Miss Mirvan and I jumped involuntarily upon the seats of our chairs: Mrs. Beaumont herself followed our example; Lord Orville placed himself before me as a guard; and Mrs. Selwyn, Lord Merton, and Mr. Coverley, burst into a loud, immoderate, ungovernable fit of laughter, in which they were joined by the Captain, till, unable to support himself, he rolled on the floor. (331)

But Captain Mirvan's constant assertions of the affinity of human and nonhuman bring the relationship back from distance to proximity:

> "Why now, Ladies and Gentlemen, I'll be judged by you all!—Did you ever see any thing more like? Odds my life, if it was n't for this here tail, you would n't know one from t'other....Come, now,...just for the fun's sake, duff your coat and waistcoat, and swop with *Monsieur Grinagain* here, and I'll warrant you'll not know yourself which is which....Well, don't be angry,—come, he sha'n't hurt

you;—here, shake a paw with him,—why he'll do you no harm, man!—come, kiss and friends!—".…

"God forbid!" cried Mr. Lovel, retreating, "I would sooner trust my person with a mad bull!"…

"Captain," said Lord Orville, "the ladies are alarmed, and I must beg you would send the monkey away."

"Why, where can be the mighty harm of one monkey more than another?" answered the Captain; "howsomever, if it's agreeable to the ladies, suppose we turn them out together?" (332)

The encounter is brought to a close by a moment of violent contact. As Captain Mirvan forces the nonhuman and the human being toward intimacy, Mr. Lovel, enraged, gives "a furious blow to the monkey." "The creature darting forwards, sprung instantly upon him, and clinging round his neck, fastened his teeth to one of his ears," at which point Lovel, "almost fainting with terror, sunk upon the floor, crying out, 'Oh I shall die, I shall die!—Oh I'm bit to death!'" (333). In this one climactic action, proximity and distance, and intimacy and violence, come together, as the nonhuman being embraces and attacks the human.

Monkeys and marriage, intimacy and violence, the nonhuman proximity to the human, and the contemporary fascination with the anthropoid ape—all of these topics link the monkey anecdote to the imaginative and cultural experience of *Evelina*'s eighteenth-century readership. This monkey belongs to the tradition of dramatic social satire, a tradition in which monkeys and marriage are consistently connected, and for which human intimacy with the nonhuman pet is a satiric trope. More broadly, the dynamic of proximity and distance and especially the climactic, violent embrace that shapes *Evelina*'s monkey anecdote reproduce a specific formal structure that characterizes the representation of the encounter with alterity elsewhere in eighteenth-century literary culture. *Evelina*'s monkey has strong ties to other images of violent intimacy that emerge from the imaginative impact of the discovery of the hominoid ape. Placing Burney's manners novel in these contexts can give us a glimpse of a distinctive and complex contemporary fantasy—a fantasy that links the monkey to the marriage plot and the violent inter-species embrace to the struggle to identify human being itself.

Marriage, Monkeys, and the Comedy of Manners

A publication entitled *London Jests* (1712), which describes itself as "a collection of the choicest joques and repartees" of the day, explains that the entourage of the fashionable lady as she makes the annual move from London to her country establishment must include "my Lady & her Monkey, the Parrot, and a French Spaniel, a young Negro, with a Silver Coller, Madam Patch and Paint my Ladies waiting Woman, and a couple of Tabby Cats."[3] The monkey, the parrot, and the lapdog, sometimes separately and often together, are frequently named as the favored companions of the woman of quality in the antifemale satire of this period. And among these privileged pets, the monkey in particular constitutes a familiar trope in the witty repartee of the comedy of manners, especially in the second generation of this dramatic subgenre that extended the tradition established during the Restoration by George Etherege and William Wycherley through the first half of the eighteenth century. George Farquhar's Archer in *The Beaux Stratagem* (1707) provides a thumbnail sketch of the coquette as a "Baggage" who "has a pert *Je ne scai quoi*, she reads Plays, keeps a Monkey, and is troubled with Vapours."[4] And Colley Cibber offers another perspective on this female pastime in *The Double Gallant* (1707), in Lady Dainty's account of pet keeping:

L.D.: How insipid wou'd Life be, if we had nothing about us but what was necessary? Can you suppose so many Women of Quality wou'd run mad after Monkeys, Squirrels, Paroqueets, *Dutch* dogs, and Eunuchs, but that they are of no manner of use in the world?[5]

The connection between the woman and the monkey in this drama serves as the basis for a range of satiric effects directed at female character and fashion, foppish male affectation, the sexual excesses of both genders, and upper-class courtship and marriage.[6] Issues of courtship and marriage consistently underpin these appearances of human-animal intimacy. For example, another Belinda, in William Taverner's play *The Artful Husband* (1735), chooses to attack her suitor through an unfavorable comparison to her monkey:

BEL: You have given me as much Pain in pursuing me, as my Monkey does in flying me, when I want his diverting Company. I'm downright angry, and so farewell.[7]

[3] *London Jests; or, A Collection of the Choicest Joques and Repartees.* (London: printed by C. B. for Tho. Norris, 1712), 85.
[4] George Farquhar, *The Beaux Stratagem*, ed. Charles Stonehill (1707; repr. New York: Gordian Press, 1967), vol. 2, 2.2, p. 138. This play was performed in 1707 and frequently revived. References to plays are to act and scene, or act, scene, and line.
[5] Colley Cibber, *The Double Gallant; or, The Sick Lady's Cure* (London: printed for Bernard Lintott, [1707]), act 3, p. 28. The play was performed during that year, according to *The London Stage*. It was revived and revised throughout the period. See *The London Stage, 1660–1800*, part 2: 1700–1729, ed. E. L. Avery (Carbondale: Southern Illinois University Press, 1960–1968).
[6] For the role of lapdogs in antifemale satire, see Ingrid H. Tague, "Dead Pets: Satire and Sentiment in British Elegies and Epitaphs for Animals," *Eighteenth-Century Studies* 42 (2008): 289–306, and Theresa Braunschneider, "The Lady and the Lapdog: Mixed Ethnicity in Constantinople, Fashionable Pets in Britain," in *Humans and Other Animals in Eighteenth-Century British Culture*, ed. Frank Palmeri (Aldershot, UK: Ashgate, 2006), 31–48.
[7] William Taverner, *The Artful Husband* (London: printed for Elizabeth Sawbridge, [1717]), act 1, p. 10. The play was performed during that year, according to *The London Stage*.

This passage ridicules the beau, Sir Harry Freelove, by comparing him to the lady's monkey. And of course it also satirizes Belinda, not only for her pursuit of her monkey but also for her tendency to conflate monkey and man. But the husband as well as the suitor can be compared to the monkey, as in Charles Molloy's *The Perplex'd Couple* (1715), where Leonora discusses with her servant Isbel the question of her marriage to a wealthy but unattractive beau:

LEON: Has he brib'd you in his Favour; or can you see a Charm in his grizly Face?
ISB: Yes I can, Madam, a thousand; for, as my Master says, Fifty thousand Pound is attended with a long Train of Charms—There's fine Cloaths, visiting Days, Parks, Plays, Operas,—
LEON: And a Wretch so homely by my Side, that he'll be mistaken for my Monkey, or rather 'twill be a greater mistake to take him for a Man.[8]

Even the male perspective projects the monkey as a substitute husband; in Farquhar's *The Inconstant* (1708), Mirabel imagines himself as a pet monkey, as he argues with his father that he should not be forced to marry:

MIR: Wou'd my Father have his youthful Son lie lazing here, bound to a Wife, chain'd like a Monkey to make sport to a Woman, subject to her Whims, Humours, Longings, Vapours and Capriches?[9]

In fact, monkeys and marriage make a consistent pair in this drama. In George Granville's comic rewriting of *The Merchant of Venice* as *The Jew of Venice* (1701), Portia, "a Rich Heiress," uses her monkey to illustrate her aversion to marrying a certain ridiculous suitor:

PORT: He has more Tricks than a Baboon: If my Bird sings, he strait falls a capering; He will fence with his own Shadow; nor is his Tongue less nimble than his Heels; I would as soon marry my Squirrel, or my Monkey.[10]

James Miller's *The Humours of Oxford* (1730) has two fashionable ladies, Clarinda and Victoria, discussing the pros and cons of marriage:

CLAR: Why, a Husband now-a-days is the only Person that can never be one's Companion for Life.
VICT: That's strange indeed!

[8] Charles Molloy, *The Perplex'd Couple; or, Mistake upon Mistake* (London: printed for W. Meares and J. Brown, 1715), 2.1, p. 30. The play was performed during that year, according to *The London Stage*.
[9] George Farquhar, *The Inconstant; or, The Way to Win Him* (1702), ed. Stonehill, vol. 1, 4.3, p. 259. This play was performed in 1702.
[10] George Granville, Baron Lansdowne, *The Jew of Venice* (London: printed for Ber. Lintott, 1701), p. 4. The play was performed during that year, according to *The London Stage*.

CLAR: But as true—for after the first Moon, 'tis the most unfashionable thing in the
    World, either to eat, drink, or lie together—and if ever you happen unfortunately to
    be alone with one another—why he pares his nails, and you play with the Monkey.
VICT: A very comfortable description of Matrimony.[11]

And in Owen Swinny's *The Quacks* (1745), when Lucinda is afflicted with the vapors, her
father, Sir Patient, offers her a monkey and a husband in the same breath:

PAT: Always sad and melancholy? Tell me the Cause of it, my pretty Dear. Discover
    your little Heart to your little Papa and tell him what disturbs it then. Shall I kiss
    thee? Don't enrage me with this Humour, but tell me the Cause, and I promise
    to do anything for you, and comply with your Inclination be it of what kind
    soever.—I can say no more.—Is there any new Fashion you have a mind to? No.
    Any Lace or Ribbon? No. Any Lap-dog, or Squirrel, or Monkey that you long
    for? Have you a mind to a Husband?[12]

The monkey often provides a means of registering a sexual critique of the coquette,
as in a one-act comedy entitled *The City Farce* (1737), where Mr. Snatch exposes the female practice of admitting gentlemen to their dressing rooms:

SNATCH: There, Madam, you see with what Spirit Miss ushers him to her Dressing
    Room—I am really of opinion, that the Introduction of Men into the Offices
    attendant on the Ladies, has had no inconsiderable Share in rubbing off the fa-
    mous old Maiden-Blush, and enabling a Lady to look a young Fellow in the Face
    with as little Concern as she peeps at her Monkey.[13]

The monkey signals the oversexed woman even more directly in Thomas Baker's *An Act at
Oxford* (1704), when Berynthia, "the Toast of the University," whose amorousness is the butt
of the play's antifemale satire, suggests that Squire Calf kiss her monkey instead of herself:

CALF: Madam, I kiss your fair Hands.
BER: Kiss my Monkey.

[11] James Miller, *The Humours of Oxford* (London: printed for J. Watts, 1730), 2.1, p. 21. The play was performed
during that year, according to *The London Stage*.
[12] Owen Swinny, *The Quacks; or, Love's the Physician* (London: printed for M. Cooper, 1745), 1.1, pp. 3–4. This play
was first performed in 1705, according to *The London Stage*, and it was published in London for Benj. Bragg in
that year, though in that copy the monkey is omitted from this passage. It was again performed in 1745; the
1745 copy, printed for M. Cooper, and including the monkey, likely reflects that performance.
[13] Weddell, *The City Farce* (London: sold by J. Roberts, 1737), 19. *The London Stage* includes no record of this play's
performance.

CALF: No, truly. I don't use to kiss Monkeys. [*Aside.*] These fine Ladies are so fond of Monkeys, Lap-Dogs, and dapper Beaus, they can say nothing else.[14]

On the other hand, in Cibber's *The Double Gallant*, the lady, rather than the beau, is the one to kiss the monkey. Lady Dainty and Sylvia are discussing the monkey that the birdman, a pet salesman, has brought to them:

BIRD: I have brought your Ladyship the finest Monkey—

SYL: What a filthy thing it is!

L.D.: Now I think he looks very Humerous and agreeable—I vow in a white Periwig he might do mischief; cou'd he but Talk, and take Snuff, there's ne'er a Fop in Town wou'd go beyond him.

SYL: Most Fops would go farther if they did not speak; but talking indeed, makes 'em very often worse Company than Monkeys.

L.D.: Thou pretty little Picture of Man—how very *Indian* he looks! I cou'd kiss the dear Creature.

SYL: Ah! don't touch him he'll bite.

BIRD: No, Madam, he is the tamest you ever saw, and the least mischievous.

L.D.: Then take him away, I won't have him, for Mischief is the Wit of a Monkey, and I wou'd not give a Farthing for one, that wou'd not break me three or four Pounds worth of China in a Morning. (act 3, p. 30)[15]

This passage equates kissing and biting in a way that seems to prefigure *Evelina*'s monkey scene. And in fact, kissing is a potential implication of the monkey trope on many occasions. Dual kissing is represented in Gabriel Odingsells's *The Bath Unmask'd* (1725), where Mr. Sprightly describes to Cleora the picture on a ladies' fan as follows:

SPRI: [The picture shows] a scornful fair, who stands exactly in your posture, madam, (*To Cle. Who turns round with a disdainful air*) kissing her monkey, with his fore paws about her neck; she embracing him with one hand, while the other is grasp'd by a beau on one knee, kissing the [monkey] behind. Was the beau design'd to represent you [another suitor on stage] or me, my lord?

CLE: I think the monkey hath the nearest resemblance of you.[16]

[14] Thomas Baker, *An Act at Oxford* (London: printed for Bernard Lintott, 1704), p. 3; 4.2, p. 41. *The London Stage* includes no record of this play's performance.

[15] William Burnaby reproduces this monkey scene in the second edition of his comedy, *The Ladies Visiting-Day*, which was performed (according to *The London Stage*) and printed in 1708. The first printed version of Burnaby's play, from 1701, does not include the scene.

[16] Gabriel Odingsells, *The Bath Unmask'd* (Dublin: printed by and for George Grierson, 1725), 3.4, pp. 34–35. The play was performed during that year, according to *The London Stage*.

Odingsells's more explicit sexual suggestion here is an indication of how the link between sexual intimacy and monkeys preoccupied writers in this period. The elegy "On the Death of a Lady's *Monkey*" (1710) explores this preoccupation very openly, in a way that helps draw out some of the insinuations raised in the monkey-kissing language of the drama. In its description of Cloe's intimacy with her monkey, the poem moves directly to the point:

> Oh how the Pretty Creature oft would creep,
> And hug his Mistress as she lay asleep,
> And hold her to him in a kind Embrace,
> Now with her Bubbies play, now stroke her Face.
> Ten Thousand little taking Tricks he'd play,
> And please his gen'rous Mistress Night and Day.[17]

This monkey makes mischief, breaks china, and of course takes the place of Cloe's husband, as the speaker warns:

> …[L]et not your Grief [for the monkey's death] exceed,
> Or more for him than for your Husband bleed,
> Tho he perhaps did more Diversion give,
> Than he who does a Dotard-like survive. (226)

The diversion named here makes it clear that the substitution of monkey for husband applies not only to the institution of marriage but also to the physical act of "Diversion" that Cloe's "Dotard" husband fails to provide.

As these last examples indicate, the trope of the lady and the monkey draws the nonhuman being into proximity or intimacy with the human. But that dynamic can take two distinct though closely related forms. On one hand, the allusion to the monkey can serve to situate the animal as a proxy for the human male sexual partner—fop, suitor, or husband—so that monkey and man sometimes seem interchangeable. This is an ontological proximity, that asks the question "What is man?" as the female characters fail to distinguish man from animal. On the other hand, the trope often places the lady in a sexualized relationship with the monkey—where kissing, embracing, and bed or closet scenes suggest another kind of human-nonhuman intimacy. This last is an experiment in inter-species connection that, as we have seen in chapter 3 in regard to the image of the lady and the lapdog, attacks a conventional or normative understanding of intimacy; in the monkey trope this attack extends directly to the institution of marriage.

The complexity of this attack can be approached through the monkey's characteristic link to another satiric device of the drama of this period, the commodity of china.

---

[17] "On the Death of a Lady's *Monkey*," *Serious and comical essays* (London: J. King, 1710), 226.

In one example, Mademoiselle Fantast, the title character in Charles Molloy's *The Co-quette* (1718), responds with a strange equivocation to the question of whether she could fall in love. She answers her servant, La Jape:

LA J: But don't you think it possible you might fall in love, Madam?
FAN: Oh, very possible. Nay, I always am in Love with one thing or other: But I can't love more than one thing at once. There's not room in a Woman's Heart for more than one Object at a time. A little while ago I was passionately in Love with my Parrot, now I begin to grow tir'd of that, I'd give anything in the World for a Monkey; and if that should be so unfortunate as to grow out of Favor, as who can answer for one's Heart, perhaps, the next thing I should take a Fancy to, may be either a Lap-Dog, a Husband, or a piece of *China*.[18]

The possibility of Mademoiselle Fantast's falling in love interchangeably with a monkey, a husband, or a piece of china illustrates the connection between the problematic of intimacy that is condensed within the monkey trope and that familiar sexual metaphor of the Restoration comedy of manners, china.

The canonical model for this familiar metaphor for sexual intimacy is the "china scene" from William Wycherley's *The Country Wife* (1675). In this scene, the locked door to Mr. Horner's bedchamber becomes the focal point for a series of urgent questions and suppositions about what may be contained behind it. Outside the door, Sir Jasper Fidget explains to Mrs. Squeamish that his wife, Lady Fidget, is within with Horner, and that she is "playing the wag with him." According to Sir Jasper, Horner will "do her no hurt," because Sir Jasper and the other male characters in the play believe him to be a eunuch. Mrs. Squeamish's interpretation of what is behind the door, however, is very different: "[H]e'll give her no quarter. He'll play the wag again with her, let me tell you. Come, let's go help her."

When Horner and Lady Fidget emerge, they use the multivalent figure of the fashionable woman's love for china to explain the contents of the closet, in a way that accounts metaphorically for their activity behind the locked door while leaving the uninitiated observers on the outside with no answers at all:

Enter Lady Fidget *with a piece of china in her hand, and* Horner *following.*
LADY FIDGET: And I have been toiling and moiling for the prettiest piece of china, my dear.
HORNER: Nay, she has been too hard for me, do what I could.

[18] Charles Molloy, *The Coquet; or, the English Chevalier* (London: printed for E. Curll, and R. Francklin, 1718), act 2, pp. 30–31. The play was performed during that year, according to *The London Stage.*

MRS. SQUEAMISH: O Lord, I'll have some china too. Good Mr. Horner, don't think to give other people china, and me none; come in with me too.

HORNER: Upon my honor, I have none left now.

MRS. SQUEAMISH: Nay, nay, I have known you deny your china before now, but you shan't put me off so. Come.

HORNER: This lady has the last there.

LADY FIDGET: Yes, indeed, madam, to my certain knowledge he has no more left.

MRS. SQUEAMISH: Oh, but it may be he may have some you could not find.

LADY FIDGET: What, d'ye think if he had had any left, I would not have had it too? For we women of quality never think we have china enough.[19]

The witty figurative ambiguity that pervades this scene expresses the imaginative fascination with the irrepressible drive toward sexual intimacy that characterizes the Restoration comedy of manners. But it also suggests a fundamental question about the nature of that intimacy—a question that arises from the pointed ambiguity surrounding its object, and that is made evident in the conjunction of a human being with a piece of china. This questioning, as we have already seen, takes two forms. First, concerning the male sexual partner: What is Horner's status? Is he a human being or a placeholder for the fashionable woman's obsession with the commodity? And second, concerning the lady herself: Is Lady Fidget, like Mademoiselle Fantast or Lucinda, actually unable to distinguish between a human being and a piece of china—or a lapdog, a parrot, or a monkey?

Susanna Centlivre's *The Busie Body* (1709) also contains a sustained closed-door scene that provides an illuminating comparison with Wycherley's china scene, with a monkey rather than china serving as proxy for the human partner. Miranda, the play's desirable heiress, conceals her suitor, Sir George Airy, behind the chimney board—the closed doorlike cover to an unused fireplace area—when her guardian, Sir George's rival, the jealous Sir Francis, arrives unannounced. To prevent discovery, Miranda claims that the closed door conceals a monkey:

MIRAN: I have a, a, a, a, a Monkey shut up there; and if you open it before the Man comes that is to tame it, 'tis so wild 'twill break all my China, or get away, and that wou'd break my Heart; for I am fond on't to distraction....

SIR FRAN: Well, well,...I won't open it; she shall have her Monkey, poor Rogue.

[19]William Wycherley, *The Country Wife*, ed. Thomas H. Fujimura (Lincoln: University of Nebraska Press, 1965), 4.3, lines 142–143, 149, 144–145, and 179–194. This play retained a prominent place in the repertory of the London theaters throughout the first half of the eighteenth century.

Outside the chimney board, a dispute arises on stage as to what lies within. Marplot, a "silly Fellow" whose role is to complicate the designs of the play's protagonists while seeking to aid them in their suits, unaware that the monkey is a ruse, offers to tame it himself:

MARPL: A Monkey, dear Madam, let me see it; I can tame a Monkey as well as the best of them all. Oh how I love the little miniatures of men.

MIRAN: Be quiet, Mischief, and stand farther from the Chimney—you shall not see my Monkey—why sure—

(*Striving with him.*)

MARPL: For Heaven's sake, dear Madam, let me but peep, to see if it be as pretty as my Lady *Fiddle-Faddle*'s. Has it got a chain?

MIRAN: Not yet. But I design it one shall last its Life-time: Nay, you shall not see it—look, [Sir Francis], how he teazes me!

SIR FRAN: (*Getting between him and the Chimney:*) Sirrah, Sirrah, let [the] Monkey alone.

Here the struggle that takes place before the closed door highlights the question surrounding the object of human intimacy, the appropriate recipient of the woman's true affection—the strange confusion between man and monkey. The ruse of the monkey thus becomes a figurative reference to marriage, and the fashionable silver collar and chain that were the essential adornment of the monkey, the lapdog, or the young African slave in this period, become the chain of matrimony.

When Sir Francis and the others leave the room, Marplot opens the door, discovers Sir George, and sounds the alarm:

MARPL: Egad, I will see the Monkey now. (*Lifts up the Board, and discovers Sir George.*) Oh Lord, Oh Lord! Thieves, Thieves, Murder!

SIR GEO: Dam'e, you unlucky Dog! 'tis I, which way shall I get out, shew me instantly, or I'll cut your Throat.

MARPL: Undone, Undone! At that door there. But hold, hold, break that China, and I'll bring you off.

(*He runs off at the Corner, and throws down some China.*)
Re-enter Sir Francis, Miranda, *and* Scentwell

SIR FRAN: Mercy on me! what's the matter?

MIRAN: Oh you Toad! what have you done?

MARPL: No great harm, I beg of you to forgive me: longing to see the Monkey, I did but just raise up the Board, and it flew over my Shoulders, scratch'd all my Face, broke yon' China, and whisk'd out of the Window.

SIR FRAN: Was ever such an unlucky Rogue!... Call the Servants to get the Monkey again....

SCENTW: Oh my Lady will be the best to lure it back; all them Creatures love my Lady extremely.[20]

"All them Creatures"—ambiguously referring both to the suitor and the monkey—repeats the indiscriminate mingling of human and nonhuman that we have seen to be characteristic of this distinctive trope, from Cibber's "Monkeys, Squirrels, Paroqueets, *Dutch* dogs, and Eunuchs," Swinny's "Lace or Ribbon... Lap-dog, or Squirrel, or Monkey,... [or] a Husband," and Molloy's "Lap-Dog,... Husband, or a piece of *China*," to "the Parrot,... French Spaniel, [and] young Negro, with a Silver Coller" of the *London Jests.* This listing of beings, so recurrent in the satiric representation of female fashion, is the rhetorical signal of a fundamental lack of discrimination between human and nonhuman. But beyond that ontological problematic is the continuing experiment in inter-species intimacy that this closet scene pursues. In asserting that "all them Creatures love my lady extremely," this scene equates the love match between Miranda and Sir George with the "love" between "my lady" and the imaginary monkey.

Unlike Wycherley's play, Centlivre's *The Busie Body* is not a social satire; it does not undercut the expressed values or motives of its protagonists, nor does it challenge contemporary assumptions about love and marriage. As its title clearly indicates, its emphasis is on stage business, and on the plots and mistakes that block the desired union of its two young couples, a union with which the play happily concludes. In this respect, the allusion in this particular scene to Miranda's fashionable monkey keeping and china collecting might seem incongruous. Nowhere else in the play is Miranda criticized for these stereotypical female excesses; her characterization is based purely on a simple romance motive—to elude the illicit and unwelcome attentions of the selfish and elderly Sir Francis, her guardian, and to marry the eligible and attractive Sir George. The appearance of the monkey trope in this context, then, indicates its imaginative durability, even where antifemale satire is not a factor. The fact that the monkey outlives the comedy of manners suggests that it carries an imaginative significance larger

[20] Susanna Centlivre, *The Busie Body* (London: printed for Bernard Lintott, [1709]), act 4, pp. 54–56. This popular play was performed in 1709, and was given 475 times in London theaters from that date until 1800. For the repertory history of *The Busie Body*, see the facsimile edition, *The Plays of Susanna Centlivre*, ed. Richard C. Frushell, 3 vols. (New York: Garland, 1982), 1:xxvii–xli.

than the forms and effects of that subgenre. Though the monkey scene in *The Busie Body* does not function as a means of attacking the affectations of the lady of quality, it still serves to problematize the marriage of Miranda and Sir George and to conflate "all them Creatures"—human and nonhuman—in a way that points toward some of the fundamental ontological questions of the day. And despite its distance from the early eighteenth-century antifemale tradition, *Evelina*'s monkey, like *The Busie Body*'s, also carries with it a means of imagining these same unconventional connections between beings, and these same disturbing questions about the ideal of marriage.

The Pet Monkey and the Hominoid Ape

Evelina's monkey trope, whose literary predecessor we have located in the early eighteenth-century comedy of manners, has an immediate context in social history. Along with the other newly prominent companion animals of this era of bourgeois pet keeping that we have noted in previous chapters, the pet monkey was a distinctive figure. The image of the monkey had been available as a subject of fable and a source of invective and exempla in European print culture from classical times, and actual monkeys became visible in Europe in the twelfth and thirteenth centuries, when they are mentioned as pets in European nunneries and monasteries, as signs of prosperity among wealthy clerics, and as performers in popular entertainments.[21] But the relatively commonplace presence of the monkey in the bourgeois household is a distinctive eighteenth-century phenomenon.

The evidence available in the literary culture suggests that, in relation to other pets, monkeys enjoyed a period of unusual visibility in the first half of the eighteenth century, during that era of "obsessive pet keeping" when urban residents experimented with a wide variety of companion animals. The monkeys in evidence in Europe at this time were most likely mainly from among the species of what we now classify as Old World monkeys, imported from the trading forts of west Africa. Along with other fashionable pets, monkeys were sold in markets or peddled to individual homes by enterprising pet sellers, who would have a variety of animals to offer to the consumer. The new owner could then employ a monkey tamer, whose task was to accustom these wild animals to human handling. Literary materials also suggest that monkeys were often dressed in human clothes or livery. A contemporary memoir describes

---

[21] Keith Thomas, *Man and the Natural World: A History of the Modern Sensibility* (New York: Pantheon, 1983), 110. H. W. Janson, in his invaluable *Apes and Ape Lore in the Middle Ages and the Renaissance* (London: Warburg Institute, 1952), describes the increase in references to the ape in the twelfth century, due to the importation of monkeys across the western Mediterranean in the pre-Crusade expansion of trade with the Middle East and Asia (30).

Mrs. Bellamy's London apartments as occupied by "never less than three or four monkeys dressed in regimentals, or as fine ladies and gentlemen."[22] Pet monkeys could also be provided with the same silver collars and chains that were advertised for the adornment of lapdogs as well as young African slaves. Monkeys make difficult, even dangerous, companion animals for humans, largely because of their biting behaviors, and—perhaps for this reason—their popularity as pets has never maintained a steady state. Unlike dogs, cats, and even exotic birds, whose presence within the home has continued on a predictable upward trajectory since the eighteenth century, the historical popularity of monkeys as pets has always been temporary and local. Thus, as the responses of the characters in *Evelina* to the arrival of that monkey suggest, monkeys were not as well tolerated in the second half of the eighteenth century, as their popularity as pets waned.

As we have seen, the new engagement with animal-kind that was prompted by the "discovery" of the hominoid apes of Africa and Asia generated a special interest in those beings that today's biological classification gathers under the designation of the Primate order. Currently, we divide the Anthropoid suborder of the Primate order into two infraorders: New World monkeys (Platyrrhini) and a group containing Old World monkeys, apes, and humans (Catarrhini). Within the infraorder of Catarrhini we place two superfamilies: Cercopithecoidea, or Old World monkeys, and Hominoidea, or apes and humans—a group that includes orangutan, gorillas, chimpanzees, bonobos, and human beings. Thus, in common parlance today, monkeys and apes are close relations, even though we recognize a special proximity between the hominoid apes and human beings. In the eighteenth century New World monkeys were not distinguished from the hominoid apes in most discourse. Despite a growing interest in the chimpanzee and orangutan, the term *monkey* was consistently used as a general designation for any animal within what we now understand to be the Anthropoid suborder. Thus the "Monkey Tribe" or "monkey kind" was said to include the orangutan as well as the baboon and the Old World monkey. Naturalists such as Buffon used the terms *monkey* and *ape* almost interchangeably; and in general, older ideas about the monkey readily mingled with the newer notions derived from recent exposure to hominoid apes.[23] Thus the conflation of the monkey with the hominoid ape, joined with its new status as fashionable pet,

---

[22] Tate Wilkinson, *Memoirs of His Own Life*, 4 vols. (York: Wilson, Spence, and Mawman, 1790), 3:214–215.

[23] See, for example, John Ash, *The New and Complete Dictionary of the English Language*, 2 vols. (London, 1775), s.v. "ape," "baboon," and "monkey."; *The Beauties of Natural History; or, Elements of Zoography* (London, 1777), section entitled "The Monkey Tribe"; and Georges Louis Leclerc, Comte de Buffon, *The Natural History of Animals, Vegetables, and Mineral*, translated from the French, vol. 1 (London, 1775–76). Buffon's translator uses *ape* and *monkey* interchangeably throughout volume 1, as well as the general term *monkey kind*. Janson describes how "the anthropomorphic qualities of the lesser simians" came to be "grafted on to the *orang-outang*," providing a composite "striking character picture" of the "monkey tribe" (*Apes and Ape Lore*, 336).

enabled this being to generate questions of ontology and at the same time to serve as the imaginative basis for an experiment with ideas of intimacy.

As we have seen, the earliest literary expressions of the culture of pet keeping in eighteenth-century social satire proposed an inter-species household intimacy that placed the lapdog in the lady's bed, and that substituted the monkey for the human husband, a substitution that is felt directly in *Evelina*. Meanwhile, the projects of human self-definition that, in chapter 2, we saw emerging in the period—from Edward Tyson's *Anatomy of a Pygmie* (1699) to James Burnet, Lord Monboddo's *Origin and Progress of Language* (1774)—can be felt even in Burney's comic monkey scene. Monboddo's argument for the proximity of human and ape holds a mirror up to human-kind, venturing to "find in [the ape]...our own features" and leading directly to the central question *"What is man?"*[24] A more violent version of this same question is involved in the anecdote of ape-human miscegenation that we have used as a point of reference in describing the development of the figure of the lady and the lapdog. As we saw in chapter 3, this anecdote arose, along with the discovery of the great ape, through European travel narrative in the seventeenth century, and became widespread in the eighteenth century as the hominoid ape captured the literary imagination.[25] In the words of Edward Long in his account of Angola, this fantasy often describes a violent embrace, as the apes "surprise" and "carry off" the human females, to "enjoy" them in their "woody retreats."[26] We have already seen how Jonathan Swift in *Gulliver's Travels* adapts this widespread miscegenation anecdote in the river-bathing scene of the voyage to the Houynhynms. In this passage, the female Yahoo, a representative of the great ape, "came running with all speed, and leaped into the water within five yards of the place where I bathed." Gulliver "was never in my life so terribly frighted.... She embraced me after a most fulsome manner....[N]ow I could no longer deny that I was a real yahoo in every limb and feature, since the females had a natural propensity to me as one of their own species."[27] The form of Swift's rendering of ape-human miscegenation here is a paradigm for the moment of contact with radical alterity. Distance alternates with intimacy, as the Yahoo views Gulliver from afar, then leaps directly upon him, and as Gulliver himself roars with fright at her embrace and then acknowledges his identity with her as "a real yahoo in every limb and feature"—an identity that echoes Monboddo's discovery of "our own features" in the mirror of the

[24] James Burnet, Lord Monboddo, *Of the Origin and Progress of Language*, 2nd ed. (Edinburgh, 1774; repr. New York: Garland, 1970), 1:313.

[25] For an account of the history of the miscegenation anecdote and a summary of critical resources, see Laura Brown, *Fables of Modernity: Literature and Culture in the English Eighteenth Century* (Ithaca, N.Y.: Cornell University Press, 2001), 236–245.

[26] Edward Long, *The History of Jamaica*, 3 vols. (London: T. Lowndes, 1774), 2:360 and 364.

[27] Jonathan Swift, *"Gulliver's Travels" and Other Writings*, ed. Louis A. Landa (1726; Boston: Houghton Mifflin, 1960), 215.

orangutan, and that highlights Monboddo's basic question *"What is man?"* The Yahoo's embrace itself condenses this dynamic, as a sudden and potentially violent gesture that joins intimacy and "terrible fright." This is the formal shape of a deeply resonant imaginative experience, whose provenance extends from drama and satire to travel literature and philosophy, and from *Gulliver's Travels* to *Evelina*.

Evelina's Monkey and the Marriage Plot

Considered in these contexts, *Evelina's* monkey anecdote repays a closer examination. We have already observed the dynamic of proximity and distance that structures this passage, as Captain Mirvan alternately brings the monkey to kiss Mr. Lovel and Lovel "retreats." That dynamic is reproduced in the rhetorical representation of the nonhuman being as, on the one hand, the "twin-brother" to the man and, on the other hand, a "monster" who "grins most horribly" and whom Lovel "would not touch…for a thousand worlds." Proximity and distance are forced into a single climactic and violent moment of intimacy at the end of this scene, as the monkey "sprung instantly upon [Lovel],…clinging round his neck" in an embrace that echoes the female Yahoo's "leaping" upon Gulliver. And like Gulliver, who "was never…so terribly frighted," Lovel is "almost fainting with terror." Meanwhile, of course, the monkey's bloody bite is a consummation predicted by the warning, "[D]on't touch him he'll bite," from the comedy of manners.

These formal and rhetorical echoes, however, are matched by ontological reverberations as well. The immediate incentive for Captain Mirvan's prank is provided by Mr. Lovel's affected adherence to fashion. Before the introduction of the monkey, Lovel demonstrates this affectation in contemplating his own appearance:

"I am often shocked to death to think what a figure I go.…I was full half an hour this morning thinking what I should put on!"

"Odds my life," cried the Captain, "I wish I'd been near you! I warrant I'd have quickened your motions a little! Half an hour thinking what you'd put on? and who the deuce do you think cares the snuff of a candle whether you've any thing on or not?" (326)

Lovel's "shocked" reaction to his own encounter with himself as he contemplates his "figure" is a comic rendering of Monboddo's and Swift's problem of identity as they contemplate the figure of the man in the mirror of the ape, as well as of the ridicule directed at the beau/monkey in the comedy of manners, when it seems impossible to distinguish one from the other. Captain Mirvan makes this confusion explicit when he suggests that Lovel and the monkey swap their coat and waistcoat, at which point he asserts to Lovel, "[Y]ou'll not know yourself which is which" (332). Mr. Lovel returns to the question of his own identity when Captain Mirvan introduces the topic of the "twin-brother," immediately before the arrival of the monkey:

[Mirvan speaking] "Pray have you e'er a brother in these here parts?"

"Me, Sir?—no, thank Heaven, I'm free from all encumbrances of that sort."

"Well," cried the Captain, "I met a person just now, so like you, I could have sworn he had been your twin-brother."

"It would have been a most singular pleasure to me," said Mr. Lovel, "if I also could have seen him; for, really, I have not the least notion what sort of a person I am, and I have a prodigious curiosity to know." (331)

Will the fop, gazing in the mirror, see himself, or a monkey? Lovel's lack of "the least notion" about who he is, "really," introduces the appearance of the monkey by means of a version of Monboddo's question *What is man?* and of Gulliver's discovery that he is a "real" Yahoo. This anxiety about human being is unique to Lovel, and to this moment in the novel just at the consummation of the marriage plot. Its expression here suggests that the monkey anecdote possesses a kind of cultural aura, a constellation of questions, problems, and ideas that cling to it, whatever its local context, and that carry a complex imaginative significance.

What is the significance of the nonhuman being, for *Evelina* or for the larger human question of the institution of marriage? This novel superimposes an immediately contemporary speculation about the structure of the natural world—which raises onto-logical questions about difference, proximity, and the nature of human being itself—on the somewhat older literary trope of pet keeping from the comedy of manners—which evokes the critique of marriage and of the social conventions that define human intimacy. In joining these two, the monkey generates an imaginative experience that exceeds the local significance either of philosophical ethnography or of social satire, or, for that matter, of the gender paradigms of domestic fiction. *Evelina*'s monkey means much more than *Evelina* can say.

For instance, retrospectively, the monkey gives new meaning to the novel's earlier experiments with gender violence—those moments when the representations of gender difference seem to exceed or to question the values and assumptions of the marriage plot. These experiments are especially focused on the female characters who are ineli-gible for marriage: Evelina's grandmother, Madame Duval, and the "two old women" at Clifton (243). The interaction between Madame Duval and Captain Mirvan is rhe-torically marked by repeated, explicit references to "violence." These references are con-firmed by several scenes of open physical attack, in which Madame Duval's violent forays are invariably countered by a definitive act of dominance by her male adversary. For instance, when Captain Mirvan tosses her into the mud and then returns to ridicule her:

> The rage of poor Madame Duval was unspeakable; she dashed the candle out of his hand, stamped upon the floor, and at last spat in his face.
>
>   This action seemed immediately to calm them both, as the joy of the Captain was converted into resentment, and the wrath of Madame Duval into fear; for he put his hands upon her shoulders, and gave her so violent a shake, that she screamed out for help....[And she] was not released till she quite sobbed with passion. (55)

Even more emphatic is the violence of the feigned robbery scene, the climax of Captain Mirvan and Madame Duval's gender war, when the Captain, pretending to be a highwayman, drags Madame Duval from her chariot, shakes and jerks her about until she is "out of joint all over," binds her with a cord, and prepares to hang her from a tree (123–124). As she is rescued by Evelina, Madame Duval, "almost bursting with passion...with frightful violence[,]...actually beat the ground with her hands" (121). Here the highwayman disguise and the threat of hanging propel the narrative into a different register from the manners mode of dancing partners and social decorum, where Evelina can register the wish that "I really think there ought to be a book, of the laws and customs á-la-mode, presented to all young people upon their first introduction into public company" (70). How is this violence relevant to the marriage plot?

Similarly, the race of the old women that is staged toward the end of the novel, and that is promoted by Lord Merton and Mr. Coverley, displays a level of violence reminiscent of those earlier brutal scenes. Again, in a strangely anomalous event, the men place bets on the two old women, who "make their appearance" as if they have been captured for the occasion. The men are drunk, they "handed...the old women to the race-ground" with "loud shouts," and "the poor creatures, feeble and frightened, ran against each other, and neither of them able to support the shock, they both fell on the ground." Ultimately, Mr. Coverley's cruel behavior falls just short of violence, when "the poor creature...too much hurt to move,...declared her utter inability to make another attempt. Mr. Coverley was quite brutal; he swore at her with unmanly rage, and seemed scarce able to refrain even from striking her" (257). Mr. Lovel's anomalous physicality and proximity to monstrousness in the monkey scene provides a context for these earlier moments when the subdued tension that conventionally accompanies the depiction of the young lady's entrance into the marriage market seems to escalate into gender war. Marriage to one of these brutal members of the male gender seems a risky business, at best.

Meanwhile, just as the monkey scene raises questions about human identity that undercut the supposedly natural union of companionate marriage, it also complicates the parallel ideology of natural gender identity. The fop, who stands at the center of *Evelina*'s imaginative encounter with difference, also stands for a different conception of masculinity from that proposed by the ideal of companionate marriage. From the earlier tradition of dramatic social satire, derived from the aristocratic cultural context of the Restoration court, the fop transmits a complex history of potential flexibility or ambiguity in regard to male sexuality. In Lovel's interaction with the monkey, then, those urgent contemporary questions about the nature of human identity are superimposed on older challenges to the naturalness or inevitability of a gendered male identity. Thus the question *"What is man?"* that is enacted in the fop's encounter with the monkey can be understood to refer to the idea of a natural masculinity as well as to the notion of a stable human being.

The introduction of the figure of the animal into the marriage plot, then, enables *Evelina* to open up a range of dissonant views of companionate marriage. One of these views emphasizes the monkey's resemblance to the beau, suggesting that Evelina is marrying an ape rather than "the best of men," and implying that the marital embrace might be an act of violence. From this perspective, the monstrousness of the monkey/fop/husband indicates an aversion to marriage even in the midst of the marriage plot. Or, alternately, in emphasizing the monkey/fop/husband's intimacy with the woman, another view constructs an experimental alternative to marriage, in which Evelina might prefer to kiss the monkey rather than her husband, and might elect an illicit intimacy with an alien, nonmasculine, or nonhuman being, rather than find satisfaction with a natural human partner. In short, the monkey attacks the institution of marriage, and at the same time he signals the problematic nature of intimacy itself as it is figured forth in the modern era, where any connection between beings generates fundamental questions of identity and difference. This imaginary animal, through its new proximity to human-kind and through its translation across literary genres, thus creates a deeply challenging cultural fantasy, which transcends its particular literary moment, defies the conventions of conduct narrative, explodes the ideals of companionate marriage, and questions the norms of human connection.

Of course it is impossible to reconcile these implications of the monkey anecdote with the affirmation of marriage, manners, and patriarchy with which *Evelina* ends. In the immediate context of the novel, the monkey is ejected from the scene, and Lovel, of course, is a secondary character whose antics are extraneous to the closure firmly pronounced by the female protagonist's final letter describing her marriage to Lord Orville: "All is over." But the intervention of the monkey in the marriage plot suggests that the affirmation of marriage is a more strenuous effort, more speculative and experimental, more richly allusive and fully contemporary, and more vitally engaged with the alien nature of gender difference than the conventions of domestic fiction seem to warrant. For contemporary readers, this is the experience of a cultural dynamism that no single meaning can begin to encompass—a dynamism created by the novel's imaginative colloquium with animal-kind.

Biography of a Spaniel

Page 5

Figure 4. James Hopwood, frontispiece to *Biography of a Spaniel*, "Elysium of Dogs" (1803).
Courtesy of the New York Public Library.

5

DOG NARRATIVE

Itinerancy, Diversity, and the Elysium of Dogs

Early in Paul Auster's novel *Timbuktu* (1999), Mr. Bones, the canine protagonist and narrative consciousness of this nonhuman testimonial to homelessness, demonstrates that he is qualified for the role of implied narrator by proving his grasp of human language:

> Mr. Bones understood.... This had been the case for as long as he could remember, and by now his grasp of Ingloosh was as good as any other immigrant who had spent seven years on American soil. It was his second language, of course, and quite different from the one his mother had taught him, but even though his pronunciation left something to be desired, he had thoroughly mastered the ins and outs of its syntax and grammar.[1]

Mr. Bones's "grasp of Ingloosh" points us both backward and forward in the historical trajectory of the modern encounter with animal-kind. Language has been a focal point in the modern approach to animals and in debates about the definition of the human in relation to the nonhuman animal since Descartes' understanding of speech as a sign of thought, and since the discovery of the great apes and the rise of the companion animal in the eighteenth century. Questions about whether animals can learn human language, and whether or how animal "language" might be related to animal mind, intentionality, or awareness, continue to be debated today, within and beyond the disciplines of primatology and comparative psychology. In the eighteenth century, new attitudes toward animals fostered a belief in animal intelligence that encouraged speculation about

---

[1] Paul Auster, *Timbuktu* (New York: Picador, 1999), 6.

the superior attributes of animal language, and about animals' abilities to speak or to engage with human language. According to Keith Thomas, in this period animals came to be compared with humans across the whole range of human capacities, including "reason, intelligence, language and almost every other human quality."[2] We have seen, in chapter 2, how James Burnet, Lord Monboddo, included theories of the orangutan's relation to language in his treatise *Of the Origin and Progress of Language* (1774). Elsewhere, Monboddo expresses the belief—apparently widely shared—that an orangutan kept by a British naturalist had learned a few words of English.[3] Thus, from the eighteenth century to the twentieth, language is a well-established signal of ontological inquiry, and of the ongoing negotiations and complexities generated by attempts to define or to defy the differentiation of species.

Mr. Bones's is a tale of itinerancy and diversity, in which random encounters and a range of experiences characterize an action that ultimately generates a unique trans-species transcendence. The canine consciousness through which the story is filtered serves to authenticate its formal arbitrariness, because canine nature is understood to be, by definition, itinerant. In fact, from Mr. Bones's perspective, the wanderings of his homeless master, Willy Christmas, merely imitate an originary canine aimlessness:

> His master was a man with the heart of a dog. He was a rambler, a rough-and-ready soldier of fortune, a one-of-a-kind two-leg who improvised the rules as he went along. They simply upped and left one morning in the middle of April, launched out into the great beyond, and saw neither hide nor hair of Brooklyn until the day before Halloween. Could a dog ask for more than that? As far as Mr. Bones was concerned, he was the luckiest creature on the face of the earth. (29)

The homeless human being here is represented as a kind of dog, possessed of a dog's heart and viewed from the dog perspective as therefore unique among nondogs—a "two-leg" who actually belongs to the four-legged species. Itinerancy, which gives the novel its shapelessness as well as its evocation of an experience outside the realm of fixed locales and firm rules, is a canine premise.

A much earlier dog narrator, Berganza of Cervantes's *El coloquio de los perros* (1613), or *The Dialogue of the Dogs*, also begins his story by addressing the issue of the surprising canine relationship to human language:

[2] Keith Thomas, *Man and the Natural World: A History of the Modern Sensibility* (New York: Pantheon, 1983), 129.
[3] James Burnet, Lord Monboddo, *Antient Metaphysics*, vol. 3 (London, 1784; repr. New York: Garland, 1977), 40.

BERGANSA: *Scipio,* I hear you speak, and I am sensible I speak to you, and yet I cannot believe it, because I think our speaking is so supernatural.

SCIP.: What you say, *Bergansa,* is very true, and this prodigy is so much the greater in that we not only speak, but with judgment, as if we were capable of reasoning, this being the only difference between brutes and men, that man is a rational, and a brute an irrational creature.[4]

Like Auster's, Cervantes's text highlights the question of language—the use of human language to render canine consciousness and the trans-species colloquium involved when an exclusively human mode of communication is attributed to a nonhuman being.[5] And again, Cervantes's speaking, reasoning canine provides the formal premise of the novella; a wanderer by species definition, Bergansa tells a story characterized by disconnected sequence. Indeed, the problematic of canine language and the idea of the range of canine experience are explicitly linked:

I have been very desirous to speak, that I may tell the things which I have kept in memory, the ideas of which, by length of time, and the variety of them, were either very much confused, or else quite forgotten: But now that I see myself so unexpectedly enriched with this divine gift of speech, I think to enjoy it as much as I can, and make the best use of it, by telling everything that I can recollect, although it may be in a confused and undigested manner; for I know not how soon this blessing which is now lent me, may be required again. (4)

This passage emphasizes the confused variety of things in the dogs' reportage, a diversity of experience that is expressed formally through the canine premise of itinerancy, and rhetorically through the problematic faculty of language.

In fact, *Timbuktu* and *The Dialogue of the Dogs* are historical bookends that together help us identify the distinctive sub-genre of the dog narrative. The dog narrative persists as a vital sub-genre to the present day, but its central premises are fully evident by 1825. Using the seventeenth- and twentieth-century texts as framing prototypes, in this chapter I will describe the development of the dog narrative in England in the

[4] Miguel de Cervantes, *A Dialogue between Scipio and Bergansa,* trans. Robert Goadby (London: Cæsar Ward, 1766), 1–2.
[5] Teresa Mangum has noted the distinctive positioning of narrator and reader in these cross-species narratives: "In the literary milieu of fictive animals like Black Beauty and Beautiful Joe, animals became impossibly positioned as fully articulate subjects with a great deal to say to their human readers and listeners." Teresa Mangum, "Dog Years, Human Fears," in *Representing Animals,* ed. Nigel Rothfels. *Theories of Contemporary Culture* 26 (Bloomington: Indiana University Press, 2002), 35–47, 35. On animal speech in fiction, the incongruities of this convention, its modes of representation, and ideas of translation and ventriloquization, see Tess Cosslett, *Talking Animals in British Children's Fiction* (Aldershot, UK: Ashgate, 2006), 66–70, 81–83.

core period of its formation from the mid-eighteenth to the early nineteenth century. Cervantes's work has a traceable influence on the premiere dog narrative of the mid-eighteenth century, Francis Coventry's *The History of Pompey the Little* (1751); thus the Spanish precedent enables us to draw out some of the implications of the eighteenth- and early nineteenth-century versions. Moving forward to Auster's *Timbuktu*, on the other hand, tests the longevity of this animal-generated literary innovation.[6] The rich and extensive connections between the twentieth-century dog narrative and that of the earlier period help establish the significance of the eighteenth century as a watershed moment in the creative impact of animal-kind on the modern literary imagination. In the history of realist fiction in this period, the dog's itinerancy generates a narrative form that diverges from the shaped action that has retrospectively come to define the rise of the novel. The dog narrative evokes a random movement through a diverse world—a movement by means of which imaginary animals create the opportunity for human speculation about boundary, diversity, and transcendence—in Bergansa's case, about the mystery of the dogs' access to language across the boundary of species; in Mr. Bones's, about the lifeways of beings who take diverse routes through our world, and about the promise of another world in Timbuktu "where dogs talked as equals with men" (108).

Cervantes's *Coloquio De Los Perros*

El coloquio de los perros was translated into English twice in the course of the eighteenth century, during the decades when translations of Cervantes's *Don Quixote* were enjoying an extraordinary popularity.[7] In 1728, Cervantes's novella appeared as *The Dogs of Mahudez* in *A Collection of Select Novels by Don Miguel Cervantes Saavedra*, translated by Harry Bridges. A new translation by Robert Goadby was published in 1766, and this time *The Dialogue of the Dogs* was the featured work, appearing with only one other of Cervantes's novellas and giving the entire volume its title, *A*

[6] Beyond *Timbuktu*, modern redactions of the dog narrative are common. One notable example, which suggests the resonance of this narrative mode even outside the English language tradition, is in Orhan Pamuk's *My Name Is Red*, where the dog narrator of chapter 3 engages the same core issues that we will examine here: the foundational question of canine speech and rationality, the effect of multiple masters, and the premise of a natural canine itinerancy that is generalized to the human world: "I'm a dog, and because you humans are less rational beasts than I, you're telling yourselves, 'Dogs don't talk.'…Dogs do speak, but only to those who know how to listen." Orhan Pamuk, *My Name Is Red*, trans. Erdağ M. Göknar (1998; New York: Vintage, 2002), 11.

[7] For a summary of the translation history of *Don Quixote* in the eighteenth century, see Julie Chandler Hayes, "Tobias Smollett and the Translators of the *Quixote*," *Huntington Library Quarterly* 67 (2004): 651–668. The seminal major study of this topic is Ronald Paulson's *Don Quixote in England: The Aesthetics of Laughter* (Baltimore: Johns Hopkins University Press, 1998).

Dialogue between Scipio and Bergansa. A second edition of this translation was issued in 1767.[8] In the period between these two translations of Cervantes's novella, the first original dog narrative in the English tradition appeared, Francis Coventry's *The History of Pompey the Little; or, the Life and Adventures of a Lapdog* (1751). Coventry's immensely popular novel went to a third edition within the year of its initial publication, and was widely read through the first quarter of the nineteenth century. By 1824 *Pompey the Little* had seen at least ten English editions, two Dublin piracies, and translations in French (1752) and Italian (1760).[9]

This influential modern dog narrative has an early eighteenth-century English precedent. In 1709, Charles Gildon published a redaction of Apuleius's *Golden Ass*, a long narrative of antique romance that was an acknowledged influence on Cervantes's picaresque form. Gildon's work, itself certainly influenced by *El coloquio de los perros*, provides for a "Modern Improvement" upon the classical original by replacing the ass who serves as the traveling frame figure in Apuleius's inset tales with a lapdog, whose wanderings through a range of social settings set in motion the peripatetic premise of the subsequent English dog narrative. As Gildon observes in his preface,

> an Ass was an Animal, that cou'd scarce come into any Place where there cou'd be any Secret Transacted, and therefore no proper Machine for the Discovery of secret Vices, and unmasking Hypocrisy. But a fine *Bologna* Lap-Dog is admitted to the Clossets, Cabinets, and Bedchambers of the Fair, and the Great, and therefore a Transformation into that Shape was more proper and Conducive to the Design than that of *Lucian* and *Apuleius*.[10]

Thus the canine protagonist emerged in the early eighteenth century as the specifically modern agent of a distinctive formal itinerary.

Coventry's and Cervantes's works were understood to be closely related. The preface to the 1766 translation of *El coloquio de los perros* notes that "it may be supposed, that the author of *Pompey the Little,* or *The Adventures of a Lapdog,* took his hint from this *Dialogue.*"[11] And this new translation of Cervantes certainly seeks to trade on the popularity of Coventry's work. *The Dialogue of the Dogs,* then, in its 1766 English redaction, can serve as an

---

[8] *A Collection of Select Novels, by Don Miguel Cervantes Saavedra,* trans. Harry Bridges (Bristol: S. Farley, 1728). *A Dialogue between Scipio and Bergansa,* 2nd ed., trans. Robert Goadby (London: S. Bladon, 1767).
[9] Robert Adams Day, introduction to Francis Coventry, *The History of Pompey the Little* (London: Oxford University Press, 1974), xiv. All references to *Pompey the Little* are to this edition.
[10] Charles Gildon, *The New Metamorphosis: or, The Pleasant Transformation: Being the Golden Ass of Lucius Apuleius of Medaura. Alter'd and Improv'd to the Modern Times and Manners* (London: Dan. Brown, 1709). Gildon's work is described as translated from the Italian by Carlo Monte Socio. It was published in a second, expanded edition in 1724.
[11] Cervantes, preface to *A Dialogue between Scipio and Bergansa,* n.p.

introduction to *Pompey the Little* and as a means of generating the core concepts through which the significance of other examples of this sub-genre can be understood.[12]

In almost every aspect of the imaginative experience that it represents, Cervantes's dog narrative engages with ideas of established order, fixed boundary, preexisting structure, and foundational system. As we have already seen, its image of speaking dogs raises the question of the boundaries between human and nonhuman: Is language ability in fact the dividing line between human and nonhuman? The idea of established genealogy is mocked at the opening of the dog's life story, when the protagonist, Bergansa, presents a canine pedigree: "I was descended from some of those mastiffs which are train'd up" in the slaughterhouse (6). This parodic foundational gesture, which becomes conventional in subsequent dog narratives, is followed by an extended evocation of disorder. Bergansa is born in Seville, a city described as "the support of the poor, and the refuge of the despised,...[whose] extent is so great, that even the rich and great ones are obscured, and...lost in it" (21). The dog narrator notes that "I once heard a wise man say that the king still had three strongholds to win in Seville: the Street of the Caza (the game market), the Costanilla (the fish market) and the Slaughter-house."[13] Even further, he is born into the slaughterhouse of Seville and raised by the "sons of noise and confusion, commonly called butchers" employed there (6). Bergansa's first master, Nicholas the Flat-nosed, teaches him to chase the bulls and employs him in traveling through the city, carrying meat to his mistress in a basket. In fact, the slaughterhouse of Seville is this text's signature locus, a site where "extravagant things...are transacted," where systems of logic and order—represented by law, political power, moral norms, and social hierarchies—do not exist. In keeping with this locale, "all that are employed there, from the least to the greatest, are a set of people...having no conscience or religion," who "make no more of killing a christian, than if they were sticking a bull." They are "the most blood-thirsty men alive," thieves and murderers, who have no "regard for the king, or his laws" (6). The "confusion" highlighted in this powerful description of the slaughterhouse is projected onto the shape of Cervantes's narrative, which is produced as a random sequence of situations, beyond which formal structures of overarching logic are emphatically missing.

---

[12] For a different genealogy, focusing on the animal narrative and tracing its use in eighteenth-century children's literature, from the early popularity of Aesop's fables through the talking animals of John Newbery's first major children's books to the fully developed didactic children's literature of the nineteenth century, see Cosslett, *Talking Animals*, 9–36.

[13] Cervantes, *The Dialogue of the Dogs* in *Six Exemplary Novels*, trans. Harriet de Onís (Woodbury, N.Y.: Barron's, 1961), 5–6. The eighteenth-century translations omit this passage, which probably, for their audience, alludes too closely to the local Spanish context of the narrative. It suggests the force and persistence with which Cervantes's text positions the dogs outside established systems of order—an impact that the eighteenth-century versions certainly reproduced at other points. Future references to this modern translation will be indicated by the parenthetical inclusion of the date.

Thus Bergansa's adventures follow one another in series, mediated only by brief expressions of transition that highlight the casual, the immediate, and the arbitrary: "I set feet to the ground, and scampered away as fast as my legs could carry me through the fields that are behind Saint *Bernardo*, not taking any particular road, but guided wholly by fortune" (9); "by good luck, I got loose one day, and without bidding adieu to anyone in the house, I ran into the street" (41); "without taking leave of anyone, [I] got through a little hole in the town-wall into the fields, and before daybreak found myself in *Mayrena*" (58); "[I] did not much like the intended journey, and so I was resolved to get loose, if I could, and afterwards put it in execution" (94–95). Leaving the slaughterhouse of Seville when his master attacks him with a knife, Bergansa runs to the countryside, where he goes to work for three shepherds, guarding a flock of sheep. Lawlessness prevails here as well, as the shepherds butcher and sell the sheep they and the dogs should be watching. Next Bergansa returns to Seville, to become the guard in the house of a rich merchant; there he witnesses the thievery of the servants and attends the merchant's children to school, where, incidentally, he learns Latin. He runs away again to a new master, a dishonest constable, who scams visitors to the city and pays off ruffians for a fee. Leaving this situation, he joins a company of soldiers on their way to Cartagena, "determined to stay with [the drummer], if he would let me, and to follow him whithersoever he went" (58–59); the drummer teaches him to dance for "the king of France" and to play tricks "very much above the capacity of any dog but myself" (59–60). A star performer, he becomes known as the "*Wise Dog*," and supports his master and six comrades "like so many kings" (61).

But in a hospital in Montilla he is taken by a witch for the son of her sorceress daughter, whose infants were transformed at birth into dogs. This incident reasserts the question of species difference that Bergansa and Scipio raised when they first considered the surprising phenomenon of their human speech. On this occasion, Scipio argues against the sorceress's species transformation, even though he continues to assert his own belief in their current, demonstrated access to human speech and reason:

> It would be the greatest folly to believe that *Camacha* ever changed men into beasts….All such things…are only lies, or the deceits of the devil; and if it seems to us now, that we have some understanding, and are capable of reasoning, being really dogs, or under the form of them, we have already said that it is a wonderful and strange thing, and what was never seen before. (87–88)

The 1766 translation omits Scipio's conclusion regarding the dogs' speech: "Even though we see it, we cannot believe it until its outcome reveals to us what we should believe" (1961, 47). Can humans become dogs through the mystery of the witch's spells? Can dogs cross the species boundary through access to human rationality? Scipio's rejection of the witch's transformation is based on the argument that the dogs' current rational conversation is "what was never seen before." The narrative here paradoxically upholds the boundary between animal- and human-kind by citing its dissolution, and dissolves that boundary while mocking the superstition that accepts such magical thinking. Indeed, the narrative presents no "outcome [that] reveals to us what we should believe."

Next Bergansa flees from the witch to join a band of thieving gypsies, then runs away to the farm of a Morisco—a converted Muslim. Then, to "seek some better fortune" (100), he finds his way to the city where he joins an acting company, becoming "a principal actor, and a great favourite of the town" (102). Finally, he takes up with the mendicant Christian, Mahudes, at the Hospital of the Resurrection in the city of Valladolid, where his dialogue is recited. And at the end of his travels, the dog narrator projects, beyond his current narrative, the unlimited vista of random experience that his tale implies: "You see how long my discourse has been? You have seen likewise, how many and different adventures I have run through; my long travels, and the many masters I have had; but all you have heard, is nothing in comparison to what I could relate to you" (103).

Bergansa's experience with the shepherds in the countryside outside Seville provides Cervantes with an opportunity for a different kind of reflection on the idea of established order—a consideration of the order afforded by literary history. The dog narrator, well versed in the Arcadian pastoral tradition that he has absorbed from his master's lady's reading, takes this occasion to compare the shepherds of his current acquaintance with those of the Arcadian myth, who "passed their whole lives in singing and playing on pipes, flutes, and other fine musical instruments;...[I had sometimes heard my mistress reading of] how the shepherd *Amfriso* sung divinely sweet the phrases of the peerless *Belisarda,* and that there was not a tree in all the mountains of *Arcadia,* under which he had not sat down to sing" (12–13). So absorbing is the Arcadian ethos that Bergansa continues at length to sketch a pastoral scene, complete with Elicio and Felicia, and with "pleasant meadows, spacious woods, sacred mountains, beautiful gardens, lympid brooks, and crystal fountains; and [with] those chaste and soft amorous expressions [of] a shepherd in despair" (15). Our loquacious dog narrator must be restrained by his companion "before," he explains, "I should have said enough of those who had deceived me so much, to have filled a volume" (15). But of course Bergansa introduces the pastoral tradition to discredit it. His direct canine experience tells him that "what [he] had heard say of the lives of shepherds, could not be true" (12). He describes the very "different lives and employments" of his shepherds, who sang "not in melodious strains" but "hoarse and untuneful"; whose music was "not the sound of pipes and flutes" but "that of two crooks struck together"; and who "passed the greatest part of the day in picking their fleas, or mending their shoes" (14). In this extended critical passage, the pleasing order of the pastoral tradition gives way before the direct experience of the canine itinerant. The dog narrative does not accept the rules and models of generic precedent, nor does it possess a literary pedigree; it introduces a mode of representation that—like the geographical site of the slaughterhouse of Seville—seems to stand apart from order, system, and genealogy altogether. Even critics who document the debt of *The Dialogue of the Dogs* to the Spanish picaresque tradition observe that Cervantes's work also differentiates itself from its most immediate picaresque predecessor, Mateo Alemán's *Guzman de Alfaráche* (1599), by evoking the much less didactic effects of the earlier *Lazarillo de Tormes* (1554).[14] The role of the dog, in particular his difference from the human species, in this case and throughout the career of the dog narrative, works to underwrite a consistent divergence from tradition and genealogy.

Bergansa's difference or apartness from norms and traditions also underwrites the tenor of his engagement with human nature. The dog protagonist's very being affords an opportunity for critical observation of human-kind—an opportunity that the subsequent canine narrative invariably exploits. In *The Dialogue of the Dogs* this critical attitude is announced directly early in the narrative by Bergansa's colleague, Scipio, who introduces what is to become a reiterated self-consciousness about the novella's satiric content:

> Having heard what a famous poet among the ancients said, *viz. That it was a difficult thing to forbear writing Satires,* I will allow you to point out faults, but not to injure or wound the character of any one, by the thing hinted at; for that satire is not good or commendable which hurts any one, though it may make many laugh; and if you can please without that, I shall think you very discrete. (11–12)

As Bergansa describes his movement through a wide urban and rural geography, he and his companion consistently feature commentary on human self-interest, pretension, pedantry, and superstition. When Bergansa comes upon a deluded, mumbling madman, lost in his own thoughts, he notes that "all [his aberrant behavior] made me conjecture, that this happy man must needs be a poet" (96). On the witch's shape-changing spells, Scipio exclaims, "Those which you think prophecies, are only foolish stories, and old women's tales...with which, the long winter nights are passed away at the fire side" (88). When his performance as the *"Wise Dog"* earns his master, the drummer, a substantial income, Bergansa comments on the way in which the drummer and his compatriots exploit their profits: "Many are in love with, and greedy of gain, only that they may spend it in good eating and drinking...[their gluttony being]

---

[14] Cervantes, *Novelas ejemplares*, ed. Jorge García López (Barcelona: Crítica, 2001), 273–283.

supported by some other means, than the profits of their respective trades" (61–62). Of the Gypsies whom he joins, he says, "In a word, they are a very wicked set of people; and although many and very wise judges have endeavoured to reform them, yet they are not in the least amended" (94).

After hearing the tale of the constable and notary who fleece visitors to the city, Scipio editorializes:

> Are there not some honest ones amongst them, who will not concern themselves with but a good cause? They do not all spin out their suits to the length of seven years, or more, and take fees of both parties, nor do they all take more than their dues, and intermeddle and foment disputes in families, to make themselves employment; neither are they all in confederacy with the judge....There are [constables], who do not associate themselves with rascally fellows and sharpers...they are not all such blustering, insolent, ill-bred, mean-spirited wretches...neither do they all pretend to take up and release people, and be both judge and advocate, just when they have a mind. (50–51)

But of course not one of these "many" just and honest men is encountered by the dog narrator in his wide wanderings. Sometimes dogs themselves are the ironic vehicles of social satire directed against human-kind, as when Bergansa joins a traveling acting company and "in less than a month," he tells us, "I became a principal actor, and a great favorite of the town" (102). And as when, in the last event of the novella, the fashionable lady's lapdog provides an instance of the insolent behavior of "little pitiful fellows...under the shadow of their masters":

> I went the other night into the house of a lady of distinction, who had in her arms a little diminutive lap dog, so small, that she might have hid him in her bosom, who, as soon as he saw me, leaped out of the arms of his lady, run at me, barking furiously, and so great was his insolence, as to bite me by the leg. I beheld him with anger, but restrained it out of respect to his lady, and said within myself: Thou little base animal, if I should catch thee in the street, I would either take no notice of thee, or I would tear thee in pieces. I reflected upon this, that even cowards and dastards are bold and insolent, when they are in favor with great men, and are the most forward to insult those that are in every respect better than themselves. (112–113)

This incident is the novella's coda, and provides a transition to the pointed social satire of the first English dog narrative of widespread popularity, Coventry's *Pompey the Little.* Cervantes's final anecdote raises the issue of the fashionable woman's indulgence of her lapdog, as well as the sexual innuendo involved in the physical proximity of the lapdog and the lady who can hide her dog in her bosom. As we have seen in chapters 3 and 4, the literary evocation of animal-kind in the eighteenth century is often connected with the representation of women, who were initially associated with the cultural practice of pet keeping. The English engagement with Cervantes's story, of which Coventry's novel is an extended indication, was stimulated by the contemporary experience of pet keeping, which gave Cervantes's speculative representation of animal-kind a direct pertinence to the newly visible connection with animal-kind. Thus, *Pompey the Little* feminizes the story of the canine protagonist and recreates it in a native English form, sharpening the satire present in *The Dialogue of the Dogs.* Indeed, satire is the eighteenth-century mode of the dog narrative. Later versions of this sub-genre offer a similar disabused perspective on human-kind, though in a moralizing rather than a satiric mode. In fact, tracking the dog narrative as a sub-genre enables us to see the continuity from Augustan social satire to expressive didacticism in the representation of animal-kind. But for the canine narrative, species difference calls human nature into question—whether in the discourse of neoclassical social satire or in that of sentimental moralism.

Coventry's *Pompey the Little*

Like *The Dialogue of the Dogs*, Coventry's *Pompey the Little* uses the random movement of the dog protagonist to generate a narrative without formal shape, whose materials demonstrate the diversity of human experience, and whose theme is a critique of human nature. *Pompey the Little* is usually associated with the eighteenth- and nineteenth-century "it-narrative" tradition, a form in which the peregrinations of speaking objects, like the "adventures of a guinea" or the "adventures of a corkscrew," express a fascination with commodities, an engagement with modern notions of economic circulation, and a concern with social commentary. The flea, the mouse, the cat, the goldfinch, the robin, and—more prominently—the dog figure as protagonists in the it-narrative tradition, and some of these stories include animal transformation or metempsychosis, which generate options for multiple animal perspectives. In the course of the nineteenth century, animal narrators come to dominate the it-narrative form. Liz Bellamy has offered a comprehensive definition of the it-narrative. She argues that these are "narratives of irresolution," which are based on the "evocation of a disordered and uncontrollable universe, devoid of structures of closure and ideological containment," and which therefore have "a subversive potential that may undermine the direct aspirations of the authors."[15] The dog narrative certainly crystallizes this experience of the undermining of established order. In fact, as we have seen, dogs evoke a distinctive relationship to order, genealogy, and boundary—a relationship that helps us grasp the imaginative impulse toward irresolution that lies behind the more diffuse form of the it-narrative. Tracking the dog narrative as a separate sub-genre, then, can bring the larger tradition of the it-narrative into sharper focus.

Pompey the Little is the first widely read modern dog narrative and one of the most influential of the eighteenth-century it-narratives, following on *The Golden Spy, The Adventures of a Shilling, The Secret History of an Old Shoe, The Genuine and Most Surprizing Adventures of a Very Unfortunate Goose-Quill, The Sopha, The Setee,* and *The Adventures of a Black Coat* (Bellamy, 135).[16] *Pompey* is not narrated by the dog himself, and it contains sustained passages of social satire only distantly connected to the perspective of the little lapdog. But the third-person narrator does sometimes enter into the consciousness of the canine protagonist, notably, in an early chapter, to ventriloquize the animal's proximity to human-kind as he engages with the "Joys and Vanities of the Town": "If he could have spoken, I am persuaded he would have used the Phrases so much in fashion, *Nobody one knows, Wretches dropt out of the Moon, Creatures sprung from a Dunghil;* by which are signified all those who are not born to a Title, or have not Impudence and Dishonesty enough to run in debt with their Taylors for Laced Cloaths" (30). Putting these human phrases into the mouth of the canine protagonist foregrounds the problem of language for the dog narrative—a problem that we have seen evoked in a similar manner in the representation of Mr. Bones's "grasp of Ingloosh" in *Timbuktu,* and Bergansa's and Scipio's amazement at the "supernatural" event of their human speech in *The Dialogue of the Dogs.* These parallels suggest that the dog narrative, in its claim to express the experience of a nonhuman being and in its violation—through nonhuman access to language—of the fundamental tenet of species difference, necessarily raises ontological questions about the nature of human-kind—questions that are closely related to this sub-genre's evocation of the social and formal irresolution of itinerancy.

Pompey, like Bergansa, is supplied with a pretentious canine genealogy at the outset of his story: "Pompey, the Son of *Julio* and *Phyllis*, was born A.D. 1735 at *Bologna* in *Italy,* a Place famous for Lapdogs and Sausages. Both his Parents were of the most illustrious Families, descended from a long Train of Ancestors" (6). Coventry repeats this parody

---

[15] Liz Bellamy, "It-Narrators and Circulation: Defining a Sub-genre," in *The Secret Life of Things: Animals, Objects, and It-Narratives in Eighteenth-Century England,* ed. Mark Blackwell (Lewisburg, Pa.: Bucknell University Press, 2007), 117–146; 123, 133. Bellamy's seminal essay contains a full bibliography of the appearance of the it-narrative between 1709 and 1900.

[16] Markman Ellis has been concerned to emphasize the idea that the canine it-narrative does not try to convey an authentic representation of canine being: "None of the literary examples [of canine narratives] constitute attempts to think like a dog or to fully inhabit the mind of an animal." See Ellis, "Suffering Things: Lapdogs, Slaves, and Counter-Sensibility," in *The Secret Life of Things,* 92–113, 105.

of genealogy in another assertion of nonhuman ancestral tradition, that of Pompey's sometime confidant, the cat Mopsa, who "was Heiress of the most ancient Family of Cats in the World....Descended from that memorable *Grimalkin* of Antiquity, who was converted into a Woman at the Request of her Master, and is said to have leapt out of Bed one Morning, forgetting her Transformation, in pursuit of a fugitive Mouse" (51). Here the dismissal of assertions of genealogical privilege and order meshes with the allusion to species transcendence—in the transformation of cat to woman and back again—that is evoked in the sorceress's transformation of humans into dogs in *The Dialogue of the Dogs.*

Compared to Bergansa's story, the transitions in Pompey's tale are even more rapid and the situations even more numerous and diverse, since, as we learn early on, "Fortune...had destined [Pompey] to a great Variety of Adventures" (17). Born into the home of a "celebrated Courtesan" of Bologna (7), Pompey is given to a fashionable gentleman on his grand tour, who takes him to England and gives him to his mistress, Lady Tempest. There, Pompey "becomes a Dog of the Town, and shines in High-life," attending the playhouse and the opera, and even learning "to play at Cards." In fact, "so forward was his Genius, that in less than three Months he was able to sit down with her Ladyship to Piquet" (30–31). Pompey moves from the world of fashion to the city; he is passed to an innkeeper, and then to a blind beggar who travels with him to Bath. These episodes include satiric portraits of the world of high fashion, bourgeois social climbing, marriage, Methodism, usury, and coffeehouse conversation. The beggar provides an experience of homeless itinerancy, while the interpolated tale told by his son includes a highwayman's narrative of adventures outside the law. Pompey returns to fashionable life, as he is given to a pair of good-natured sisters, sold to a prosperous widow milliner, stolen by a lord, given to a penniless poet, and then passed to a Cambridge scholar. In these episodes, Coventry ridicules female folly, doctors, lawyers, modern science, education and pedantry, poetry, and the contemporary theater. Finally, Pompey returns to the world of female fashion, as he is rediscovered by his original mistress, Lady Tempest, and returned to her London residence, where, in his fourteenth year, he is "gathered to the Lapdogs of Antiquity" (200).

Though its range of reference remains wide, as we have suggested, Pompey's social critique highlights female fashion and folly, including the sexual excesses that are central to the eighteenth-century representation of pet keeping. But *Pompey the Little* also reproduces the core materials and concerns of *The Dialogue of the Dogs,* including a great deal of the social satire, some of the images of experience outside systems of order and hierarchy, and much of the ontological questioning about species boundaries and the definition of the human. This last concern is especially emphasized on two occasions in this text. One night, Pompey accompanies one of his masters, Mr. Rhymer, a destitute and talentless poet, to "a dirty little dog-hole of a tavern," where he witnesses a debate between a "free-thinking writer" and a *"Fleet* parson" on animals' capacity for reason—a debate that is directly inspired by the presence of the participants' dogs: "By odd luck, every one of these great advancers of modern literature, happened to have a dog attending him; and as the gentlemen drew round the fire after supper in a ring, the dogs likewise made an interior semi-circle" (169). The freethinker advances precisely the argument that Bergansa and Scipio introduce at the beginning of *The Dialogue of the Dogs*—he argues that animals are "capable of reasoning" (*Coloquio,* 1): "I have a curious thesis now by me,...those dogs there put me in the head of it....I undertake to prove that brutes think and have intellectual faculties....I go farther...and maintain that they are reasonable creatures, and moral agents" (171). The parson counters with the conventional theological defense of the uniqueness of the human soul—a uniqueness based on the idea of the human participation in the divine and the consequent absolute distinction between animal- and human-kind: "Sir, you may be ashamed to prostitute the noble faculty of reason to the beasts of the field....What is reason, sir?...why reason, sir, is a most noble faculty of the soul, the noblest of all the faculties. It discerns and abstracts, and compares and compounds, and all that" (171). Both the parson and the freethinker are objects of ridicule, of course, but their extended discussion reproduces one of the central ontological debates of the period, in this case specifically accommodated to the context of canine-human colloquium.

Earlier in the novel, the problem of species difference is raised through the evocation of another satiric manifestation of the same contemporary debate. Lady Sophister, whether through "caprice or vanity of being singular," has taken "a fancy into her head to disbelieve the immortality of the soul, and never came into the company of learned men without displaying her talents on this wonderful subject" (35). Pompey witnesses her confrontation with two physicians on this topic of the soul, as his mistress, Lady Tempest, "guessing that her female friend was going to be very absurd, resolved to promote the conversation for her own amusement" (36). Lady Sophister makes use of a sketch of Locke's idea of matter to summarize a current strain of thinking on the problem of species difference:

> You know Mr. *Locke* observes, there are various kinds of matter....Well, out of this matter, some you know is made into roses and peach-trees; then the next step which matter takes, is animal life; from whence you know we have lions and elephants, and all the race of brutes. Then the last step, as Mr. *Locke* observes, is thought and reason and volition, from whence are created men, and therefore you very plainly see, 'tis impossible for the soul to be immortal. (37).

Their argument ultimately turns to Pompey himself, whom Lady Sophister cites as an immediate example of her argument:

"You say, I think, Sir,…that a multitude of opinions will establish a truth. Now you know all the *Indians* believe that their dogs will go to heaven along with them; and if a great many opinions can prove any thing to be true, what say you to that, Sir?…For instance, now, there's lady *Tempest*'s little lapdog"——"My dear little creature," said lady *Tempest*, catching him up in her arms, "will you go to heaven along with me? I shall be vastly glad of your company, *Pompey*, if you will." (39)

Both of these instances provide a strong intellectual context for Coventry's dog narrative; they express the vital contemporary engagement with theological, philosophical, and scientific ideas about the intersection of animal- and human-kind. Thinking on the topics of animal intelligence, orangutan language, and the similarities between human and chimpanzee anatomy accorded with and supported adjustments in the concept of the Platonistic chain of being, in which the principles of continuity and plenitude began to take precedence over doctrinal notions of the separation of man from animal-kind. Like Lady Sophister's interpretation of Locke, these new views of the chain described differences in the hierarchy of beings as fluid blendings in which one species merged into the next or formed a hybrid relationship with those contiguous to it. Soame Jenyns's "On the Chain of Universal Being" (1790) illustrates the reasoning on which Lady Sophister is drawing:

> The various qualities with which these various Beings are endued, we perceive without difficulty, but the boundaries of those qualities, which form this chain of subordination, are so mixed, that where one ends, and the next begins, we are unable to discover….The manner by which the consummate wisdom of the divine Artificer has formed this gradation, so extensive in the whole, and so imperceptible in the parts, is this:—He constantly unites the highest degree of the qualities of each inferior order to the lowest degree of the same qualities, belonging to the order next above it; by which means, like the colours of a skilful painter, they are so blended together, and shaded off into each other, that no line of distinction is anywhere to be seen.[17]

Closely related to these developments in the concept of the chain of being was the debate about animal souls, in which the Cartesian analogy between animal and automaton—decisively distinguishing man from beast in this regard—met increasing resistance from a wide range of perspectives, including the neoclassical tradition of theriophily that privileged animals above men, popular or Pythagorean ideas of metempsychosis,

[17] Soame Jenyns, "On the Chain of Universal Being," in *Disquisitions on Several Subjects* (London: J. Dodsley, 1782), 2, 8.

the arguments of rationalizing theology, and the rise of the new humanitarianism.[18] Henry St. John, Viscount Bolingbroke's comment on this matter illustrates the currency of this debate and the prevalent attitude in the mid-eighteenth century:

Absurd and impertinent vanity! We pronounce our fellow animals to be automates, or we allow them instinct, or we bestow graciously upon them, at the utmost stretch of liberality, an irrational soul, something we know not what, but something that can claim no kindred to the human mind. We scorn to admit them into the same class of intelligence with ourselves, tho it be obvious…that the first inlets, and the first elements of their knowledge, and of ours, are the same.[19]

And John Hildrop's *Free Thoughts upon the Brute-Creation* (1742–1743), another widely read contribution to the ongoing debate, rejects Cartesianism for animals by claiming that, since animals existed in the Garden of Eden, "there seems to be a strong Presumption, that in the Intention of their Creator in their original Frame, and their Relation to the universal System, they were to be Partakers of that Blessing and Immortality which was the Privilege of the whole Creation."[20] Speculation about animals' immortality even included the notion that their resurrected souls might be "transmitted to some Peculiar Habitations, perhaps in Saturn, Mars, or Jupiter."[21]

Coventry's novel clearly mocks the pedantic or foolish interlocutors who engage in these debates within the narrative. But the satiric undercutting here functions like the paradoxical critique of superstitious belief in species transformation in *The Dialogue of the Dogs*. For both works, ridiculing the issue of species transformation or transcendence does not result in a simple resolution to the problems that the text proposes—that

[18] For an account of the debate about animal souls, see Thomas, *Man and the Natural World*, 139–142; and Christine Kenyon-Jones, *Kindred Brutes: Animals in Romantic-Period Writing* (Aldershot, UK: Ashgate, 2001), 15–27. For a summary of the religious arguments regarding animal souls and of the developing new ideas of humanity, see David Perkins, *Romanticism and Animal Rights* (Cambridge: Cambridge University Press, 2003), 27–41. For the French theriophilist movement of the period, which was influential in England, see George Boas, *The Happy Beast in French Thought of the Seventeenth Century* (1933; New York: Octagon Books, 1966). Ingrid H. Tague describes the treatment of animal souls and of metempsychosis in pet epitaphs, concluding that "the view that animals might have immortal souls like humans was not that of the majority, but ideas that stopped short of this position were common." See Tague, "Dead Pets: Satire and Sentiment in British Elegies and Epitaphs for Animals," *Eighteenth-Century Studies* 42 (2008): 289–306, 299.
[19] Henry St. John, Viscount Bolingbroke, *The Works of the Late Right Honorable Henry St John, Lord Viscount Bolingbroke* (London: David Mallet, 1754), 352–353.
[20] John Hildrop, *Free Thoughts upon the Brute-Creation* (London: R. Minors, 1742), 2:40. Reprinted in *Animal Language, Animal Passions and Animal Morals*, ed. Aaron Garrett (Bristol: Theommes Press, 2000), vol. 1. For a summary of materials on animal thought, animal souls, and the development of animal rights, see Garrett's introduction to this facsimile collection.
[21] William Coward, *The Just Scrutiny; or, A Serious Enquiry into the Modern Notions of the Soul* (London: John Chantry, [1705?]), 97. Also cited in Thomas, *Man and the Natural World*, 139.

a dog can be the protagonist or the narrator of a novel, that a human can become a dog, that a dog can be possessed of a human soul, or that a human and a dog can be united in another realm of existence. And in this latter example from *Pompey the Little*, the evocation of a shared afterlife, the human assertion that "I shall be vastly glad of your company" in that other realm, and the concluding image of Lady Tempest's embrace of Pompey demonstrate the prominent role played by the transcendence of species difference within the sub-genre of the dog narrative. Indeed, the idea of the potential union of dog and human in a different realm of existence is a common theme in the moral and didactic dog narratives of the turn of the nineteenth century—a theme that develops out of the tropes of transformation that we have identified in Cervantes. Those later works emerge from and reproduce the most distinctive experiences evoked by canine fiction in this early phase of its development—its attention to diversity, its problematization of alterity, and its encounter with the "supernatural." But for these works, that supernatural transcendence of the everyday is expressed through the representation of an afterlife or another world.

The Rise of the Dog Narrative

In the first two decades of the nineteenth century, dog-protagonist narratives become a popular sub-genre. The satiric tradition is represented by an English translation of a French imitation of *Pompey the Little*, published in 1804 as *The History of a Dog. Written by himself, and published by a gentleman of his acquaintance.*[22] The canine narrative in this period is sentimentalized and increasingly moralized, however, and several of these works are intended for the consumption of children. Early in the eighteenth century, beginning with Locke's advocacy of Aesop for the education of children, animal stories began to be published for a juvenile audience. By the early nineteenth century, original stories of animals had come to dominate the growing children's trade. In fact, as Tess Cosslett demonstrates, "the animal story was central to the rise of a separate children's literature" (10).[23] But well beyond the active juvenile market, the dog-protagonist narrative also attains a wide and deep provenance throughout the nineteenth century, while the broader literary appearance of the dog extends to a range of other forms. Teresa Mangum argues that

---

[22] Charles Augustin de Bassompierre Sewrin, trans., *The History of a Dog. Written by himself, and published by a gentleman of his acquaintance* (London: Minerva-Press, 1804). This is a translation of Pigault LeBrun, *Histoire d'un chien, écrit par lui-même et publiée par un homme de ses amis* (Paris, 1802).

[23] For accounts of animals in children's literature from the eighteenth to the early nineteenth century, see also Kenyon-Jones, *Kindred Brutes*, (51–78) and Harriet Ritvo, "Learning from Animals: Natural History for Children in the Eighteenth and Nineteenth Centuries," *Children's Literature* 13 (1985): 72–93.

more than any others, it was the canine point of view that took center stage in a host of Victorian novels. Self-proclaimed autobiographies of show dogs, hunting dogs, lost or escaped dogs, and neglected, even tortured dogs took the form of novels, of short stories published in periodicals and collected in anthologies, and of poetry written about and to dogs. (35)

And Barbara T. Gates has documented the steady rise of the animal biography—including anecdotes and chronicles, pet stories and parables of natural history—to a height of popularity in the 1890s.[24] This engagement with the literary representation of dogs coincides with and contributes to the rapid development of the humanitarian movements in this period. James Turner outlines what he emphasizes as a "startling upsurge of animal welfare activity in the decade after 1800."[25] The most long-lived and influential institutional outlet for animal advocacy, the Society for the Prevention of Cruelty to Animals, was founded in London in 1824, and its U.S. equivalent followed in 1866.

Looking forward for a moment to the canonical texts of the fully developed humanitarian movement of the second half of the nineteenth century, Anna Sewall's *Black Beauty* (1877) and (Margaret) Marshall Saunders's *Beautiful Joe* (1894), we can find in those later works a direct debt to the earlier canine narrative's formal premises of itinerancy and diversity. These major humanitarian statements are emanations of the dog narrative that we have traced from the eighteenth century, and whose provenance in the early nineteenth century we will shortly examine. Significantly, the horse autobiography *Black Beauty* is a variant of the canine narrative, sharing its random movement from place to place as well as its privileging of animal access to human intelligence or prescience. *Black Beauty*, in fact, is an imitation of the original English horse autobiography, *Memoirs of Dick, the Little Poney, Supposed to be Written by Himself* (1800), which was published at the turn of the century among the group of popular dog narratives of that period. The anonymous author of *Dick* also published, within the year, *The Dog of Knowledge; or, Memoirs of Bob, the Spotted Terrier: Supposed to be Written by Himself. By the author of Dick the Little Poney* (1801). The dog narratives of the early nineteenth century, then, represent a core group whose influence extends to those later canonical humanitarian texts.

Of this core group, the first is the novel, *Biography of a Spaniel* (1797), published by the Minerva Press in an anonymous collection entitled *Interesting Tales Selected and Translated*

---

[24] Barbara T. Gates, *Kindred Nature: Victorian and Edwardian Women Embrace the Living World* (Chicago: University of Chicago Press, 1998), 220–230.

[25] James Turner, *Reckoning with the Beast: Animals, Pain, and Humanity in the Victorian Mind* (Baltimore: Johns Hopkins University Press, 1980), 24. For an account of the humanitarian movements and attempts at protective legislation, see Turner, 15–38, and Hilda Kean, *Animal Rights: Political and Social Change in Britain since 1800* (London: Reaktion Books, 1998), 13–38. For a broader account of early nineteenth-century attitudes toward animals, see Perkins, *Romanticism and Animal Rights*.

from the German.[26] It is not clear that these were translations at all; certainly several of the stories appear to be English originals. The author is most likely a Mrs. Showes, who wrote three other novels that were published over the next four years by Minerva. The stories included in the *Interesting Tales* were not intended for children, but *Biography of a Spaniel*, along with one other tale from the collection, was reissued in 1803 in a smaller format with a new frontispiece, a copperplate engraving by James Hopwood illustrating the "Elysium of dogs" described in the opening of the story. This imprint was certainly intended for a juvenile audience, and was perhaps designed to share in the success of the two new dog narratives just issued by rival presses—*Keeper's Travels in Search of His Master* (1798) by Edward Augustus Kendall, and a work we have already noted, *The Dog of Knowledge; or, Memoirs of Bob, the Spotted Terrier* (1801).[27]

Thus the rise of the dog narrative is a prominent cultural and publishing event of these decades. *Keeper's Travels* saw "immediate success and…prolonged popularity" and ran to sixteen editions by 1879.[28] This work was issued by Elizabeth Newbery, a publisher instrumental in promoting the burgeoning business of juvenile publications, and is dedicated to an "infant in arms."[29] But its evocation of the Jacobin rhetoric of "rights" in the dedication led to questions about *Keeper's* appropriateness for a young audience, and it lacks the extended didacticism typical of later children's works.[30] *The Dog of Knowledge* is similarly dedicated "To the Lovely Children of the most noble Marquis of W——," but again, its extensive and even bitter social critique seems more relevant to an adult audience. In fact, one contemporary reader comments, "If we had not learnt from the dedication, and from the prefatory advertisement…that this Book was written for young people, we should have ranked it among Novels."[31] In these two works, we can see the continuing relevance of the dog narrative to an adult audience, even while this sub-genre is recruited for the juvenile book trade.

Elizabeth Fenwick's *The Life of the Famous Dog Carlo* (1804?), which was issued by another publisher of books for children, Benjamin Tabart, is more clearly and consistently oriented toward what we would now call a young adult audience than *Keeper's Travels* and

---

[26] *Interesting Tales Selected and Translated from the German* (London: Minerva Press, 1797).
[27] For information on the publication history of *Biography of a Spaniel*, see Judith St. John, preface to *Biography of a Spaniel, To which is annexed The Idiot, a Tale* (Yorkshire: S. R. Publishers; New York: Johnson Reprint Corporation, 1969) vii–x. All references to *Biography of a Spaniel* will be to this reprint edition.
[28] St. John, preface, ix. See also the introductory essay to *The Dog of Knowledge*, in The Hockliffe Project, De Mountfort University, http://www.cts.dmu.ac.uk/AnaServer?hockliffe+0+start.anv, cat. no. 0179B. All references to *The Dog of Knowledge* will be to the following edition: *The Dog of Knowledge* (London: J. Harris, 1801).
[29] Edward Augustus Kendall, dedication to William Webb Kendall, *infans in brachia*, in *Keeper's Travels in Search of His Master* (London: E. Newbery, 1798). All references to *Keeper's Travels* will be to this edition.
[30] See the introductory essay to *Keeper's Travels in Search of His Master* (1817), in The Hockliffe Project, cat. no. 0153.
[31] Sarah Trimmer, *The Guardian of Education* (1802–1806), vol. 1 (1802), 327–328. Cited in the introductory essay to *The Dog of Knowledge*, The Hockliffe Project, cat. no. 0179B.

The Dog of Knowledge, since *Carlo* features sympathetic adolescent human figures as Carlo's various masters.[32] The original Carlo, however, enjoyed a popularity that extended well beyond a juvenile audience. Fenwick's novel *Carlo* is based on a contemporary dramatic production featuring a dog-actor as Carlo. This was a two-act comedy by Frederic Reynolds, *The Caravan; or, the Driver and His Dog* (1803). The play was so successful on the London stage that Richard Brinsley Sheridan called the dog "the author and preserver of Drury Lane Theatre."[33] *Cato; or, The Interesting Adventures of a Dog of Sentiment* (1816), by Mary Pilkington, provides numerous set-piece moralizing anecdotes for the instruction of youth, including lessons about obedience to parents, love of siblings, the dangers of firearms, charity to the poor, kindness to animals, and the cruelty of hunting, among others.[34] And Mary Elliott, in her *Confidential Memoirs; or, Adventures of a Parrot, a Greyhound, a Cat, and a Monkey* (1821), directly addresses "the young reader" and hopes that "in the course of this little Work, the readers may have traced a similarity in the situations and circumstances described to those of their own experience."[35]

Of these texts, *The Dog of Knowledge* and *Biography of a Spaniel* most clearly reproduce the specific materials that distinguish *The Dialogue of the Dogs* and *Pompey the Little.* Like their canine predecessors, both of these dog narrators take up with itinerant beggars and pompous, penniless poets, and both offer critiques of religion, female fashion, and social excess. Even more specifically, in both of these works the dog protagonist demonstrates an extraordinary ability to learn certain tricks that—like Bergansa's career as a *"Wise Dog"* when he is taught to jump for the king of France, or Pompey's "Genius" in learning to play piquet—are advertised as the canine version of "academic studies" (*Biography of a Spaniel,* 12). The "dog of knowledge" learns to pick pockets, perform card tricks, and dance in a harlequin's jacket (*Dog of Knowledge,* 36), and he is "fit to play at cards with a Jonas" (*Dog of Knowledge,* 55). The dog narrator of *Biography of a Spaniel* learns to "jump over a stick for King Frederic," finding "the solid advantages that learning gives; for at every cook-shop and public-house…my talents were rewarded" (12–13). Both of these works blend social satire—in which we can see the debt to Cervantes and Coventry most directly—with an exemplary sentimentalism that features the faithful dog as its model. *The Dog of Knowledge* ends with three anecdotes illustrative of canine loyalty and a poem describing the Christian lessons represented by the dog and designed

[32] For the publication date of *The Life of the Famous Dog Carlo,* see the introductory essay to *The Life of the Famous Dog Carlo,* The Hockliffe Project, cat. no. 0162. All references to *Carlo* are to the following edition: Eliza Fenwick, *The Life of the Famous Dog Carlo* (London: Tabart, 1809).

[33] Richard Brinsley Sheridan, cited in the introductory essay to *The Life of the Famous Dog Carlo* in The Hockliffe Project.

[34] *Cato; or, The Interesting Adventures of a Dog of Sentiment* (London: J. Harris, 1816). All references to *Cato* will be to this edition.

[35] Mary Elliott, *Confidential Memoirs; or, Adventures of a Parrot, a Greyhound, a Cat, and a Monkey* (London: William Darton, 1821), 246, 249. All references to *Confidential Memoirs* are to this edition.

"to inculcate a love of animals in general, and of dogs in particular" (179). And *Biography of a Spaniel* closes with a sentimental scene of conjoined human-dog mortality, to which we will return. The compatibility of social satire and affective moralism within these two narratives indicates the nature of the relationship between Cervantes and Coventry on the one hand, and the affective canine narrative of the early nineteenth century on the other. Even when satire turns to sentiment, the imaginative premise of the dog narrative, in its exploration of species difference, supports a critique of the present and a projection beyond the realities or injustices of the here and now. In other words, when dogs are at the center of the story—whether as satirists or as moralists—they lead the reader to a critical view of human-kind and, beyond that, to the contemplation of another realm of existence.

These early nineteenth-century dog narratives introduce an addition to the sub-genre in the form of sentimental canine achievements. *Biography of a Spaniel* provides a new trope, which becomes persistent in the canine narrative from the early nineteenth century to the twentieth, that of saving children from danger—in this particular case, saving a child from drowning. The spaniel rescues Betsey from the river, when she falls in "without uttering a word" (47). Children are subsequently saved from a watery death in *Keeper's Travels* and, repeatedly, in *Carlo.* The latter rescues directly reproduce the actions of the dog-hero of the popular play that *Carlo* imitates, where the original Carlo dives onstage into a water tank to preserve "the lovely child of the Marquis of Cala-trava," in a star role reminiscent of Bergansa's acting career as a "great favourite of the town."[36] These canine feats diverge in tone from the activities of Bergansa and Pompey, but they subscribe to the same assumption promulgated in those earlier texts: that the dog protagonist is endowed with special abilities that enable him to rival or even exceed the accomplishments of human-kind.

But beyond these specific resemblances, the dog narratives from the first quarter of the nineteenth century share the core tenets of the form that we have defined in the works of Cervantes and Coventry. As we have seen, the dog protagonist, as he moves from master to master, enacts a formal itinerancy, and his wanderings assert the diversity of human experience. This itinerancy is indicated rhetorically through expressions of arbitrary transition: "He ran hastily along, without stopping to notice anything" (*Keeper,* 13); "Late at night, perceiving the street quiet, and summoning courage to depart, he left the house, unobserved, and continued his journey" (*Keeper,* 30); "I ran *zigzag*, not knowing which way to take, till the sight of a village ... fixed my wavering resolution" (*Biography of a Spaniel,* 19); "I ran as fast as I could, without looking back, ... when I supposed myself out of danger of being overtaken, I slackened my pace, and continued my peregrination

[36] Introductory essay to *The Life of the Famous Dog Carlo* in The Hockliffe Project.

leisurely, undetermined which way to take" (*Biography of a Spaniel*, 31); "Observing the door not quite shut close,...I ran down stairs into the street" (*Carlo*, 18); "I ran a great distance" (*Cato*, 115); or, in a reflective vein, "This is terribly changing work; I fear I shall never have a settled home" (*Confidential Memoirs*, 104).

The diversity of experience that the canine world provides emerges through the dog's connection with prosperous masters on the one hand, and with beggars, Gypsies, minstrels, soldiers, and other itinerants on the other. In *Biography of a Spaniel*, the dog narrator, in addition to his time with his master the beggar, is "*aid-de-camp* to the General of an army of Gypsies" (60). Cato and his young master move among the London lower classes, befriending a blind boy and his entire blind family, and Cato himself later lives with an apple-stall woman in her cellar. Carlo gathers with the poor outside a Spanish monastery where, he says, "I lived for some time, daily ringing the monastery bell, and receiving my provisions like any friendless and destitute person" (57). Julio of the *Confidential Memoirs* is stolen by dognappers, who introduce him to a different manner of living, "To be cooped up in such a wretched habitation!" he complains, "I who had been accustomed to houses of the first style, whose feet had never yet touched a dirty floor" (88). And the "dog of knowledge" accompanies one master, a soldier, to Jamaica, where, he tells us, "I felicitated myself on being born a dog, and not a negro." This new experience causes the dog to offer an innocent critique of slavery; he is puzzled that the "negroes" seem to be "born to subjection," since "they walked on two legs like the rest of the species, and seemed to me to differ in nothing; but in the colour of their skin and the contour of their face" (*Dog of Knowledge*, 70–71).

Many of these dog protagonists also reproduce the trope of mock genealogy that links the experience of diversity to a parodic undercutting of ideas of established hierarchy. The "dog of knowledge" claims that "the family of the Terriers, from which I am paternally descended, are as ancient as any in the kingdom" (*Dog of Knowledge*, 4). The dog narrator of *Biography of a Spaniel* worries that

> more is not in my power to say about [my father], for this part of my genealogy remains wrapped in eternal darkness; but I comfort myself with the reflection that many of Adam's descendants' fate is similar to mine in this respect, and that the space which contains their names in the parish-register would have been a blank, had it not been the fashion to fill it up with a name at random. (8)

Cato confirms that "my father [was] a small terrier...my mother, a handsome spaniel [who] possessed many good qualities" (*Cato*, 2). In the first sentence of *Carlo*, Carlo says, "I am descended, both by the father's and mother's side, from the noble race of New-foundland dogs" (3). And Julio of the *Confidential Memoirs*, in establishing his reputation, claims that "my mother had been a favourite of a great cardinal" and "my birth-place was a palace" (52).

The paradox of canine language also continues as a theme in these texts. To justify dog authorship, canine rationality or intelligence must be foregrounded. In *Keeper's Travels* the reader is informed that "the understanding of dogs…surpasses that of all other animals, except man and the elephant" (65). *Biography of a Spaniel* accounts for the dog narrator's ability to speak by removing him from the known world, where reality might constrain such conjectures about animal abilities, and setting him in an afterlife on an island in a sea on the moon, "the appointed Elysium of dogs" (3). This unusual imaginary realm emerges directly from contemporary speculation about animal souls, which sometimes placed them on a remote heavenly body—Saturn, Mars, Jupiter, or the moon. Thus situated, the dog narrator observes that "had I, whilst in the lower regions, possessed the power of speech as I do now, without doubt I should have found a biographer" (5–6). Carlo is taught his letters by his youthful master, who thinks he is playing a game of "make believe" with his pet dog: "He would take an old spelling book, and make believe to teach me my letters.—He had no idea that a dog could really learn his letters, but I soon knew all their forms" (*Carlo*, 11).

Language is further emphasized in the sentimental dog narrative through the evocation of a common canine-human discourse of affect—not that dogs speak like humans, but that dogs and humans both speak to each other in the universal language of nature. The idiom of sentiment is often cited as a trans-species mode of communication—a superior language that registers universal values. Thus *Keeper's Travels* cites "that universal language which is every where understood, by the inhabitant of every region, and by all orders of beings. For nature has so finely tuned the ears of all her creatures, that the sounds of misfortune, and of sorrow, never fail to win attention: and with such skill has she set the notes, that they cannot be misconceived" (6–7). Similarly, in *Biography of a Spaniel*: "The language of humanity is adapted to the comprehension of other animals, as well as to that of human beings, and…I," says the narrator, "understood it" (48).

By posing the fundamental question of whether dogs can cross the species boundary through access to human language, or whether humans and dogs can communicate directly in some universal language, the canine narrative opens itself up to the representation of a transcendent realm. As we have seen, in *The Dialogue of the Dogs* and *Pompey the Little* the transcendental is contained within the oblique modes of satire and parody—in Berganza's encounter with the sorceress who claims to have changed him from human to animal at his birth, and in Pompey's embrace by Lady Tempest as she expresses the wish that he accompany her to heaven. But these later sentimental texts bring that realm fully to consciousness—in dream, in lyric, or in the direct evocation of a liberated world beyond the here and now. Toward the end of *Keeper's Travels*, the dog protagonist, near death, dreams of a reunion with his master: "He fancied that this friend of his life was endeavouring to rescue him from his misery. He thought that his warm hand was on his neck. He thought that he dug away the perishing snow. The idea became still less distinct: he even thought himself relieved from his misery. He fancied himself in the arms of his master. He was happy" (136). This trope recurs frequently in canine fiction. The protagonist of *Biography of a Spaniel* recollects a favorite mistress in a dream: "Often, in my dreams, did I fancy myself near the dear child [Betsey], attempting to lick her hand—but was always prevented by her withdrawing herself, and casting a sorrowful but affectionate look at me" (60). And in the course of his wanderings, Cato says he "fell asleep, and dreamed that I met my beloved Henry, who, delighted to see me, took me in his arms, and with the greatest kindness, carried me home.... [But] my happiness had been only a dream" (77–78).

The Dog of Knowledge puts this transcendental reunion into lyric form. At the end of his story, Bob's voice slips from first to third person, to narrate the dog narrator's own death: "Having now no farther services to perform than the reciprocal interchanges of duty and love,...the reader can know little more of Bob than that he lived to such an age, and that, when he was no more, the tear of affection bedewed his verdant grave" (178–179). Then the dog narrator continues, after his own death, to "take a respectful and final leave" of the reader by quoting a poem by Samuel Jackson Pratt, a popular writer on humanitarian topics. Bob's canine voice thus uses human discourse to recite, from "beyond the grave," a lyric rendition of the transcendent realm in which true sensibility—canine and human—resides:

> But wouldst thou see an instance yet more dear,
> A touch more rare—thy dog may still afford
> The example high—go read it on the bier,
> If chance some canine friend survives his lord;
>
> Awhile survives his latest dues to pay,
> Beyond the grave his gratitude to prove,
> Moan out his life in slow but sure decay,
> Martyr sublime, of friendship and of love! (183)

The proof of canine gratitude is also proof of a realm beyond the present one—a realm in which the dog can indisputably lay claim to human virtue.

At its conclusion, *Biography of a Spaniel* dramatizes this transcendental rapprochement of human and animal by giving us the simultaneous death of dog and human, the trans-species union of their souls, and a glimpse into their prospective afterlife. The dog narrator has bitten a boy who sought to steal him away from his destitute and blind master:

A few minutes after I saw two men approach us, with guns in their hands, who, by their dress, I supposed to be the ministers of justice:—they were so, and employed by the Town Major, whose son I had bit, to punish my crime. I had time enough to escape; but, instead of doing so, I crept closer to my master—who, when he was told the danger I was in, bent over me—thinking, by so doing, he should be able to protect me. But his effort was vain—for the mercenary slaves fired; and the same ball that passed through my head, penetrated his heart.— "Bury us together!"—was the last sound I heard with my mortal faculties, and likewise the first my aerial substance comprehended. Our shades met—we tried to embrace, but an invisible power tore us asunder; yet as the spirit of my friend ascended, it called to me, and said—"We shall meet again!"

CONCLUSION.

"Yes, so you will," re-echoed the united voices of the whole society [of the Elysium of dogs], who, with silent admiration, had listened to the stranger's relation. (92–93)

Though their souls meet for a moment, their full reunion is distanced by "an invisible power"—the force of difference which the "united voices" of the speaking dogs reject in their chorus, "so you will."

When and where will distance be replaced by that trans-species embrace that the spaniel and his master attempt, and that Lady Tempest anticipates in *Pompey the Little?* The dedication to *Keeper's Travels* locates that emblematic embrace in a future produced by political revolution. In fact, a contemporary reader condemned Kendall's novel as a Jacobin work: "We have long been used to hear of the RIGHTS OF MAN, and RIGHTS OF WOMEN; but the levelling system, which includes the RIGHTS OF ANIMALS, is here carried to the most ridiculous extreme."[37] Indeed, Kendall's dedication, and his justification for the novel as a whole, evokes the language of rights in explicit contrast to the language of sensibility or "compassion":

Many exertions are now making to obtain our compassion for the various animals for whom, in common with ourselves, the rain descends, and the sun shines: and I doubt not a rapid alteration of the opinions of mankind will reward these endeavours: but I cannot help anticipating the time, when men

---

[37] Sarah Trimmer, *The Guardian of Education*, (1802–1806), vol. 1 (1802): 400. Cited in the introductory essay to *Keeper's Travels* in The Hockliffe Project, cat. no. 0153. See also Cosslett, *Talking Animals*, 35, and Kenyon-Jones, *Kindred Brutes*, 64–65, for an account of the political critique of *Keeper's Travels.*

shall acknowledge the RIGHTS; instead of bestowing their COMPASSION upon the creatures, whom, with themselves, GOD made, and made to be happy!—If any part of their condition is to be compassionated,—it is that they are liable to the tyranny of man.... It is not ... for [Keeper] alone, I plead—nor for the race of DOGS only, but for the whole breathing world! I shall be fortunate if I contribute to the happiness of any one of those whom I am proud to call my fellow-creatures. (iv–vi)

By using or ventriloquizing human language, by occupying the traditionally human-centered role of literary protagonist, by wandering through the diverse world of human experience, by occupying the place of the displaced or the dispossessed as well that of privilege or fashion, and by undercutting claims to genealogical hierarchy and social regulation, the imaginary dog creates a unique cultural opportunity to consider an alternative to the structures and limits of the present day. Kendall seizes that opportunity for the ends of political revolution. For others, it remains an open-ended speculation, a fantasy whose final form is not yet realized. Toward the middle of the century, Margaret Scott Gatty, in *Worlds Not Realized* (1856), a didactic animal-advocacy novel, has her main character describe for his children the transcendent Elysium of dogs from *Biography of a Spaniel:*

> The charm of [that novel] was, that at the beginning, there was a picture of a scene in the moon;—a sort of Paradise to which dogs were supposed to go when they died. It was the custom in that happy place, for each dog, on his arrival, to relate his adventures upon earth; and the picture represented a circle of dogs, sitting as you are sitting now; in front of a spaniel, the hero of the tale, who was talking to them, as I am talking to you now; and telling them the history of his life. Over this picture I used to pore with the deepest interest, trying by looking into it to discover what sort of a place the moon-paradise was; and wondering by what means the poor dog, who, according to the book, had just been shot dead in the street, could have got there!...You must not suppose that I was left in such ignorance as seriously to believe that such a place as the moon-paradise existed. People told me it did not, and I submitted. But I used to try and forget that it was all nonsense, whenever I took up my book again; and sometimes I pleased myself by thinking, that as nobody knew what was in the moon, there was just a loop-hole of possibility that the dog-paradise might be there after all.[38]

[38] Mrs. Alfred Gatty [Margaret Scott Gatty], *Worlds Not Realized* (London: Bell and Daldy, 1856), 168–169.

This reader, like others, might be brought to submit to the norms of everyday orderliness, to the idea that only humans can talk, and to the assumption that a dog who is dead in the street cannot ascend to a world beyond the here and now. But the canine narrative continues to work against those norms, returning its reader repeatedly to that "loop-hole of possibility" of a realm where the boundaries and constraints of this world are thrown off.

Auster's *Timbuktu*

Timbuktu opens that same loop-hole, in a way that responds to the tradition of the dog narrative and especially its evocation of the Elysium of dogs, and that helps us appreciate the sustained impact of these formative early literary experiments that mark the rise of the animal in the modern imagination. Mr. Bones's first master, Willy, teaches the dog that

> once your soul had been separated from your body, your body was buried in the ground and your soul lit out for the next world....There was no doubt in the dog's mind that the next world was a real place. It was called Timbuktu....At one point, Willy described it as "an oasis of spirits." At another point he said: "Where the map of this world ends, that's where the map of Timbuktu begins." (48–49)

Willy and Mr. Bones have been "wandering the streets of Baltimore without a map" (8), on a final fruitless pilgrimage, as Willy moves toward his own imminent death and Mr. Bones composes an extended canine tribute to his homeless master: "Had he been capable of smiling, he would have smiled at that moment. Had he been capable of shedding tears, he would have shed tears. Indeed, if such a thing were possible, he would have been laughing and crying at the same time—both celebrating and mourning his beloved master, who was soon to be no more" (34). This tribute to the homeless, the itinerant, the "one-of-a-kind two-leg who improvised the rules as he went along" propels the text to the representation of a world beyond boundaries and systems—for Willy first, and ultimately for Mr. Bones and Willy together.

The conclusion of *Biography of a Spaniel* anticipates the staging of Willy's death and provides a model for *Timbuktu*'s movement toward this transcendent realm. The canine protagonist of that earlier novel, like Mr. Bones, shares the itinerant life of his master, now a blind beggar, as he "patiently waited for death" (88):

> With a joy that even my present power of utterance can but faintly express, I followed the infirm protector of my helpless youth through the streets, where

his piteous moans could barely procure him the scanty means of subsistence; yet every morsel of bread or bone of meat the hand of charity put into the wooden bowl he carried under his arm, he shared with me. It was more for his sake than my own that I lamented the penury we lived in, and grieved at the hardness of heart the affluent shewed when they drove him from the door without relieving his wants. (87)

Both of these texts use the premise of the dog narrator to make visible and even to celebrate the existences of those human beings whose lives are conducted outside the regulated and accepted structures of society. And both represent the imposition of that regulated structure on these unaccepted human beings as an occasion to contemplate a transcendence of boundaries and of difference. We have already seen how, at the conclusion of *Biography of a Spaniel*, the dog and the beggar are approached by the "two men…with guns in their hands," town policemen come to keep order in the streets. Willy's life ends with a similar confrontation between itinerancy and established order: "A police car pulled up…and two large men in uniforms climbed out. One was white and the other was black, and they were both sweating in the August heat, a pair of wide-hipped cops out on Sunday patrol, carrying the instruments of the law around their waists: revolvers and handcuffs, billy clubs and holsters, flashlights and bullets" (67).

As in *Biography of a Spaniel*, the arrival of the two policemen heralds Willy Christmas's death, though instead of dying on the streets, Willy is transported to the indigents' ward of Our Lady of Sorrows Hospital and dies there seventeen hours later. In both these spectacles of the encounter of itinerancy and order, the mapless world of the itinerant is sited in the street, the forces of order are marked by the potentially violent "instruments of the law," and their encounter propels the narrative into a transcendent realm. In effect, Willy dies twice for Mr. Bones, the first time in a dream, in which Mr. Bones sees the two policemen approach and "knew that this was it, that the dreaded moment was suddenly upon them,…licked Willy's face, whimpered a brief farewell as his master patted his head for the last time, and then took off, charging down North Amity Street as fast as his legs could take him" (67). In this first dream, an extraordinary second dream of metamorphosis transforms Mr. Bones into a fly, enabling him to follow his master to the hospital ward and to witness Willy's last hours as well as his last words, which "as one might have expected,…were about Mr. Bones" himself (76).

When he awakes from these embedded dreams, Mr. Bones finds himself still on the street, still at the side of his master. It is in the next scene that he faces Willy's real death, which occurs exactly as in his dream:

Mr. Bones realized that it was happening in precisely the same order as be-fore….This was his real and authentic life, and because you got to live that life only once, he knew that they had really come to the end this time. He knew that the words tumbling from his master's mouth were the last words he would ever hear Willy speak....A police car was inching its way down the street....Mr. Bones didn't have to look to know what it was, but he looked anyway. The car had pulled up alongside the curb, and the two cops were getting out, patting their holsters and adjusting their belts, the black one and the white one, the same two jokers as before. Mr. Bones turned to Willy then, just as Willy was turning to him....Willy looked him in the eyes and said, "Beat it, Bonesy. Don't let them catch you." So he licked his master's face, stood stock-still for a moment as Willy patted his head, and then he sprinted off, flying down the street as if there were no tomorrow. (78, 83)

We have seen the canine dream of his master to be a trope of species transcendence in the dog narratives that precede *Timbuktu*. For the dog protagonist in this novel, the dream sequence offers a partial transcendence both of difference and of death. As a fly, Mr. Bones is given a magical ability to accompany Willy on his final journey, an ultimate intimacy with human-kind that even the canine narrator cannot achieve. Meanwhile, awakening from his dream of death at the side of his beloved master makes even this "real and authentic" death potentially relative: "So befuddled was Mr. Bones for the next little while that he wasn't sure if he was really in the world again or had woken up in another dream" (77). This layering of the transcendental and the authentic is realized in a series of subsequent dreams in which Mr. Bones is reunited with Willy and takes his final trip to Timbuktu to meet his master.

Like the earlier canine protagonists, Mr. Bones expresses the change from master to master and place to place in the rhetoric of arbitrary transition characteristic of the dog narrative from the time of *The Dialogue of the Dogs*: "charging down North Amity Street as fast as his legs could take him," for example, and "flying down the street as if there were no tomorrow." Or when he leaves the city of Baltimore, "he had no idea where he was going, but he knew that he had to keep on running until his legs gave out on him or his heart exploded in his chest....He kept on running for three days" (113, 114). Just like Bergansa, Mr. Bones lays claim to an "infinity" of experiences: "There might not have been many advantages to living with Willy, but no one could accuse Mr. Bones of not having traveled. He had been everywhere, and in his time he had seen just about everything" (162). And Mr. Bones's adventures include many of the basic tropes of the canine narrative—he is shot at, starved, and frozen in the snow; he is down and out as the companion of Willy but "dandified, turned into a bourgeois dog-about-town" in his suburban life with the Joneses (142). And though he does not rescue her, he is the special confidant of Alice, a precocious eight-year-old who locates his literary heritage for us herself—even citing the theme of canine child rescue—as she pleads with her mother to give Mr. Bones a home: "'Remember that book you used to read to me when I was little? The red one with the pictures in it and all those stories about animals? There was a dog in there that looked just like this one. He rescued a baby from a burning building and could count up to ten. Remember, Mama? I used to love that dog'" (131–132). Willy Christmas describes Mr. Bones as "the dog of dogs, an exemplar of the whole canine race" (40), and Alice, too, seems to see Mr. Bones—Sparky, to her—as an embodiment of the prototypical dog of literary imagination.

As the end of the narrative—and the end of Mr. Bones's travels—nears, the celebration of Willy's unregulated existence, the transcendence of species difference, the paradox of dog language, and the promise of Timbuktu come together in a way that looks back to those "stories about animals" that Alice remembers and that we have canvassed from the early nineteenth century. In two vivid dreams, Mr. Bones approaches a reunion with his itinerant master and finds the prospect of Timbuktu confirmed. These are dreams of "impossible and beautiful things," of a world of "strangeness and beauty...beyond the boundaries of hard fact" (120, 174). They are dreams in which the dog protagonist "suddenly found himself able to speak" (121), and converses with his master "as clearly and smoothly as any two-leg yapping in his mother tongue" (176). The dog's accession to human language proves to Mr. Bones that these dreams have taken him to join Willy in Timbuktu, since he knows that in that other world "man's best friend would stay by the side of man after said man and said best friend had both kicked the bucket. More than that, in Timbuktu dogs would be able to speak man's language and converse with him as an equal" (49).

And yet the promise of these dreams, for Mr. Bones and for Willy, is "no more than a prelude to something far more important" (175)—Timbuktu itself. In the final scene of the novel, Mr. Bones runs onto the highway to play the "venerable, time-honored sport" of dodge-the-car, expecting that "with any luck, he would be with Willy before the day was out" (180–181). His last thought as he launches himself toward the Elysium of dogs provides a final tribute to Willy's eloquence, his outlandish inventions, and his extravagant and unbounded imagination: "All he had to do was step into the road, and he would be in Timbuktu. He would be in the land of words and transparent toasters, in the country of bicycle wheels and burning deserts where dogs talked as equals with men" (180). The words, toasters, wheels, and deserts, and the leap of imagination beyond the boundary of species, are the furniture of the homeless Willy's extraordinary, improvisational, and unaccepted mind. As Timbuktu finally comes into sight, Mr. Bones enables us to recognize it as the imaginative landscape of the "man with the heart of a dog," Willy Christmas himself.

Two centuries after *Biography of a Spaniel*, *Timbuktu* testifies to the strength and continued relevance of the dog narrative to the modern imaginative experience. All the defining components of the sub-genre are on display: the grounding but problematic premise of canine access to human discourse or human processes of thought, the transgression of foundational structures of order, the engagement with the diversity of human experience, and the trip beyond the accepted and regulated world of the here and now. Why should the dog's story be so compelling? Perhaps because of the scope and complexity of its impact on the human being who imagines it—an impact that embraces the literary, the social, and the metaphysical. In terms of the literary conventions of the novel, the dog narrative presents an implicit challenge to the shaped structure and the mundane representational realm of realist fiction. In regard to our encounter with the social world, the dog seems to give us a unique way to process human diversity, and to acknowledge human difference. In reference to the metaphysical, the Elysium of dogs speaks for itself. Lying "beyond the boundaries of hard fact" (174), it indicates the speculative space that animal-kind lends to the human imagination.

INDEX

animal souls, 19, 68, 69, *112*, 127–29, 135

animal studies, alterity and identity in, 14–16

"The Animal That Therefore I Am (More to Follow)" (Derrida, 2002), 13, 14

animals, terms for, 2n2

animals as other, 11–12

animals in literature. *See* literary animals

Animals' Rights Considered in Relation to Social Progress (Salt, 1892), 25

anthropological approaches to animals, 17–18

Anthropomorpha (Linnaeus, 1760), *26*, 32, 34–35

Anthropomorphism, Anecdotes, and Animals (Mitchell, Thompson and Miles, eds., 1997), 16

anthropomorphization of animals. *See* alterity and identity

apes. *See* hominoid apes

Apuleius, 117

Arbuthnot, John, 43–46, 50, 53

Arcadian pastoral tradition in dog-narratives, 120–21

archaeological approaches to animals, 17–18

Aristotle, 7–8, 38, 40, 45, 51

Armstrong, Philip, 20, 23–24, 49n41, 62n59

Arnold, Matthew, ix

The Artful Husband (Taverner, 1735), 95–96

Ash, John, 105n23

Ashworth, William B., 18–19, 33n16

Augustan satire, 76, 77, 123

Austen, Jane, 91

Auster, Paul, ix, 113–16, 124, 139–43

automata, Cartesian view of animals as, 8–9, 10, 14, 113, 128

Baker, Steve, 11–12

Baker, Thomas, 97–98

Barbot, John, 31

Barrett Browning, Elizabeth, 7, 65–67, 88–89

Bassompierre Sewrin, Charles Augustin de, 129n22

The Bath Unmask'd (Odingsells, 1725), 98–99

Battell, Andrew, 30, 32, 33–34, 59

"Bavius," Mr., 72

Beautiful Joe (Saunders, 1894), 130

The Beaux Stratagem (Farquhar, 1707), 95

Beeckman, Daniel, 30–31

Bellamy, Liz, 123, 124n15

Bentham, Jeremy, 24

Bilger, Audrey, 92n1

Biography of a Spaniel (Minerva Press, 1797), 130–40, 143

Black Beauty (Sewall, 1877), 130

Blackmore, Richard, 42–43, 54–55, 58

Boas, George, 128n18

Boehrer, Bruce, 14n24

Bolingbroke, Henry St. John, Viscount, 128

Bontius, Jacobus (Jakob de Bondt), 27, 33, 34–35, 38

Boosey, Edward J., 68n6

Boreman, Thomas, 31, 33, 46–47n37, 54–55, 59

Bosman, William, 31

boundaries and order, dog-narratives addressing problems of, 118–19, 120–21, 123–24

Braidotti, Rosi, 14n24

Braunschneider, Theresa, 70–71n10, 71n11, 95n6

Breydenbach, Bernhard von, 33, 35

Bridges, Harry, 116

Brobdingnagians in Swift's *Gulliver's Travels* (1726), 52

Broberg, Gunnar, 32, 35

Brown, Laura, 48n39, 86n33, 88n37, 106n25

Brown, Thomas, 73

Browning, Robert, 66

Brutus (Lucius Junius Brutus), 45

Buffon, George-Louis Leclerc, Comte de

 fables and natural history, relationship between, 22

 on hominoid apes, 27, 31–34, 42n31, 52, 56

 monkey and ape, interchangeable use of, 105

 on natural or savage man, 47–49, 50, 52

 Peacock's *Melincourt* and, 5

 Shelley's *Frankenstein* influenced by, 59, 61

Burnaby, William, 98n15

Burnet, James. *See* Monboddo, James Burnet, Lord

Burney, Frances. See *Evelina*

Burroughs, Edgar Rice, 6

dreaming dogs, 135–36, 140–41, 142
Dryden, John, 22, 76

Edwards, George, 35
elegies and epitaphs for pets, 20, 68, 71, 99,
    128n18
Elliott, Mary, 132, 134–35
Ellis, Markman, 70, 80n27, 86, 124n16
Elysium of dogs, concept of, *112*, 131, 135,
    137, 138, 139, 142, 143
"Elysium of Dogs" (Hopwood, 1803), *112*, 131
emblematic view of animals, 18–19, 22
Empedocles, 8
environmentalism, alterity and identity in, 11
"An Epistle to a Friend, with a Setting Dog"
    (Reeves, 1780), 77
"An Epitaph upon My Lady M———'s Lapdog"
    (Mr. "Bavius," 1731), 72
epitaphs and elegies for pets, 20, 68, 71, 99,
    128n18
Epstein, Julia, 92n1
Etherege, George, 95
Evelina (Burney, 1778)
    as conduct novel or novel of manners, 91–92
    description of monkey scene in, 93–94
    marriage plot, introduction of monkey into,
        21, 107–10
    social and historical context of, 104, 105, 106
exotic animals, as pets, 68

fables and natural history, relationship between, 22
*Fabulous Histories, Designed for the Instruction of Children,
    Respecting Their Treatment of Animals* (Trimmer,
    1796), 7
Farquhar, George, 95, 96
Fenwick, Elizabeth, 131–32, 133, 134, 135
Ferrier, Susan, 79–80
Fidelity (Wordsworth, 1805), 7
Flush: A Biography (Woolf, 1933), 66
"Flush or Faunus" (Barrett Browning, 1850),
    65–67, 88
fops and foppishness, monkeys as means of
    addressing, 93–94, 107–8, 110
Foucault, Michel, 18

Four-Footed Friends (Taylor, 1828), 7
Fox, Christopher, 53n43
Fox, Stephen, 74–75
Frankenstein (Shelley, 1816), 21, 23, 28, 59–63
Free Thoughts upon the Brute-Creation (Hildrop,
    1742–1743), 128

Game, Thomas, 54
Gates, Barbara T., 7n6, 24n38, 130
Gatty, Margaret Scott, 138
Gay, John, 22, 43, 72–73
the gaze, 72, 83, 85
gender issues
    lapdogs. *See* ladies and lapdogs
    modesty of hominoid apes, 31, 33, 38–39,
        53, 56, 57, 63
    pet monkeys. *See* monkeys and companionate
        marriage
    pets and pet keeping, 69, 77
genealogies, canine and feline, 118, 124–25,
    134–35, 138
General Character of the Dog (Taylor, 1804), 7
Geoffroy-Saint-Hilaire, Étienne, 33
Gesner, Conrad, 18, 32n16, 33, 41
Gildon, Charles, 117
Gleanings of Natural History (Edwards, 1758–1764),
    35
Goadby, Robert, 116
Golden Ass (Apuleius; Gildon's 1709 redaction),
    117
The Golden Trade (Jobson, 1623), 33, 46
gorillas. *See* hominoid apes
Gould, Robert, 70n9
Granville, George, 96
great apes. *See* hominoid apes
Greenfield, Susan, 92n1
The Guardian of Education (Trimmer, 1802-1806),
    131n31, 137n37
Guattari, Félix, 11, 13
Gulliver's Travels (Swift, 1726)
    Anatomy of a Pygmie and, 46–47, 50–52, 53
    Brobdingnagians in, 52
    hominoid apes and, 27–28, 43, 46–53,
        58, 87–89

Hoppius, Christianus Emanuel, 34

Hopwood, James, *112*, 131

horse autobiographies, 130

"Hottentots," 21, 31, 47–49, 52, 87, 89

Houpt, Katherine, ix–x

Houyhnhnms in Swift's *Gulliver's Travels* (1726), 49

human-alienating and human-associative positions. *See* alterity and identity

humanitarian movements and literary animals, 5, 24–25, 86, 128, 130, 137–38

The Humours of Oxford (Miller, 1730), 96–97

Huxley, Thomas H., 34n20, 35n22

identity with animals. *See* alterity and identity

Iliad (Homer; Pope's translation of 1715-1720), 40

Images of Animals (Crist, 1999), 15–16

imaginary animals. *See* literary animals

The Inconstant (Farquhar, 1708), 96

Interesting Tales Selected and Translated from the German (Minerva Press, 1797), 131

inter-species intimacy, 6. *See also* ladies and lapdogs; monkeys and companionate marriage

fantasy of inter-species miscegenation, 1, 5–6, 86–89, 106

inversion of affections, ladies and lapdogs displaying. *See* ladies and lapdogs

itinerancy as feature of dog-narratives, 114, 116, 118–20, 123, 125, 133–34, 138, 139–42

"it-narrative" tradition, 123–24

Janson, H. W., 5n4, 20, 28, 29, 30n8, 33, 87n34, 104n21

Jenyns, Soame, 127

The Jew of Venice (Granville, 1701), 96

Jobson, Richard, 33, 46

Johnson, Samuel, 69

Journey to the Holy Land (von Breydenbach, 1486), 33

Judeo-Christian views on animals, 8n8

Juvenalian antifemale satire, 76

Kafka, Franz, 6

Keeper's Travels in Search of His Master (Kendall, 1798), 2, 131, 133, 135–36, 137–38

Keeton, William T., 10

Kendall, Edward Augustus, 2, 131, 133, 135–36, 137–38

Kennedy, John S., 10

Kenyon-Jones, Christine, 17n29, 24n38, 128n18, 129n23, 137n37

Kete, Kathleen, 68n5

King Charles spaniels, 69, 74

King Kong (1933 film), 6

"Knowing and Acknowledging" (Cavell, 1969), 10

ladies and lapdogs, 21, 65–89

alterity and identity between, 67

Browning, Elizabeth Barrett, and Flush, 7, 65–67, 88–89

Cervantes's *El coloquio de los perros*, 122–23

classical mythology involving, 65–67, 88, 89n38

in comedy of manners genre, 94–95

in Dickens, 81–85, 89

the gaze between, 72, 83, 85

The History of Pompey the Little (Coventry, 1751). See *The History of Pompey the Little*

in narratives of sensibility, 77–81

"Nude with Dog" (Courbet, 1861), *64*

as part of general cultural phenomenon, 67–70

powerful literary resonance of, 85–89

in satiric poetic tradition, 70–77, 89, 123

sexual aspects of, 67, 70–79, 85–89, 122–23, 125

The Ladies Visiting-Day (Burnaby, 1708), 98n15

language. *See* speech and language

"The Lap-Dog" (Thompson, 1731), 72

The Lay-Monastery (Blackmore, 1714), 42–43, 54–55

Lazarillo de Tormes (anonymous, 1554), 121

le Comte, Louis Daniel, 39

LeBrun, Pigault, 129n22

CPSIA information can be obtained
at www.ICGtesting.com
Printed in the USA
LVOW03s2044160817
545251LV00005B/379/P

9 781501 713552